Secrets of Practical Chess

John Nunn

First published in the UK by Gambit Publications Ltd 1998. Reprinted 1998.
Copyright © John Nunn 1998
The right of John Nunn to be identified as the author of this work has been asserted in accordance with the Copyright, Designs and Patents Act 1988.

A copy of the British Library Cataloguing in Publication data is available from the British Library.

ISBN 1 901983 01 3

DISTRIBUTION:
Worldwide (except USA): Biblios Distribution Services, Star Rd, Partridge Green, West Sussex, RH13 8LD, England.
USA: BHB International, Inc., 41 Monroe Turnpike, Trumbull, CT 06611, USA.
For all other enquiries (including a full list of all Gambit Chess titles) please contact the publishers, Gambit Publications Ltd, 69 Masbro Rd, Kensington, London W14 0LS, England
Fax +44 (0)171 371 1477. E-mail 100561.3121@compuserve.com.

Edited by Graham Burgess
Typeset by John Nunn
Printed in Great Britain by Redwood Books, Trowbridge, Wilts.

10 9 8 7 6 5 4 3 2

Gambit Publications Ltd
Managing Director: GM Murray Chandler
Chess Director: GM John Nunn
Editorial Director: FM Graham Burgess
Assistant Editor: GM John Emms
German Editor: WFM Petra Nunn

Contents

Introduction   5

1 At the Board   7
  Decision-making   7
    The Tree of Analysis revisited   7
    Evaluation functions   14
    When to analyse   18
    DAUT   21
    Safety-nets   26
    When the tactics *have* to work   28
    Implicit commitments   30
    Positional thinking   34
    The method of comparison   44
    Making your opponent think   46
  Oversights and blunders   49
    Warning signals   51
    'Hard-to-see' moves   55
  Time-trouble   59
  Laziness   62
  Determination   63

2 The Opening   67
  Building a repertoire   67
  Using opening books   69
    Books on offbeat openings   70

3 The Middlegame   82
  Good positions   82
  Bad positions   88
  Attack   98
    'Inviting everyone to the party'   98
    Over-sacrificing   103
  Defence   105

4 The Endgame	112
King and Pawn endings	112
Opposition	112
The Réti manoeuvre	117
Triangulation	118
Expect the unexpected	120
Chess is more than counting	122
Rook endings	124
Rook and Pawn vs Rook	125
The extra Pawn	128
Positional advantage	135
Minor-piece endings	138
Knight endings	139
Bishop vs Knight endings	141
Bishop endings	143
Queen endings	147
Queen and Pawn vs Queen	147
The extra Pawn	152
Common endings without Pawns	155
Rook vs minor piece	155
Rook and minor piece vs Rook	158
Quick-play finishes	164
5 Using a Computer	166
Game databases	166
Playing programs	169
Index of Names	174
Index of Openings	176

Introduction

This book is aimed at players who are primarily interested in improving their results. If you are prepared to lose nine games in order to score one brilliant victory, then it is probably not for you. However, most players are motivated at least partly by over-the-board success – the thrill of winning is one of the attractions of chess, and most players feel very satisfied when their rating improves.

The level at which one plays is governed by a number of vague and poorly understood factors. The first is what one might term 'natural talent'. By this I mean that combination of factors which sets an upper bound to the level one can achieve by training and practice. One cannot list precisely which factors are relevant, but one may divide the possible factors into two classes. The first class consists of non-chess-specific elements such as general intelligence and memory. The second class involves a mesh of inter-related chess factors such as the age at which one learnt the game, early chess education and so on.

By the time anyone gets around to reading this book, the 'natural talent' factor will probably be immutable, which brings us to other factors which are more under one's control. These determine how closely one approaches the ceiling imposed by one's 'natural talent'. It is my belief that most players never get anywhere near their natural ceiling, and that considerable improvement is possible with appropriate education, training and practice. Most chess books aim to help readers improve their chess. An opening book, for example, will give general plans and concrete analysis, both to help the reader prepare his chosen openings and, after a game, to compare the course of the game with established theory. Clearly, concrete knowledge is an important factor in establishing chess strength; someone who has a detailed knowledge of rook and pawn endings will have an advantage over someone who does not. An assiduous program of self-training is bound to have a positive effect. In 1977, Jon Tisdall explained to me his plan for becoming a grandmaster. He had estimated how many hours of study were required to advance by one rating point. Multiplying this by the difference between his current rating and the grandmaster level gave the total number of hours of study required. I laughed, and pointed out that with each advance, the number of hours required to gain the next point would probably increase, and so he might never make it. However, his plan proved justified, because in 1995 he did indeed gain the grandmaster title.

There are few players who can conduct a training program stretching over decades, and indeed time limitations apply to virtually all players. In practice this restricts the amount of improvement possible on the 'chess knowledge' front. In this book I will give advice on how to use the time available for chess study most efficiently, for example by distinguishing essential knowledge from optional knowledge, and advising on the construction of an opening repertoire.

The third factor, which is the main focus of this book, is the efficiency with which one applies the first two factors while actually sitting at the board. A detailed knowledge of rook and pawn endings won't help a bit if one has an attack of blind panic; an encyclopaedic memory is valueless if one is regularly seized by an uncontrollable impulse to sacrifice a piece unsoundly. Chaotic and muddled calculation; misjudgements; oversights; lack of confidence (or overconfidence!); lack of determination – these and many other negative influences all serve to whittle away one's playing strength. Such problems are not at all easy to solve, firstly because players very often do not realize what they are doing wrong and secondly because they imagine that there is nothing they can do to improve matters.

This book includes a description of various common failings at the board. I think that many readers will reach a particular section and suddenly think "Yes, that's exactly the mistake I always make." Recognizing the problem is already the first step towards solving it. An awareness of when one is most likely to go wrong enables one to take special care in these 'danger situations'. Eventually, by concentrating on a particular weakness, it is often possible to eradicate it completely.

Since many of the matters dealt with in this book are psychological in nature, there will be quite a few examples from my own games – I can personally testify that muddled thinking occurs at grandmaster level! Where I have covered a familiar topic, I have made an effort to replace, whenever possible, the standard time-worn examples with excerpts from contemporary play.

Of course, this book, while containing much useful advice and information, cannot hope to go into detail about every aspect of the game. My aim has been merely to start the reader along the upward path of self-improvement. I hope that *Secrets of Practical Chess* will help readers to improve their results and produce more satisfying games.

John Nunn
Chertsey, 1997

1 At the Board

Decision-making

The Tree of Analysis revisited

The so-called 'Tree of Analysis' was popularized in Kotov's famous book *Think Like a Grandmaster*. The analysis of any chess position has a tree-like structure. There are various alternatives in the current position, which form the main branches. Each alternative permits a range of replies, which form slightly smaller branches, and so on. Since there are, typically, dozens of legal moves in an average chess position, a tree including every legal move rapidly becomes too dense for human beings to handle. Of course, it isn't necessary to consider every legal move, since a considerable percentage of these legal moves are nonsensical, and this tends to thin the tree somewhat. Nevertheless, even if there are only five reasonable possibilities at each ply (we will borrow a term from the computer chess world and call half a move a *ply*), after three whole moves there are 15,625 'leaves'. It follows that analysing solely by means of an analytical tree is only possible when the number of reasonable possibilities for the two players is limited – in practice this means tactical positions and certain types of endgame. However, one constructs some sort of analytical tree in thinking about almost any position; in less tactical situations, where the opponent's replies are much less predictable, one would not rely solely on the 'tree' but also take other factors into consideration.

It follows that the 'Tree of Analysis' is a very important method of chess thinking; computers have shown that it is possible to play very strongly using practically nothing else. Kotov's book described in detail the mental processes involved in concrete analysis. If we assume that White is to move, then Kotov recommended that White form a list of 'candidate moves' which he is trying to decide between, making sure that the list is complete. For each of these, White creates a list of possible replies by Black and so on, following each branch in turn until a definite evaluation can be given. Kotov specifically warned against jumping from branch to branch; he thought that you should analyse each candidate move until it can be definitely evaluated, and only then move on to the next one.

The following example, which I have taken from Colin Crouch's interesting book *Attacking Technique*, is given as an exercise. It can be solved by Kotov's method, although this does not mean to say that you will find it simple.

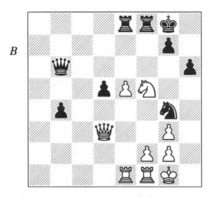

L. Psakhis – D. King
London (Lloyds Bank) 1994

Black actually blundered a piece away with **31...♘xe5??** 32 ♕xd5+ ♕e6 33 ♖xe5, but 31...♖xe5 is better. Crouch then remarks "The attempt at a tactical refutation ... with **32 ♘e7+** does not quite succeed: **32...♖xe7 33 ♖xe7 ♖xf2 34 ♕xd5+ ♔h7!** 35 ♕e4+ ♖f5+! 36 ♔h1 ♘f2+ 37 ♖xf2 ♕xf2 38 ♖f7 ♔g6 39 ♖xf5 ♕xf5 40 ♕xb4 with a draw." Your task is to choose a move after 34 ♕xd5+ *(D)* in this line. The diagram is given at the top of the next column and the solution may be found on page 14.

It is interesting to see how Kotov's method for, as he put it, teaching 'human beings to analyse with the accuracy of a machine' compares with the way machines actually calculate.

In Figure 1 we see a stage in the computer's analysis of a position, with

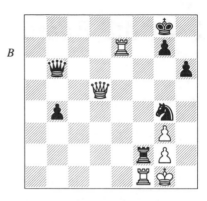

L. Psakhis – D. King *(analysis)*

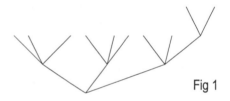

Fig 1

many branches removed for the sake of clarity. The computer analyses by a process of 'iterative deepening'. Let us suppose it is analysing a position in which it has to choose between 40 legal moves. It will analyse all legal sequences of moves to a particular depth, taking some branches deeper, especially those with forcing sequences involving checks or captures. This will allow it to attach a numerical evaluation to all the 40 possibilities. Based on its evaluation, it will re-order the 40 moves to put the most promising ones (i.e. those with the highest evaluation) first. Then it will go one ply deeper, again analysing all possible legal sequences, and devoting more time to those moves early in the list.

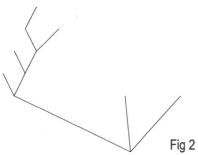

Fig 2

Figure 2 shows a human being analysing according to Kotov's recipe. He has listed three candidate moves and is in the process of analysing the first of these. He has not started analysing the other two.

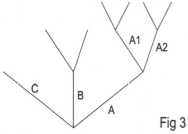

Fig 3

Figure 3 shows how a human actually thinks. He has started analysing move A and discovered line A1. He wasn't especially impressed by it, so switched to analysing move B. He didn't like that move either, so he returned to his analysis of A, adding line A2 to his earlier efforts. He has either not got around to move C, or has simply forgotten about it.

More recent authors, such as Tisdall (see the Introduction!) in *Improve*

Your Chess Now, have discussed the pros and cons of Kotov's recommendations, but my concern is to give practical advice and not to get involved in an academic discussion.

There are several problems which can arise as a result of Kotov's method. The most obvious is that it can be extremely inefficient. Let us suppose that you are analysing a possible combination 1 ♗xh7+ ♔xh7 2 ♘g5+. There are two defences, 2...♔g6 and 2...♔g8. You start analysing 2...♔g6; it is very complicated, but after twenty minutes you decide that White has the advantage. Then you start looking at 2...♔g8. After a couple of minutes it becomes obvious that this refutes the sacrifice. The upshot of Kotov's inflexible approach is that you have lost twenty minutes' thinking time, solely on account of the bad luck of having chosen the wrong move to analyse first. A more rational approach would be to spend a couple of minutes looking at each of the two alternatives. It is possible that this will reveal one of them to refute the sacrifice, at which point ♗xh7+ can be abandoned. It is also possible that the preliminary analysis will show one of them to be a clear-cut loss, in which case you can switch attention to the other one in the confidence that it is definitely the critical line. If both are unresolvable within a short time, then this is in itself useful information. It shows that the task of determining whether the sacrifice is sound or not will require a substantial time investment. Then the decision is really whether it is worthwhile putting in the effort to analyse deeper. We will revisit this question of whether or not to analyse in the next section.

A second problem with Kotov's method is that it fails to take into account the synergistic effect of analysing several lines. The analysis of move A and that of move B are very often not independent of one another. Suppose you have rejected move A, but when analysing move B you suddenly notice a tactical possibility. It makes sense to return to move A to see if the same possibility is applicable there.

Here is a simple example:

J. Gunst
Das Illustrierte Blatt, 1922

Clearly White has to move his bishop, so there are three possibilities. You look at 1 ♗xd7, and note that 1...♚c7 wins one of the two minor pieces by a fork. The next move is 1 ♗b7, but this leads to the same result after 1...♚c7. Finally, there is 1 ♗a6, which avoids the king fork, but after 1...♚c7 White nevertheless must lose a piece, as the knight is now trapped. This is all in accordance with Kotov's method. While looking at this last line, however, you notice a surprising point: after 1 ♗a6 ♚c7 White can try 2 ♚c5!?, with the idea that 2...♚xb8 3 ♚d6 ♚a8 4 ♚c7 leads to mate by 5 ♗b7#. Having spotted this, it is certainly worth noting that it might be possible to utilize it in the previously analysed lines. This jumping back is not in accordance with Kotov's method. Sure enough, after 1 ♗b7 ♚c7 White can play 2 ♗a6, and again Black cannot take the knight.

So which line is correct? The answer is that 1 ♗a6 ♚c7 2 ♚c5 fails to 2...d6+ 3 ♚d5 ♚xb8, and now 4 ♚xd6 ♚a8 5 ♚c7 is stalemate. White must prevent Black giving up his d-pawn, and so 1 ♗b7! ♚c7 2 ♗a6! is the right line (2...d6 allows the knight out).

Spotting a new idea may even cause you to change your list of candidate moves. Here is an example *(D)*:

White has just played 19 ♖g1-g5. Black was threatening 19...♘d3+ followed by 20...♘c5+, but now this threat is nullified, because on the discovered check White can take on f5. Moreover, 20 ♖xf5 gxf5 21 ♖g1 is a serious threat.

My initial thought was the safety-first 19...e6, but after 20 hxg6 fxg6 21 ♖dg1 the position is just unclear, so I

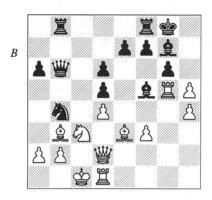

A. Kuligowski – J. Nunn
Wijk aan Zee 1983

started looking for alternatives. My eye was suddenly caught by a tactical idea. After 19...♗h6 the most obvious reply is 20 ♖xf5, but then I wondered if some combination of ...♗xe3 and ...♘xa2+ might force mate. After some thought I established that 20...♘xa2+! 21 ♘xa2 (21 ♗xa2 ♗xe3) 21...♕xb3 22 ♗xh6 ♕xa2 wins for Black, and concluded that after 19...♗h6 White would have to sacrifice the exchange on g5. The resulting positions appeared to give Black some advantage. The game continued:

19...♗h6! 20 ♖dg1 ♗xg5 21 ♖xg5 e6 22 hxg6 fxg6 23 h5?!

After 23 ♕g2 ♖f6 24 h5 White would have had better chances of counterplay, although Black retains a large advantage with 24...♘c2.

23...♖b7 24 ♕g2 ♖g7 25 h6 ♖b7 26 ♖xf5 exf5 27 ♕xg6+ ♔h8 28 ♕g2

After 28 ♗g5 ♕xd4 Black defends.

28...f4 29 ♗g1 ♖g8 0-1

However, having noticed the possibility of ...♘xa2+ in the variation with ...♗h6, I should have gone back to see if this affected my list of candidate moves. The key point is that the capture on a2 becomes possible once the white queen no longer guards b2, and so the move 19...♗c2!! *(D)* springs to mind:

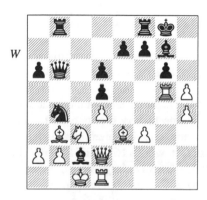

White is now completely helpless, for example:

1) 20 ♘xd5 ♘xa2+ 21 ♔xc2 ♕xb3+ 22 ♔b1 ♖b7 23 hxg6 f5 wins for Black.

2) 20 ♖dg1 ♘xa2+ 21 ♘xa2 ♕xb3 22 ♕xc2 ♕xa2 is also decisive.

3) 20 hxg6 ♘xa2+ 21 ♔xc2 (21 ♘xa2 ♗xb3) 21...♕xb3+ 22 ♔d3 ♘xc3 23 bxc3 ♕c4+ 24 ♔c2 ♕a2+ 25 ♔d3 ♖b2 wins the queen.

There are also some types of chess calculation which have nothing to do with the 'Tree of Analysis'. One of these is the 'goal-seeking' approach. Here is an example:

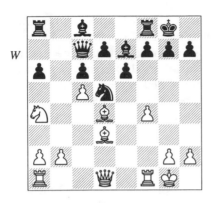

G. Kuzmin – E. Sveshnikov
USSR Ch, Moscow 1973

The position seems tailor-made for a double bishop sacrifice on h7 and g7, the only problem being that it doesn't work: 16 ♗xh7+ ♔xh7 17 ♕h5+ ♔g8 18 ♗xg7 ♔xg7 19 ♕g4+ ♔h7 20 ♖f3 (of course White can give perpetual check) 20...♘xf4 21 ♖xf4 f5 defends. In order to win, White has to isolate the element that makes the sacrifice fail (i.e. the possibility of ...♘xf4) and ask a 'What if...' question, in this case 'What if I could deflect the knight away from d5?'. Then the solution becomes obvious:

16 ♘b6! ♘xb6

It does not help if Black moves his rook, for example 16...♖b8 17 ♘xd5 cxd5 18 ♗xh7+ ♔xh7 19 ♕h5+ ♔g8 20 ♗xg7 ♕xc5+ 21 ♔h1 ♔xg7 22 ♕g4+ ♔h8 23 ♖f3 ♕c2 24 f5! ♕xf5 25 ♖xf5 exf5 26 ♕h3+ (had Black played 16...♖a7, White would now have 26 ♕d4+) followed by ♕g3+ and the rook on b8 falls.

17 ♗xh7+ ♔xh7 18 ♕h5+ ♔g8 19 ♗xg7 ♔xg7 20 ♕g4+ ♔h7 21 ♖f3 1-0

You can never find a move like 16 ♘b6! by using the tree of analysis (unless you are a computer) because it makes absolutely no sense except as part of the whole tactical operation, and therefore will not make it onto your list of 'candidate moves'.

Here is a more sophisticated example.

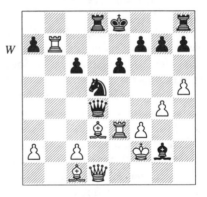

V. Anand – J. Lautier
Biel 1997

There are so many pieces hanging that it takes a few moments to grasp what is going on in this position! White is set to lose the exchange on e3, but the bishop on g2 is trapped, so it looks as if the most likely outcome is a position with, for example, two bishops against a rook and two pawns. However, Anand had an imaginative tactical idea, namely to sacrifice his queen with the astonishing move 20 ♗g6. Unfortunately, after 20 ♗g6 ♕xd1 21 ♖xe6+ Black can just run with his king by 21...♔f8 22 ♗a3+ (22 ♖xf7+ ♔g8) 22...♘e7 23 ♗xe7+ ♔g8 and White is losing. Now White can ask 'What if I had a pawn on h6?'. Then the line with ♖xf7+ would lead to mate as ♖xg7+ followed by ♗a3+ would be possible.

20 h6!! gxh6?

Black apparently hadn't seen Anand's idea at all, or he would have tried 20...♘xe3, although White retains the advantage after 21 ♗xe3 ♕e5 22 hxg7 ♖g8 23 ♕c1!. Of course, the variation 20...g6 21 ♗xg6 represents the fulfilment of White's idea.

21 ♗g6!! ♘e7

Now that h6 is available for White's bishop, the line 21...♕xd1 22 ♖xe6+ ♔f8 23 ♗xh6+ ♔g8 24 ♗xf7# ends in mate.

22 ♕xd4 ♖xd4 23 ♖d3! ♖d8 24 ♖xd8+ ♔xd8 25 ♗d3! 1-0

The tree of analysis is certainly a useful technique in tactical positions, but it should be used flexibly and supplemented by other types of chess thinking. One has to strike a balance between the rigid application of Kotov's principles and jumping from one variation to another too much. In particular, I favour the 'quick scan' approach, looking briefly at all the major lines to see if any can be quickly resolved. With any luck, this will be enough to settle the analysis; if not, at least you know where the tricky areas lie.

The most common errors in 'tree' analysis are:

1) Forgetting to analyse a move completely. This is surprisingly easy to do. After spending twenty minutes analysing defences A and B to your intended sacrifice, you decide that it is sound and play it. The instant your hand has left the piece you remember defence C, which you had noticed but not analysed.

2) Confusing similar lines. If you are jumping about a lot between rather similar variations, then it is easy to get mixed up as to which position came from which line. In other words, although you have the positions clear in your mind, the links between them which form the branches of the 'tree' have become muddled. You may need to start rebuilding the 'tree' in your mind from scratch when this happens.

While a certain amount of mental discipline can greatly increase the efficiency of your tactical analysis, a great deal still depends on 'natural talent'. It would be quite easy to overlook the whole idea of ♗g6 in the Anand-Lautier position above, and in this case a wonderfully organized tree of variations will not help you. But then, Lautier missed it too, so at least you would not be alone.

Now we return to the exercise on page 8. Here is the diagram again:

B

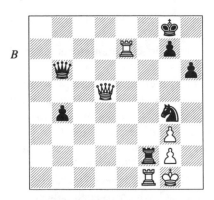

L. Psakhis – D. King (analysis)

Crouch's 34...♔h7 is actually the weakest of the three king moves, and leads to a draw, as in his analysis.

Initially I thought that 34...♔h8 was winning, since any check on the eighth rank is met by ...♖f8+, and otherwise White has no defence to the threats against his king. However, Fritz found an incredible defence: 35 ♖e8+ ♖f8+ 36 ♔h1 ♖xe8? 37 ♖f8+! ♖xf8 (after 37...♔h7 38 ♕f5+ Black is worse) 38 ♕g8+! forcing stalemate. Therefore, Black would have to play 36...♘f2+ 37 ♖xf2 ♖xe8, with a large advantage although no forced win.

The final move, 34...♔f8, is actually the strongest and leads to a forced win for Black, although it appears the least likely move because it self-pins the f2-rook. White can only try 35 ♖e2 ♖f6+ 36 ♖ff2 (36 ♖ef2 ♖xf2 37 ♕a8+ ♔e7 38 ♕e4+ ♔f6 wins) 36...♖xf2 37 ♕a8+, but there is no perpetual check: 37...♔f7 38 ♕e8+ (38 ♕d5+ ♔f6) 38...♔f6 39 ♕e7+ (39 ♕f8+ ♔g6)

39...♔f5 40 ♕f7+ (40 ♕d7+ ♔g5) 40...♔g5 41 ♕xg7+ ♔h5 winning.

Evaluation functions

When computers analyse a position, they create a tree of analysis, and then use a rather crude evaluation function to assess the position at the end of every branch. Then, by working backwards, they can evaluate the current position and establish what they consider to be the optimal line of play. If a computer had a perfectly accurate evaluation function, then it would not need to analyse the position more than one ply ahead – it could simply evaluate the position after each legal move and choose the one with the highest evaluation. The effect of analysis is to increase the accuracy of the fairly primitive evaluation function.

Humans tend to analyse in a different way, but they still use an evaluation function. While they may not think they have an advantage of 0.32 pawns, it is quite normal to think 'Well, at the end of this line I have a slight/fair/clear/crushing advantage.' After looking at various lines the human decides on the best. This process is rather similar to that performed by the computer.

However, the human also typically uses an evaluation function in a different way. If you think that you have an advantage in the current position, then you automatically reject moves which allow your opponent total equality.

This type of reasoning is very common and is extremely useful in rapidly cutting down the number of moves that you have to consider, but it also has its dangers. It is almost the reverse of the computer's logic; instead of using the analysis to evaluate the position, the 'evaluation' is used to prune the analysis tree. However, because the initial 'evaluation' is not based on concrete analysis of the current position, it is inherently unreliable. Typically, players simply carry over their evaluation from the preceding move and use it as a starting point for the next one. If the evaluation is inaccurate, then all kinds of odd things can start to happen. Suppose you have three possible moves, A, B and C, and believe that you have the advantage. You analyse A and decide that it leads to equality; B the same. You then conclude that C must be the correct move with very little analysis. If the position is in fact equal, then C may actually lead to a disadvantage, although you do not realize this immediately. Then, because you tend to carry over evaluations from one move to the next, you repeat this exercise in defective logic the next move. The upshot is a whole string of inaccurate moves; this is, in fact, what commonly known as 'losing the thread of the game'. If you experience 'losing the thread', try afterwards to trace the problem back to its root cause; surprisingly often, the source of the error was a faulty evaluation.

Y. Seirawan – J. Nunn
Brussels World Cup 1988
King's Indian Defence

1 d4 ♘f6 2 c4 g6 3 ♘c3 ♗g7 4 e4 d6 5 f3 0-0 6 ♗e3 ♘c6 7 ♘ge2 a6 8 d5 ♘e5 9 ♘g3 c6 10 a4 cxd5 11 cxd5 e6 12 ♗e2 exd5 13 exd5 ♖e8 *(D)*

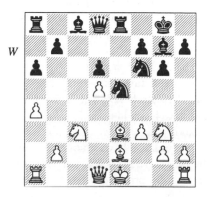

I was very happy with the result of the opening. It seemed to me that 8 d5 was premature, giving Black a target to aim at with ...c6 and ...e6. In the diagram position, I felt that the move f3 was not only a loss of time, but even served to weaken White's dark squares, especially e3. It is thanks to this that White cannot castle (allowing the e3-bishop to be exchanged by ...♘c4 and ...♘e3 would really be bad for White). Therefore I assessed the position as slightly better for Black, but this was just wrong. Perhaps White has not played the opening in optimal style, but a small inaccuracy by White is not enough to hand Black the advantage; he has equalized, but no more.

14 ♕d2

Not unexpected, since 14 0-0 ♘c4 is bad (as mentioned above) and 14 ♔f2 ♕c7 15 ♕b3 (preventing ...♘c4) 15...♕e7! creates unpleasant pressure along the e-file.

14...♕e7

My first thought was to continue 14...♕c7 15 0-0 ♘c4 16 ♗xc4 ♕xc4, but then I saw that White could more or less force a draw by 17 ♘ge4 ♘xe4 (17...♕b4 18 ♘xf6+ ♗xf6 19 ♘e4 ♕xb2 20 ♖ab1 ♕e5 21 ♗f4 ♕d4+ 22 ♔h1 even favours White) 18 ♘xe4 ♕b3! 19 ♗d4! ♕xd5 20 ♖fd1 ♕xd4+ 21 ♕xd4 ♗xd4+ 22 ♖xd4 ♖e7 23 ♘xd6.

I could also have simply developed by 14...♗d7 15 0-0 ♖c8, but once again this hardly promises Black more than equality.

15 ♔f2

Of course 15 0-0? ♘c4! and 15 ♗d4?! ♘c4 are fine for Black, but the fact that White had to play this artificial-looking king move seemed to justify my earlier assessment. I was now quite excited about various tactical possibilities involving a bishop or knight moving to g4, but at the moment no such idea is effective.

15...h5

Continuing my plan to 'punish' White for his opening play. Since there was no immediate tactical blow, the only way to keep the momentum going seemed to be by pushing the h-pawn.

16 ♖he1 *(D)*

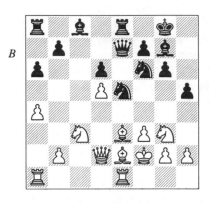

The rook emerges so that it will not be blocked in when the knight has to retreat.

16...h4 17 ♘f1

After 17 ♘ge4 ♘h7 (17...♘eg4+!? 18 fxg4 ♘xe4+ 19 ♘xe4 ♕xe4 20 ♗f3 ♕c4 is also possible) 18 ♔g1 f5 White has to retreat with loss of time.

17...♘h5? *(D)*

Up to this point Black has not made any real error, but now his desire to play for the advantage leads him badly astray. Originally I intended 17...h3, thinking that after 18 g4 there would be some combination based on taking the g4-pawn. Now I discovered that there was no such combination. I became frustrated by my inability to find a continuation consistent with my earlier active play. The result was the very weak text-move, based on a trap which doesn't even work!

The right plan was 17...♘h7 (preventing ♗g5) 18 f4 ♘g4+ 19 ♗xg4 ♗xg4 20 ♗d4 ♗xd4+ (20...♕f8 21 ♘e3 favours White) 21 ♕xd4 ♕f6 22 ♕xf6 ♘xf6 leading to a roughly equal ending, but of course this was not acceptable to me.

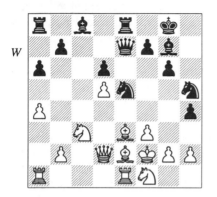

W

18 ♔g1

After 18 ♗g5, I intended the pawn sacrifice 18...♕c7 19 ♗xh4 ♕c5+ 20 ♘e3 ♗h6 21 ♘e4 ♘g4+ 22 fxg4 ♖xe4, but after 23 ♗f3 ♖d4 24 ♕c3 Black is struggling to find any compensation for the pawn. Perhaps 19...♕b6+ 20 ♘e3 ♗h6 is better, but even so 21 ♘cd1 is unclear. In fact the mundane 18...♗f6 19 ♗xf6 ♕xf6 20 ♘e4 ♕e7 is probably best.

18...h3

Now 18...♗d7?! is bad after 19 ♗g5! ♗f6 20 f4 ♗xg5 21 fxg5 ♘g7 22 ♘e4, heading for f6 so, to avoid losing the h4-pawn to ♗g5, the pawn has to advance.

19 g4

Cutting off the h3-pawn.

19...♘f6

The sacrifice 19...♘xg4 20 fxg4 ♗xc3 21 bxc3 ♕e4 is refuted by 22 ♗f3! ♕xf3 23 gxh5, so the knight has to retreat with loss of time.

20 ♗d4

Threatening 21 f4.

20...♕f8 21 ♘g3 ♘h7 22 g5

Sealing the h7-knight out of play.

22...f6 23 f4 ♘g4 24 ♘ce4 ♗d7
(D)

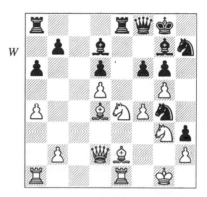

W

White now made the very weak move 25 gxf6?, which allowed the dead knight on h7 back into the game; after many complications the game ended in a draw.

Had Seirawan continued 25 ♕d1 f5 26 ♗xg7 ♕xg7 27 ♗xg4 fxg4 28 ♕d2 then Black would have been in trouble. The d6-pawn is under fire and the h7-knight can only emerge in the distant future. Even the solid 25 ♖f1 would have given White a clear advantage.

In this example the chain of events was: a bad assessment of the position, resulting in over-ambitious play by Black; then avoidance of drawing lines, leading to the awful 17...♘h5?. Black only got back on track after his position had severely deteriorated.

When to analyse

One question which Kotov did not really cover is whether to analyse at all, or how much to analyse. Yet this is of great practical importance. One might end up playing better moves if one could analyse for an unlimited time, but games played before the introduction of chess clocks (and some postal games) show that this is not necessarily the case. Too much analysis can easily lead to fatigue and confusion. These days the tendency is towards faster and faster time-limits, and this means that apportioning one's thinking time becomes ever more crucial.

When analysing a given position, it is fair to say that one almost always sees more in the first five minutes than in the next five minutes. The five minutes after that is even less productive, and so on. I have observed that if a player spends more than 20 minutes over a move, the result is almost always a mistake. The normal decision-making process should not take longer than this, even in fairly complex situations. There will, of course, always be exceptions to any such empirical law, but in this case they are fairly rare. If a player takes a long time over a move, the reason is usually either indecision or inability to find a satisfactory continuation. It is very unusual for the position to be so complicated that it really demands more than 20 minutes' thought.

If you have thought about a position for some time and are still unsure what to play, then it is essential to be ruthlessly pragmatic. You have to ask yourself whether further thought is really going to help you make a better decision. Suppose your lengthy cogitation is the result of indecision; for example, say there are two moves, both of which have roughly equal merit. If you have not been able to decide between them up to now, it is reasonable to suppose that there is in fact little to choose between them. Considerable further thought might eventually reveal some tiny difference, but it is rare that this expenditure of time is worthwhile. First of all, it is easy to be wrong when dealing with such fine distinctions and secondly, gaining an infinitesimal advantage is of little value if the result is that you run into time-trouble and blunder away a piece. Games are decided by very small advantages far less often than is usually supposed. There are players, such as Capablanca and Karpov, with the ability to convert a small advantage into a win on a regular basis, but this talent is rare even amongst grandmasters. Games in which the players make errors and the advantage swings back and forth are far more common; in the end the decision comes about as a result of a serious mistake. My advice is to obey your instinctive feeling as to which of the two moves is better or, if you don't have any preference, just choose at random. I have occasionally been tempted to toss a coin at the board, but despite the undoubted psychological impact on the opponent, this does seem rather unsporting.

If you are unable to find a satisfactory continuation, then once again it usually does not help to think on and on hoping for a miracle. Of course, if it is a question of coming up with something or resigning, then you may as well continue, but this is uncommon. Usually, you are better off playing what appears to be the least unfavourable continuation and saving the time for accurate defence and possible counterplay later on. It is worth noting that if you are generally unhappy with your position, then this might well be colouring your assessments. Before choosing a move, it is probably worth having a quick review of the alternatives and the reasons why you deemed them unsatisfactory, to see if they are really as bad as you imagine. It is not unusual suddenly to find that your intended equal continuation is slightly worse for you; you then look at more and more unfavourable possibilities, become deeply depressed about your position, and forget that the first line you looked at wasn't actually all that bad.

Another common time-waster is instinctively to want to play a certain move and then to spend a long time trying to back up this intuitive feeling with concrete analysis. Don't do this. If your intuition is telling you strongly to play move X, then you will probably play it in the end anyway and further thought is only going to waste time. The situation which represents the worst of all worlds is when you want to play X, but can't find any objective reason for doing so; then you analyse and analyse until you find some half-baked and dubious reason why X is a good move. Then you end up playing a dubious move *and* spending a lot of time. However, it is usually worthwhile spending a few minutes trying to find something concrete *wrong* with your intuitive choice, because positional intuition doesn't insure against the possibility that it might be bad for tactical reasons. If, during these few minutes you don't find anything wrong, then you should just play the move.

The following game is a successful example of playing (almost!) without calculation.

J. Nunn – P. van der Sterren
Bundesliga 1995/6
Ruy Lopez

1 e4 e5 2 ♘f3 ♘c6 3 ♗b5 a6 4 ♗a4 ♘f6 5 0-0 ♗e7 6 ♖e1 b5 7 ♗b3 d6 8 c3 0-0 9 d3 ♘a5 10 ♗c2 c5 11 ♘bd2 ♖e8 12 ♘f1 h6 13 ♘g3 ♗f8 14 d4 exd4 15 cxd4 cxd4 16 ♘xd4 ♗b7 17 b3 d5 18 e5 ♘e4 (D)

Black's inferior handling of the opening has left him with an offside knight on a5. The idea of ...d5 and ...♘e4 is to offer a pawn in order to free his position.

W

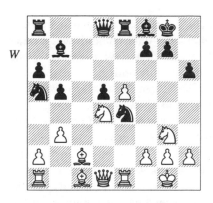

19 ♗b2

I did consider taking the pawn by 19 ♘xe4 dxe4 20 ♗xe4 ♗xe4 21 ♖xe4 ♕d5 22 ♕e2 (but not 22 ♕g4 ♖xe5 23 ♖xe5 ♕xe5 24 ♗xh6 f5 25 ♕f4 ♗d6 26 ♕xe5 ♗xe5 27 ♗e3 f4 and Black wins) but I instinctively didn't like it. White's pieces are badly tangled up, while Black's development problems are solved. It seemed to me that it would be very hard to put the extra pawn to good use in such a position. Looking back on it, I think this line would also have been somewhat better for White, since Black still has trouble using his knight effectively. The more dynamic game continuation is at least as good, and presents Black with difficult decisions.

In general, White would be quite happy for Black to exchange knights on g3, as then he would have an automatic attack by ♕d3 (meeting ...g6 by e6). However, I was not prepared to spend a tempo on forcing it by playing 19 f3. Moreover, this move both weakens the a7-g1 diagonal and blocks the

d1-h5 diagonal, along which White might like to move his queen.

19...♕b8

After 19...♖xe5 20 f3 ♗b4 21 fxe4 ♗xe1 22 ♕xe1 ♕b6 23 ♔h1 White has a large advantage since an assault on g7 is not far away.

The text-move was unexpected, but the point is clear: if White takes three times on e4, then Black just plays ...♖xe5.

20 e6

A key moment. I thought for a few minutes about the direct 20 ♕g4, when Black has almost no choice but to play 20...♕xe5. Then it looks as though there must be a tactical possibility using the long diagonal, but I could only see one idea: 21 ♘df5 ♕xb2 22 ♘xh6+ ♔h7 23 ♘xf7 ♕xc2 24 ♖xe4 dxe4 25 ♘g5+, followed by ♕h5. However, even a quick glance is enough to show that the analysis of this line will be very complicated: in the middle Black can try 24...♖xe4, or he may decline the second piece and play, for example, 23...♕f6.

Here is a case in which a quick scan of the other possibilities is much better than the twenty minutes or so which would have been required to assess this double piece sacrifice. I first looked at 20 ♘gf5 ♖xe5 21 ♕g4 g6, but there seemed to be nothing clear. Then the text-move occurred to me and I was at once attracted to it. After 20...fxe6 21 ♘xe4 dxe4 22 ♗xe4 ♗xe4 23 ♖xe4 Black has a miserable position; the e6-pawn is weak, the a5-knight remains offside and White can step up his pressure with natural moves such as ♕g4 and ♖ae1. Best of all, it is simple and risk-free.

Home analysis shows that the double piece sacrifice leads to a draw: after 25 ♘g5+ ♔g8 26 ♕h5 in the above line, Black can respond 26...e3! and White has nothing more than perpetual check.

20...♕f4

Another rather unexpected move.

21 ♘xe4 dxe4 22 g3

Again a simple choice. In order to avoid losing the pawn on e4, Black's queen must move onto the long diagonal, but then White has various tactical ideas based on moving the d4-knight.

22...♕e5

After 22...♕f6 23 ♕d2 b4 24 ♗xe4 Black will be lucky to escape with only the loss of a pawn.

23 ♕g4

It is important to take into account any finesse which might make the win easier. Here White has the choice between 23 ♕e2 and 23 ♕g4 h5 24 ♕e2. The latter is clearly superior for two reasons. Firstly the protruding pawn on h5 is a weakness, as it will be undefended; secondly, the weakening of the g5-square may allow White to occupy it later with his knight, creating a permanent danger to Black's king. This is an example of the method of comparison (page 44).

23...h5

There is nothing better. 23...♗b4 24 ♖e2 is no different, while 23...fxe6 24

♗xe4 ♗xe4 25 ♖xe4 ♕f6 26 ♖f4! ♕g5 27 ♕xg5 hxg5 28 ♖e4 is similar to the game, but with Black's kingside pawns even weaker.

24 ♕e2 fxe6 25 ♗xe4 ♕xe4 26 ♕xe4 ♗xe4 27 ♖xe4

An ideal outcome. Black will inevitably lose the e6-pawn within a couple of moves (e.g. 27...♔f7 28 ♖ae1 ♗b4 29 ♖f4+) and he remains with an offside knight.

27...♖ac8

If White takes on e6 immediately, then this rook will penetrate to c2. However, there is no rush.

28 ♖ae1

Threatening to take twice on e6 with the rooks, thereby leaving the d4-knight to cover c2.

28...♗b4 29 ♖1e2 ♗c3 30 ♗xc3 ♖xc3 31 ♖xe6 1-0

This may appear a little premature, but Black will lose the a6-pawn as well, and there is no point continuing with two pawns less.

DAUT

This acronym means: if in doubt, 'Don't Analyse Unnecessary Tactics'.

Tactical analysis is an error-prone activity. Overlooking one important finesse can completely change the result of the analysis. If it is possible to decide on your move on purely positional considerations then you should do so; it is quicker and more reliable. There are, of course, many positions in which concrete analysis is essential, but even in these cases you should not analyse specific variations more than necessary.

The following example is a marginal case.

J. Nunn – M. Přibyl
Bundesliga 1995/6
Giuoco Piano

1 e4 e5 2 ♘f3 ♘c6 3 ♗c4 ♘f6 4 d3 ♗c5 5 0-0 d6 6 c3 0-0 7 ♘bd2 a6 8 ♗b3 ♗a7 9 h3 ♘d7 10 ♗c2 f5 11 exf5 ♖xf5 12 d4 ♖f8

Black has played the opening in a rather provocative manner, aiming to open the f-file and create counterplay by attacking f2. However, the cost has been retarded development.

13 ♘e4

After 13 d5 ♘e7 14 ♘g5 ♘f6 15 ♘de4 ♘f5 White has secure control over e4, which would warm the heart of anyone who plays against the King's Indian. Unfortunately for White, the black bishop is on a7 rather than g7, and the pressure on f2 gives Black reasonable counterplay.

13...exd4 *(D)*

With quite a few of White's pieces pointing at Black's naked kingside, there is clearly potential for a forcing continuation, but which move should he choose? 14 ♘eg5, 14 ♘fg5, 14 ♗b3+ and 14 ♗g5 are all reasonable continuations. I would regard this as a borderline case for deciding whether to spend the time to analyse everything thoroughly. The position does

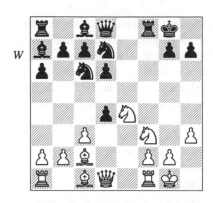

indeed look promising on purely strategic grounds, but the wide range of moves at White's disposal indicates that a complete analysis will be very time-consuming.

In the end I decided on a straightforward forcing continuation which gives White a slight positional advantage. In fact White could have secured a larger advantage by another line, but that is the risk one takes in making a decision not to look too deeply into a position. However, I would certainly have taken my time had there not been an advantageous alternative.

14 ♘eg5

Here is an analysis of the other possibilities:

1) 14 ♗g5 ♕e8 15 ♖e1 ♘de5 16 ♘xd4 ♗xh3! 17 gxh3 ♗xd4 18 cxd4 ♘f3+ 19 ♔g2 ♘xe1+ 20 ♕xe1 ♘xd4 and Black is slightly better.

2) 14 ♕d3 ♘ce5 15 ♘xe5 ♘xe5 16 ♘f6+ ♕xf6 17 ♕xh7+ ♔f7 defends.

3) 14 ♗b3+ ♔h8 15 ♘fg5 ♕e7 (not 15...♘de5 16 ♘xh7!) 16 ♘e6 (16

♕h5 g6 17 ♕h6 ♘f6 and 16 ♘xh7 ♕xe4 17 ♘xf8 ♘xf8 18 ♕h5+ ♘h7 19 ♕f7 ♗xh3 20 gxh3 dxc3 are fine for Black) 16...♘f6 17 ♘xf8 ♕xe4 18 ♖e1 ♕h4 19 ♘e6 dxc3 and Black has two pawns for the exchange – the position is unclear.

4) 14 ♘fg5! and now:

4a) 14...d5 15 ♘e6 (15 ♕h5 h6 16 ♘e6 is also good) 15...♕e7 16 ♘4g5 ♘f6 17 ♘xf8 wins the exchange.

4b) 14...♘de5 15 ♘xh7! ♖f5 16 ♘eg5 d3 17 ♗b3+ (17 ♗xd3 ♘xd3 18 ♕xd3 is unclear as the knights have no way back from their advanced positions) 17...d5 18 g4! ♖f7 19 ♘xf7 ♘xf7 20 ♕xd3 ♘ce5 21 ♕xd5 ♕xd5 22 ♗xd5 ♔xh7 23 ♖e1 and now, with ♖+2♙ vs 2♘, White has the better ending.

4c) 14...dxc3 15 ♕h5 (15 ♘e6 ♕e7 16 ♘xf8 cxb2 17 ♗xb2 ♘xf8 is unclear) 15...h6 16 ♕g6 with a decisive attack.

4d) 14...h6 15 ♘e6 ♕e7 16 ♘xf8 ♘xf8 17 ♖e1 ♗e6 and Black has a pawn and a slight lead in development for the exchange, but this does not provide sufficient compensation.

14...♘f6 15 ♕d3 g6

After 15...h6 16 ♘h7 ♖e8 17 ♕g6 White has a winning attack, so this move is forced. However, the weakening of the dark squares around Black's king is serious when his dark-squared bishop is far away on the queenside.

16 ♘xd4 ♘xd4 17 cxd4 d5

This is almost forced, or else Black cannot complete his development, for example 17...♗f5 fails to 18 ♕b3+ and 19 ♗xf5. Now, however, 18...♗f5 is a threat.

18 ♘xh7! (D)

Definitely best. The net effect of this is to exchange the h7- and d4-pawns, further eroding the defences of the black king.

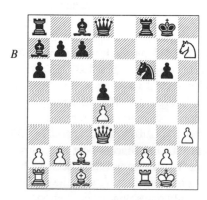

18...♗f5

Not 18...♔xh7 19 ♕xg6+ ♔h8 20 ♗g5 with a decisive attack, for example 20...♕e7 21 ♖ae1 ♕g7 22 ♗xf6 ♖xf6 23 ♖e8+ ♖f8 24 ♖xf8+ ♕xf8 25 ♕h7#.

19 ♘xf6+ ♕xf6

Forced, as 19...♖xf6 20 ♕b3 ♗xc2 21 ♕xc2 ♗xd4 22 ♗g5 costs the exchange.

20 ♕b3 ♗xc2 21 ♕xc2 ♗xd4 22 ♗h6 ♖f7 23 ♖ad1

This position is the almost forced consequence of White's decision at move 14. The immediate threat is 24 ♖xd4, and the d4-bishop is pinned against the d5-pawn.

23...♖h7? (D)

A serious error, which costs Black the game immediately. Other moves:

1) 23...♔h7 24 ♗e3 ♗xe3 25 fxe3 ♕e7 26 ♖xf7+ ♕xf7 27 e4 dxe4 28 ♕xe4 is unpleasant for Black. The b7-pawn is attacked, and White threatens both 29 ♖f1 and 29 ♕g4, followed by 30 ♖d7.

2) 23...c5 24 ♗e3 ♗xe3 25 fxe3 ♕c6 26 ♖xf7 ♔xf7 27 e4! d4 (White wins a pawn after 27...dxe4 28 ♖f1+ ♔g7 29 ♕c3+ ♔g8 30 ♖f6 ♕e8 31 ♕c4+ ♔g7 32 ♖e6 ♕d7 33 ♕xe4 ♕d4+ 34 ♕xd4+ cxd4 35 ♖d6) 28 ♕c4+ ♔g7 29 b4! with strong pressure.

3) 23...♗xb2 24 ♖xd5 ♖e8 25 ♖fd1 ♗e5 is Black's best line. However, I still prefer White because his king is completely safe, while Black's has only one pawn for protection.

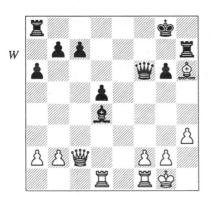

Here is a case in which it most definitely is worthwhile looking for a forced win! After the sacrifice on d4 Black will have no pawns at all defending his king. White only needs to switch his bishop to the long diagonal, or bring his rook into the attack, and the game will be over. The lines are quite straightforward and forcing, so there is little possibility of error.

24 ♖xd4! ♕xd4 25 ♕xg6+ ♔h8 26 ♖e1

Black is helpless against the threat of 27 ♖e8+.

26...♖d7

The only way to limp on. Now White can win two pawns by 27 ♖e8+ ♖xe8 28 ♕xe8+ ♔h7 29 ♕xd7+ ♔xh6 30 ♕xc7, but Black has a passed d-pawn and in a queen ending a strong passed pawn can counter-balance the loss of several pawns. At any rate, White would have to take care, so it is worth looking for a killer move.

27 ♕h5! ♕d3

There are simply too many threats. 27...♔g8 28 ♖e3 is hopeless, and after 27...♕c4 28 ♗f4+ ♔g8 29 ♖e8+ White wins the black rook for nothing.

28 ♖e6

Once the rook enters the attack it is all over.

28...♖g8 29 ♗g7+! ♔xg7 30 ♕h6+ 1-0

It is mate next move.

Quite apart from the possibility of miscalculation, there are psychological traps lying in wait for the avid calculator. Suppose that, in a slightly favourable position, you see a sharp and complicated line; it takes you half an hour to investigate all the variations which may arise, but you discover that the upshot is at best 'unclear'. It is then incredibly hard to write your analysis off as a waste of time and start thinking about alternative ideas. Eventually you convince yourself to play the tactical line with an argument like 'well, he probably won't find his way through all the complications, and even then he doesn't have any advantage'. Thus you end up playing a move which is objectively not the best, and it is amazing how often one's opponent does indeed find his way through the complications once they have been forced on him.

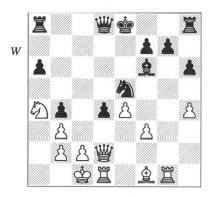

V. Anand – G. Kamsky
Linares 1994

In this position a great deal depends on White's mobile e- and f-pawns. If he can set them moving by f4 and e5, gaining tempi with both moves, then Black will be dead lost. At the moment, however, Black threatens a fork on f3.

Anand decided that forcing through f4 and e5 was so important that he was prepared to sacrifice the rook on g1 to achieve it. The game continued with the complex tactical variation 19 f4! ♘f3 20 ♕g2 ♘xg1 21 e5 0-0 22 ♗d3! ♗xe5! 23 fxe5 ♕xh4 24 ♖xg1 ♕f4+ 25 ♔b1! ♕xe5. Even for a grandmaster, working one's way through this line is far from easy, but that is not the end of it. In the resulting position Black has a rook and three pawns for a bishop and a knight, on paper a considerable material advantage. However, Anand showed that after 26 ♘c5! White's initiative prevents Black from co-ordinating his pieces. He went on to win very nicely.

One can hardly criticize Anand's choice, as it did give him the advantage in a very forcing way, but for ordinary mortals (and normal GMs such as myself) this continuation would be a distinct leap in the dark. If faced with the diagram position, it would be reasonable to spot 19 f4 and think "Well, that may be good, but it's very complicated. I'll analyse it if I have to, but is there another line which gives me the advantage and involves less risk?" The move 19 ♗e2 is natural; it threatens f4 and e5 without any sacrifice at all. Black cannot blockade White's pawns with 19...g5 because 20 hxg5 hxg5 21 ♕xb4 (or 20 ♕xb4 gxh4 21 ♖xd4) is very good for White. Anand did not play this move because of 19...d3, which is indeed the only reasonable reply. However, White can then continue 20 ♕e3! and Black is in big trouble. The threat of f4 and e5 is renewed, and the pawn on d3 is hanging. The continuation might be 20...♗xh4 21 ♗xd3 ♕c7 22 ♘b6 ♘xd3+ 23 ♖xd3 ♖d8 24 ♖xd8+ ♕xd8 25 ♘d5 and Black is losing. He cannot castle owing to 26 ♕xh6, the g7-pawn is hanging, White threatens ♕c5 and the bishop is dominated by the powerful centralized knight. This variation is fairly straightforward to calculate, and probably not really necessary as after 22 ♘b6 it is already clear that White stands very well. Thus White could have gained at least as much advantage as in the game with the simple move 19 ♗e2. It is easy to imagine that having calculated the difficult and attractive line with 19 f4, White was not eager to find an equally good simple alternative, even though moves like 19 ♗e2 and 20 ♕e3 are child's play to someone such as Anand.

Safety-nets

When you are thinking about a complex and lengthy tactical line, especially one involving sacrifices, it helps to have a *safety-net*, i.e. an alternative line which you can adopt if, half-way through your intended continuation, you discover that it doesn't work.

The simplest type of safety-net is when you have a perpetual check in hand *(D)*.

This looks like a fairly normal Najdorf Sicilian, but Shirov found an imaginative tactical idea.

17 ♖f5! ♗c8

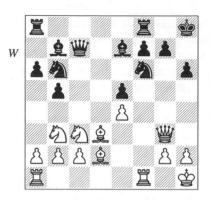

A. Shirov – B. Gelfand
Dos Hermanas 1996

This does provoke the following combination, but Gelfand probably did not realize how dangerous the coming sacrifice would prove to be. 17...b4 would have been a safer alternative.

18 ♖xe5!

This involves the sacrifice of a whole rook.

18...♗d6 19 ♗f4 g5?!

After 19...♗xe5 20 ♗xe5 ♕d8 21 ♖f1 (21 ♗c7 ♘h5!) Black would come under very strong pressure, for which he has only a minute material advantage as consolation.

Shirov did not analyse 19...♘c4!?, but perhaps this would have been a way for Black to reach a reasonable position. The main line runs 20 ♖c5 (20 ♗xc4 bxc4 21 ♘d4 g5! is much better for Black than the game, as without the bishop on d3 White's threats are far less dangerous) 20...♗xf4 21 ♖xc7 ♗xg3 22 hxg3 ♘xb2 and White has an active rook, but his pawns are shattered. The position should be at least equal for Black.

20 ♖c5!

The stunning point of White's combination.

20...gxf4 21 ♕h4 ♝xc5 22 ♕xf6+ ♚g8 *(D)*

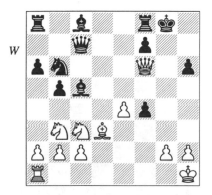

The first critical moment. White has no trouble forcing a draw, for example by 23 ♕xh6, when Black has no reasonable way to prevent perpetual check (23...♕d6 24 ♕g5+ ♕g6 25 ♕xc5 is very good for White).

Shirov now thought carefully about the various options for playing on. This raises the question as to why he embarked on the combination if he had no idea how he was going to continue at this stage. The answer is that even a leading grandmaster such as Shirov is human. We are already six moves away from the start of the combination, and it is not possible to calculate complex tactics accurately an indefinite distance ahead. Very forcing

variations can indeed be carried much further, but in this position there are numerous options for both players, and this increases the complexity by a large factor.

Shirov based his sacrifice largely on intuition. In this position, with Black's king seriously exposed, he must have felt that there would very likely be a way to play for a win. Moreover, at the back of his mind there was the comforting knowledge that if in fact there was no winning attempt, he had the safety-net of perpetual check to fall back on.

23 ♘xc5 ♕xc5 24 e5!

A risk-free method of playing for a win. This introduces the d3-bishop into the attack, and possibly the c3-knight as well, while all the time retaining the option of perpetual check.

24...♝b7?!

Gelfand slips up and now gets into serious trouble. The critical line was 24...♘d7! 25 ♕f5 and now:

1) 25...♖d8? 26 ♕h7+ ♚f8 27 ♕xh6+ ♚e8 (27...♚e7 28 ♕h4+ ♚e8 29 ♘e4 ♕xe5 30 ♖e1 wins) 28 ♘e4! ♕c7 29 ♘d6+ ♚e7 30 ♘f5+ ♚e8 31 e6 winning.

2) 25...♖e8! 26 ♕h7+ ♚f8 27 ♝e4 (once again, White has a draw by 27 ♕xh6+ ♚e7 28 ♕g5+ ♚f8, but can play on without risk) 27...♘b6 (it is essential to cover d5; 27...♖b8 loses to 28 ♘d5!) 28 ♕xh6+ ♚e7 29 ♖d1 (29 ♕xb6 ♕xb6 30 ♘d5+ ♚e6 31 ♘xb6 ♖b8 gives White no advantage) and now:

2a) 29...♖b8 30 ♕f6+ ♔f8 31 ♖d5! ♕c7 (31...♘xd5 32 ♘xd5 wins) 32 e6! ♖xe6 33 ♖d8+ ♕xd8 34 ♕xd8+ ♔g7 35 ♕g5+ ♔f8 36 ♕xf4 with a clear advantage for White.

2b) 29...♗e6! 30 ♕f6+ ♔f8 31 h4 and it is still possible for Black to go wrong, for example 31...♖ac8 32 h5 ♕f2 33 h6 ♘d7 34 ♕g7+ ♔e7 35 ♕g5+ f6 36 exf6+ ♘xf6 37 ♘d5+ ♗xd5 38 ♗xd5 and White wins. However, after 31...♕f2 32 h5 ♖ad8! 33 ♖xd8 ♕e1+ 34 ♔h2 ♕g3+ the game finally ends in perpetual check, although oddly it is Black who gives it!

Although he could have reached a draw, the task confronting Gelfand was enormous. He had to defend very accurately for a long time against an opponent who has taking absolutely no risk, since he always had a perpetual check in reserve.

25 ♕xh6 f5 26 exf6 ♖f7

The only defence, as 26...♕c7 27 ♕g5+! ♔h8 28 ♖e1 would be hopeless.

27 ♕g6+ ♔f8 28 ♕h6+ ♔g8 29 ♖f1! ♖e8 30 ♕g6+ ♔f8 31 ♕h6+ ♔g8

Now Shirov could have played 32 ♗h7+ ♖xh7 33 ♕g6+ ♔f8 34 ♕xh7 ♗xg2+ 35 ♔xg2 ♕c6+ 36 ♖f3 ♕xf6 37 ♘e4. After 37...♕g7+ 38 ♕xg7+ ♔xg7 39 ♖xf4 ♘c4 40 ♘c5! Black would have been two pawns down in the ending.

Shirov chose a different continuation and won after further complications.

When the tactics *have* to work

If you initiate tactics which involve a large commitment and have no safetynet, then you have no margin for error at all. Thus you have to be absolutely sure that your idea works, and it is probably worth double-checking everything before you commit yourself.

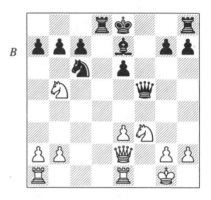

A. Yusupov – L. Portisch
Tunis Interzonal 1985

In this position Black has already moved his king and so cannot castle kingside. White has just attacked the c-pawn with ♘b5 and 18...♗d6 would be a normal reply. Yusupov certainly has some compensation for the pawn as Portisch's king is stuck in the centre, but Black's pieces are fairly well placed and he is, at any rate, not worse. However, Portisch now decided to play a combination.

18...a6?

The idea is that if White takes on c7 then his knight will be trapped.

19 ♘xc7+! ♔d7

There is no way back; after 19...♔f7 20 ♖f1 ♔g8 21 ♘d4 ♕e5 22 ♘cxe6 White wins a pawn and Black's h8-rook is blocked in.

20 ♘xa6 ♖a8

The immediate acceptance of the piece is bad for Black after 20...bxa6 21 ♕xa6 ♖b8 (21...♖c8 22 ♕b7+ ♖c7 23 ♖ad1+ ♗d6 24 ♖xd6+ ♔xd6 25 ♖d1+ ♕d5 26 ♕b3 ♖b8 27 ♖xd5+ exd5 28 ♕c3 is very good for White) 22 ♖ed1+ and now:

1) 22...♔c7 23 ♖ac1 ♗c5 (23...♖b6 24 ♕a7+ ♖b7 25 ♖xc6+ ♔xc6 26 ♘d4+ ♔c7 27 ♖c1+) 24 ♘d4 ♖b6 25 ♕a4 ♗xd4 26 ♕a7+ ♖b7 27 ♕xd4 and wins.

2) 22...♗d6 23 ♖ac1 ♖hc8 24 ♖c3 and there is no way out of the d-file pin. White wins by some combination of ♖cd3 and ♕a3.

Portisch was certainly aware that taking the knight with the b-pawn would expose his king too much, and the text-move was the point of his idea. He aims to take the knight with a piece, leaving the b7-pawn to defend his knight and provide his king with adequate defence.

21 ♖ed1+ ♔c8 (D)

The critical moment. Portisch has staked the game on his ability to take the knight with a piece. If he fails, then he will inevitably lose because the concessions he has made in order to trap the knight are so large. He has been prepared to go a pawn down (two pawns have been sacrificed, but he

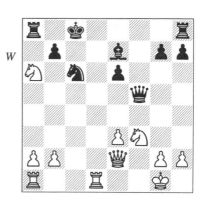

was a pawn up in the diagram position) and, just as important, he has been prepared to expose his own king seriously. In view of the total lack of any safety-net, Portisch should have made absolutely sure that there was no hole in his calculations.

22 b4!

Yusupov pinpoints the flaw in the whole concept. Black does not now win a piece and his position has been irreparably damaged.

22...♖xa6

After 22...bxa6 White wins by 23 ♖ac1 ♔b7 24 ♖xc6 ♔xc6 25 ♘d4+.

23 b5 ♖a3 24 bxc6 b6

Trying to keep some lines closed. 24...bxc6 loses to 25 ♖ac1 ♗c5 26 ♘d4 ♕e5 27 ♕c4! and the attack breaks through.

25 ♖ab1 ♗c5

Black's position is hopeless owing to his fatally exposed king. The finish was **26 ♖b3 ♖a5 27 ♕c4 ♖xa2 28 ♖xb6 ♗e3+ 29 ♔h1 ♗xb6** (or 29...♕d5 30 ♖b8+ ♔xb8 31 ♕b4+ ♔c7 32 ♕b7+ ♔d6 33 ♕d7+ ♔c5 34

罝xd5+ exd5 35 響e7+ 含xc6 36 響xe3)
30 響xa2 含c7 31 罝d7+ 含xc6 32 響a4+ 含c5 33 ⑤d2 1-0

Implicit commitments

Almost every move in chess involves some sort of commitment. A pawn move cannot be reversed and with each advance the pawn permanently loses the ability to control certain squares. Even a piece move is a commitment; if the piece turns out to be badly placed on its new square, it may have to go into reverse, with consequent loss of time. However, the degree of commitment is important. A piece sacrifice involves a greater degree of commitment than a natural developing move. We have already discussed the more obvious types of commitment earlier. However, there is a more subtle type of commitment, which we call *implicit commitment*. Very often, a certain type of commitment is bound up in a player's choice of opening. A player as White adopting the Velimirović Attack in the Sicilian (one of the main lines of which runs 1 e4 c5 2 ⑤f3 ⑤c6 3 d4 cxd4 4 ⑤xd4 ⑤f6 5 ⑤c3 d6 6 盒c4 e6 7 盒e3 盒e7 8 響e2 a6 9 0-0-0 響c7 10 盒b3 0-0 11 g4) is committing himself to an all-out kingside attack, which may involve sacrifices, and if he is hesitant about giving up material then he has simply chosen the wrong opening. Of course, this is an extreme example – there are few opening variations as one-sided as the Velimirović

Attack, but the same general principle applies in many openings. For example, it is not unusual for a player to seize a long-term strategic advantage in return for piece activity or a lead in development. In this case the player with the better development has taken on an implicit commitment to undertake rapid action. Advantages such as a lead in development are inherently temporary, because when the opponent has brought out all his pieces the advantage disappears. A common mistake is to take on such a position, but not to appreciate that the long-term chances lie with the opponent. The result is a fatal lack of urgency. Here is an example.

J. Nunn – J. Mellado
Leon 1997
French Defence

1 e4 e6 2 d4 d5 3 e5 c5 4 c3 響b6 5 ⑤f3 盒d7 6 盒e2 盒b5 7 c4 盒xc4 8 盒xc4 dxc4

I had noticed in my database a game won by my opponent with this rather offbeat line (instead of the usual 8...響b4+). Players are often unduly affected by the result of a game. If a player has won a game with a particular line, he will very often repeat exactly the same line, even if it is rather dubious. After looking at 8...dxc4 before the game, I quite liked the resulting positions for White, so I decided to go down the same variation.

9 d5 ⑤e7

Black does not completely equalize after 9...exd5 10 ♕xd5 ♘e7 11 ♕xc4.

10 d6

This is the critical continuation. In Mellado's earlier game White had played 10 ♘c3, which allows Black to swap everything on d5, with a more or less equal position.

10...♘ec6 11 0-0 *(D)*

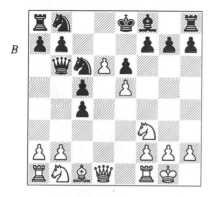

This is a typical case of implicit commitment. The extra pawn is not relevant, as White will win back the c4-pawn in a few moves. The key factor is that Black has allowed White to drive a wedge into the middle of his position. The protected passed pawn is not going to promote in the near future – there are simply too many pieces on the board for that – but it is an asset both in the middlegame and in the endgame. In the middlegame it stifles the activity of Black's pieces and cuts communication between the queenside and kingside. This could help White to mount a kingside attack, for Black's queenside pieces would have trouble feeding across to the other side of the board. In the endgame the pawn is more likely to promote, as there are fewer pieces available to keep it under control. Black would probably have to assign one piece to keep a watchful eye on the pawn, leaving him a man short elsewhere. The only caveat here is that White should not exchange too many pieces in an endgame, since then Black could use his king as the blockading piece.

In return for White's long-term asset, Black's minor pieces can converge to attack the e5-pawn and for some time White will be tied down to its defence. Moreover, Black's development is quite good, especially as White will have to invest some time in regaining the pawn on c4. However, these compensating factors are all temporary, and given time White will complete his development and reorganize his forces to defend e5 efficiently. Black has therefore taken on a heavy implicit commitment either to keep White off-balance or to convert his temporary advantages into something more permanent before White puts his house in order. If Black has not achieved something concrete within the next half-dozen moves, then we can safely predict that he will be in trouble.

White, on the other hand, can content himself with more modest play. All he need do is consolidate his position and bring all his pieces into play and Black will 'automatically' be worse. Of course, this might have been quite difficult if Black had continued accurately, but nevertheless White's position is easier to play. He has a very clear-cut aim, while Black must try to generate counterplay 'somehow', i.e. he has to formulate a plan from scratch, whereas White's plan is handed to him on a plate. This is a typical situation in such 'long-term advantage vs piece play' situations. The piece-play side has much more work to do, at least to begin with, to find the best plan. If he succeeds, then the other side may also have to think carefully about how to contain his opponent's counterplay, but if he does not succeed the game can be quite easy.

To my surprise, Black spent very little time over the next few moves and only started to think when he was already in considerable difficulties. Evidently he did not appreciate that this is the critical phase of the game and ordinary developing moves will not be enough.

From all this we can learn an important lesson. At the end of the opening, spend a few minutes deciding whether one player has the better long-term chances. This may be obvious simply from the opening variation chosen (for example, in the Exchange Ruy Lopez it is obviously White who has the better long-term chances), but if it is at all unclear then it is worth spending time on this question. The strategy for the two players may then be quite clear: one side must aim to consolidate and contain his opponent;

the other must play to stir up trouble quickly.

11...♘d7 12 ♖e1 g6 13 ♘a3

The first task is to regain the pawn on c4.

13...♗g7

Black cannot hang on to the pawn by 13...♕a6 14 ♕e2 b5 because 15 b3 breaks up the queenside pawn structure and regains the pawn in a more advantageous way.

14 ♘xc4 ♕a6 15 ♕e2 (D)

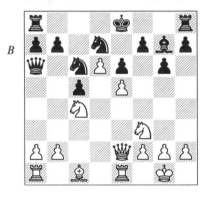

15...0-0?

A natural move, but one which allows White to consolidate his central pawns. Black should have continued 15...b5 16 ♘a3 (relatively best, as White must not block in his bishop) 16...♖b8 (after 16...♘cxe5 17 ♘xe5 ♗xe5 18 ♘xb5 0-0 19 a4 White has some advantage; Black cannot take on d6 because of the d-file skewer, so White manages to support his dangerous passed pawn) 17 ♗f4 0-0 and White has more difficulties than in the game because his knight is offside at a3. After 18 ♖ad1, for instance, Black can continue 18...c4 and try to plant a knight on d3 (for which White will probably have to give up the exchange).

16 ♗f4 ♘b6

If now 16...b5, then White replies 17 ♘cd2; thanks to Black's inaccurate 15th move, the knight can retreat to the centre rather than to a3.

17 b3

White must not allow the exchange of queens. His own queen is well placed in the centre of the board, while Black's is marooned on the queenside, so such an exchange would clearly favour Black.

17...♘d5

The transfer of the knight to d5 has blocked the d-file and prevented White backing up his pawn with a rook at d1, but it has also relieved the pressure on the e5-pawn.

18 ♗g3

Now the defects of Black's earlier play start to become apparent. Certainly he has developed his pieces, but he has done nothing to prevent White doing the same. All other things being equal, the position will favour White because of his superior structure. More and more, Black struggles to find constructive moves. He can only undermine White's pawns by ...f6, but then White would swap on f6, leaving the e6-pawn hopelessly weak.

18...h6

Black wants to prevent White supporting his d-pawn by a later ♗h4,

covering the queening square, but we can already see that Black is running out of ideas.

19 ♕e4

A typical move from the player who has time on his side. It does not create any immediate threat, but tidies up White's position by unpinning the c4-knight. Black also has the worry that the white queen might now switch to the kingside and form the basis of a direct attack.

19...♖ac8 20 h4

Both relieving White's back rank (his king would be very safe on h2) and making another threatening gesture against Black's king.

20...b5 21 ♘e3 (D)

White aims to open the d-file by removing Black's best-placed piece, the blockading knight on d5.

21...♘cb4?

The correct plan is indeed to use the second knight to restore the d-file blockade, but this move is a tactical error which leads to the loss of material.

21...♘xe3 22 ♕xe3 ♘b4 was the right way to put the plan into action. After 23 ♖ac1 ♘d5 24 ♕e2 c4 25 bxc4 bxc4 26 ♘d2 ♕xa2 27 ♖xc4, for example, Black has avoided any immediate disaster, but White's long-term advantages remain intact. As the pieces are exchanged, the d-pawn poses a more and more serious danger, while Black's bishop on g7 is practically dead.

22 a3! ♘c3 23 axb4 ♕xa1 24 ♕c2 (D)

Winning two knights for a rook and a pawn. This might not be decisive except for the fact that the structure of the position very much favours minor pieces over rooks.

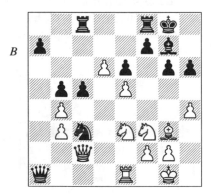

24...♕a3 25 ♕xc3 cxb4 26 ♕d3 ♖c3 27 ♕xb5 ♖xb3 28 ♘c4 ♕a2 29 ♘a5

The most convincing win. White positions his knights both to prevent the advance of the b-pawn and to move to c6 or b7, assisting the advance of the d-pawn. 29 ♘fd2 ♖d3 30 ♕xb4 a5 would be less clear.

29...♖b2 30 ♘d4 ♖d2 31 ♘ab3 ♖b2 32 ♕xb4 ♕a6 33 ♕c3 ♖a2 34 ♘c5 ♕c8 35 ♖c1 ♕a8 36 ♕b3 ♖d2 37 ♕b4 ♖a2 38 ♕b7 ♖d2 39 ♕xa8 ♖xa8 40 ♘cb3 1-0

Positional thinking

Although precise analysis plays some part in most chess situations, positional thinking is just as important. Even in sharp situations, positional factors can still play a major part; for example, there is little point in playing a combination winning the exchange if the result is a position riddled with weaknesses (see Sax-Stean on page 105).

Unfortunately, if you have little natural talent for it, positional thinking is one of the most difficult aspects of chess to learn. One often hears of how a certain player has a 'natural feel' for the pieces and instinctively puts them on the right squares. This is either an innate ability or something which is learnt by experience. If you have played over and studied thousands of games, and seen all the different patterns and plans which can arise from the main openings, then you already have a good start when it comes to positional play.

Most players do not have the time for this sort of study and must focus their efforts where they will do the most good. This really means concentrating on the types of middlegame position which can arise from your opening repertoire. Most openings give rise to certain distinctive central pawn structures. Some pawn structures are particular to just one opening. Look, for example, at the following diagram:

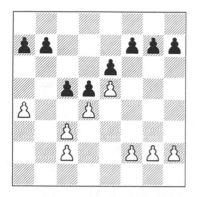

You don't need to see the position of the pieces to know that it's almost certainly a Winawer French. On the other hand, look at the following diagram:

It could be virtually anything: Caro-Kann, 2 c3 Sicilian, Queen's Gambit

Accepted, Nimzo-Indian, etc. If such pawn structures arise in your repertoire, it pays to look not only at games with 'your' opening, but at others which give rise to identical central pawn structures. If you have a database program with a 'position search' facility, then you can use this to find which openings result in a particular pawn structure.

Once you have identified the main pawn structures relevant to your openings, then try to find games resulting in these structures. Once again, a database program makes this easy. If there are too many games to play over, then restrict yourself to games by grandmasters – there is no point playing over games in which the players adopt quite inappropriate plans. It is much better if the games are annotated, preferably with words rather than symbols. Languageless annotations are fine for displaying tactical analysis, but when it comes to explaining the plans for both sides, there is no substitute for a clear explanation in words by someone who really understands the opening. Opening books which emphasize general ideas and plans may also be of help.

For each pawn structure, try to play over about fifty games. This should be enough to give you an idea both of the typical plans adopted by both players, and of which plans tend to succeed. The idea is not really to learn what to play in specific positions, but to see what the two players are trying to do, and how each side tries to frustrate the other's plans. By looking at all these games in quick succession, you will notice connections and similarities between them which would not be apparent if you looked at them over a period of months. When these positions arise in your games, you will then have a much better idea of what you should be trying to do.

Even grandmasters depend on this type of knowledge, and if they are thrown into unfamiliar territory, then they immediately start to play much less strongly. The following game is an illustration of this, but it also demonstrates a second valuable lesson: the importance of sticking consistently to a plan.

M. Adams – A. Onishchuk
Tilburg 1997
Two Knights Defence

1 e4 e5 2 ♘f3 ♘c6 3 ♗c4 ♘f6 4 d3 ♗e7 5 0-0 0-0 6 a4 d6 7 ♘bd2

Adams is playing this quiet system in a slightly unusual way. White normally plays c3 at some stage, so as to preserve his c4-bishop from exchange (he can meet ...♘a5 by ♗b5, and then drop it back to a4 and c2 if Black chases it with his pawns). Adams has countered the threat of ...♘a5 in a different way, by playing a4. This not only enables him to maintain the bishop on the a2-g8 diagonal, but may also form the basis of a space-gaining operation on the queenside. A third

point, which comes into play later in the game, is that White's a1-rook may emerge via a3.

Of course, this slightly unusual idea is hardly enough to win the game by itself, but it puts Onishchuk off his stride. Instead of the normal patterns in this system, he has to work out a plan for himself. As we shall see, Adams has a much better grasp of the requirements of the position.

7...♗e6 8 ♖e1 ♗xc4 9 dxc4!

Once again taking the chance to steer the game along original paths. The mechanical reply would be 9 ♘xc4, when the knight could later drop back to e3. However, Adams chooses a different move, which greatly strengthens his grip on d5. He has already formulated his plan for the next phase of the game: to increase his control of the light squares as much as possible, with particular reference to d5 and f5. Rather unusually, this is the only plan he needs to win the game! The first step is to transfer his knight from d2 to e3.

9...♖e8 10 ♘f1

Preparing ♘e3, taking aim at both critical squares.

10...♗f8?

A definite error. One of White's problems is that the immediate ♘e3 is impossible because the e4-pawn would be hanging. Thus White would have to spend some time preparing ♘e3. By allowing White to play ♗g5 and ♗xf6, Black not only lets White solve the problem of developing his bishop, but also allows ♘e3 without loss of time. Already one can see the outlines of a good knight vs bad bishop position shaping up.

Black should have played 10...h6. He need not worry about 11 ♘g3 ♗f8 12 ♘f5, because the knight can be expelled by 12...♔h7 followed by ...g6.

11 ♗g5 h6

Having played ...♗f8, it would have been psychologically very difficult to return to e7, although that might have been the best choice. The move played ultimately turns out to weaken Black's kingside.

12 ♗xf6 ♕xf6 *(D)*

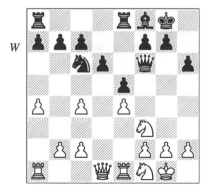

13 ♘e3 ♕e6

White has now completed the first step of his plan.

14 a5

In this static position, it is possible to create plans stretching over a relatively long time, since the pawn structure is likely to remain unchanged. The text is a typical positional move. White would be hard-pressed to come up with a concrete line in which a5 turned out to be a useful move, but he must look to the long term. Given that he is aiming for light-squared control, the possibility of a6, forcing ...b6, would be helpful. Black can, of course, prevent this by playing ...a6 himself, but this would not be without possible defects. White will at some stage play ♘d5, and Black would like to be able to expel the knight with ...c6. If he has already played ...a6, then the knight can settle on b6.

Thus Black is presented with a choice of evils, which never makes for an easy decision.

14...♘e7 15 ♖a3

Another useful move. Once again, White is looking forward to the day when Black will have to play ...c6, leaving his d6-pawn weak. Now the rook can come to d3, stepping up the pressure against d6 without loss of time. The firepower could even be increased by ♖e1-e2-d2. Note that when one is lining up the heavy artillery along an open or half-open file, it is usually better to have the rooks in front of the queen. Here White can achieve this ideal formation very efficiently.

Both these ideas (gaining a queenside space advantage and developing the rook via a3) were already inherent in White's 6th move, so Adams's play has been very consistent.

15...g6?!

Black would like to improve the position of his bishop, but he is being unrealistically optimistic. He will almost certainly have to play ...c6 at some stage, and then the bishop will be needed on f8 to protect the pawn on d6. If Black could force through ...f5 he would gain some counterplay and thereby justify ...g6, but against Adams's accurate play it proves impossible to realize this plan.

It would have been better to play 15...c6 at once; after 16 ♖d3 ♖ad8 17 ♖e2 ♘g6 everything would be defended and White would have to find a further 'mini-plan' to improve his position.

16 h4!

An excellent and unexpected move. Unlike the advance of the a-pawn, the aim is not so much to gain space as to weaken Black's kingside pawns. If he replies 16...h5, then 17 ♘g5 ♕f6 18 ♘d5 ♘xd5 19 cxd5 leaves White with the advantage. Black cannot expel the knight by ...f6 because it would just hop into e6; the best he could do would be to exchange it off with ...♗h6, but White would retain the advantage because of his queenside space advantage.

16...♗g7

Black ignores the h-pawn, but after h5 and hxg6 White has achieved two notable objectives: preventing Black's possible counterplay by ...f5, and creating a new weak pawn at g6.

17 h5 ♖ad8

Again a difficult choice. 17...gxh5 18 ♘h4 is clearly bad, and now it is rather late for 17...c6, as 18 ♖d3 ♖ad8

19 ♖e2 b6 20 axb6 axb6 21 hxg6 fxg6 22 ♖ed2 ♘c8 23 b4, followed by b5, gives White control of the central d5-square.

18 a6

Forcing a further slight weakening of the light squares.

18...b6 19 ♘d5 ♖d7 20 hxg6 fxg6 21 ♘h4!

Planning ♖g3, when the weakness of g6 will force ...g5, giving White the f5-square. There is little Black can do to counteract this plan.

21...c6 22 ♘xe7+ ♖exe7 23 ♖g3 g5 24 ♘f5 (D)

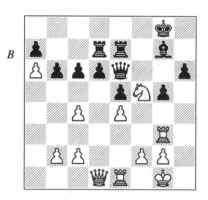

An ideal position for White. Six of Black's seven pawns are positioned on dark squares, and the knight occupies a beautiful outpost; in addition the pawn on d6 is weak. Black is lost.

24...♖f7 25 ♖d3 ♗f8 26 b3 d5

This desperate bid for counterplay costs material, but in any case White could step up the pressure easily enough, for example by ♖e2-d2.

27 ♕g4 ♔h7

27...dxe4 28 ♘xh6+ wins the exchange.

28 cxd5 cxd5 29 ♘xh6! ♕xg4

Or 29...♕xh6 30 ♖h3 winning the queen.

30 ♘xg4 ♗c5 31 ♖e2 1-0

Black will be two pawns down for nothing.

There comes a point in the vast majority of games when your acquired knowledge will be exhausted and you will have to rely on your own resources. This point normally arises in the early middlegame. The next step is to formulate a plan. You may already have some idea of the options available from your opening study; this will help you to narrow your search. In any case, it is time for some serious thought; the plan you choose now will go a long way towards defining the whole shape of the struggle to come. In some positions, for example, those with a blocked centre, it may be appropriate to construct a long-term plan which may require ten or twenty moves to execute. More likely, your plan will be much shorter-range, lasting perhaps five moves. This applies particularly in relatively open positions.

Here are some tips on making a plan:

1) Make sure your plan is beneficial. There is no point aiming for a target which does not actually enhance your position. Typical misguided plans are: attacking on the wrong part of the board; aiming for the exchange of the wrong pieces; committing yourself to weakening pawn advances.

2) Make sure your plan is realistic. There is no point in embarking on a five-move plan if your opponent can wait for the first four moves, and then stop your plan by playing one move himself.

3) Make sure your plan is not tactically flawed. Even if what you are aiming for is worthwhile, this will not help if your opponent can mate you while you are executing it.

Having decided on a particular plan, you have to strike a balance between consistency and flexibility. On the one hand, pointless changes of plan are very damaging. If you play two moves of one plan, then three moves of another, then four moves of a third, you will probably be back more or less where you started! The ideal situation occurs when you formulate a plan and, while you are executing it, your opponent does little either to prevent it or to develop counterplay. Then you can produce an elegant positional game which is dominated by a single strategic thread. However, games like this normally only arise between players of very different strengths (the Adams-Onishchuk game above is an exception in this respect). More often your plan will be blown off course because your opponent will interfere with it in some way. While consistency is a virtue, sometimes you have to be as pragmatic as a politician in changing your plan. If your opponent has blocked Plan A, but at the cost of creating a weakness elsewhere on the board, it would be foolish to stick to your original intention, ignoring the new situation. Instead you should rethink your strategy. Most games are like this: the players formulate a series of mini-plans and strike a balance between forwarding their own plans and interfering with those of the opponent. Eventually the balance is upset, either by one player's plan succeeding decisively, or by the game dissolving into tactics.

J. Nunn – V. Hort
Wijk aan Zee 1982
Giuoco Piano

1 e4 e5 2 ♗c4 ♘c6 3 ♘f3 ♗c5 4 c3 ♘f6 5 d3 a6 6 0-0 d6 7 ♘bd2 0-0 8 ♗b3 ♗a7 9 ♖e1 ♗e6 10 ♘c4 h6 11 a4

White has adopted a quiet opening system which avoids an early d4 in the hope of playing it at a more effective moment later. While this system is very solid, it has the defect that if Black plays in equally solid style, the game may simply peter out to a draw.

White's last move aims for a5, gaining space on the queenside and awaiting a more favourable moment for the thematic move ♘e3 (aiming at the squares d5 and f5). Readers will already be familiar with this type of strategy from the Adams-Onishchuk game given above.

11...b5?!
Weakening the queenside like this appears rather dubious. 11...♖e8 is a more solid alternative, which has been played in a number of games.

12 ♘e3 ♕d7 (D)

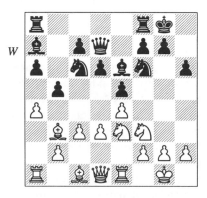

The game has now deviated from known theory, so it is time for White to think about his long-term plan and immediate 'mini-plan'. Since the position is still fairly fluid, it is difficult to create any long-term plans; trying to anticipate what will happen more than a few moves ahead is fruitless, as too many things might happen to throw a plan off course. However, the mini-plan is much easier; as mentioned earlier, one of White's ideas in this opening is to play d4 in the middlegame, when it may be more awkward for Black. White cannot play d4 immediately, as Black could take on b3 and then on d4, so 13 ♗c2 is indicated. Then d4 will be a real inconvenience, as Black must meet the threatened fork by d4-d5.

13 ♗c2 ♖fe8 14 d4 exd4

A major concession by Black, giving up his strong-point in the centre.

15 ♘xd4

White could perhaps have played 15 cxd4, although it is more complicated after either 15...d5 16 e5 ♘e4 (when 17 ♘xd5 ♘xf2 18 ♘f6+ gxf6 19 ♔xf2 fails to 19...♘xd4) or 15...♘b4 16 ♗b1 c5 (16...d5 17 e5 ♘e4 18 ♘xd5 ♘xf2 19 ♘f6+ gxf6 20 ♔xf2 fxe5 is unclear) 17 d5 ♗g4 18 ♘xg4 ♘xg4 19 h3 ♘e5 20 ♘xe5 ♖xe5.

15...♘xd4?!

After this White's advantage is safe. Black would have preferred not to make this exchange, but he was probably worried about the pressure on b5. However, he could have made a bid for counterplay by 15...b4!?.

16 cxd4 c6

The first mini-plan is over and has achieved a definite success, but now it is time for the next. White has a permanent advantage in his greater central control, if only he can maintain his 'two abreast' centre intact. Thus his next mini-plan should consist of consolidation. The immediate problem is the e4-pawn; Black need only move his e6-bishop to attack it awkwardly. White cannot defend it by ♕f3, because the queen must defend the d-pawn. One solution is to play f3, but the weakening on the a7-g1 diagonal is ugly, especially in view of the lurking bishop on a7 – Black would have good chances for counterplay by means of a timely ...c5.

17 h3!

The start of an alternative plan for supporting e4, based on ♘f1-g3. White first of all rules out the possibility of ...♗g4, which might be annoying once the e3-knight has moved away.

17...♕c7 18 ♘f1 ♗d7 *(D)*

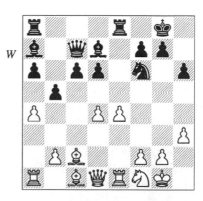

Now e4 is defended, and at first sight a natural continuation would be 19 ♘g3, further covering the central pawn and making a move towards Black's king. However, one should always take into account the opponent's intentions and see if there is a possibility to frustrate them. Black's recent moves, removing the bishop from e6, suggest that he intends to play ...c5. After 19 ♘g3 c5 20 d5 c4, for example, Black activates his queenside majority while White, thanks to the bishop on a7, has trouble getting his own central majority moving.

19 b4!

A very ambitious move, which is only justified because White's central structure is already secure. Now if

Black ever plays ...c5, White will reply bxc5 and d5, gaining a massive central majority. Moreover, the c1-bishop can now move to b2, setting up further latent threats against Black's kingside. In a sense, this move falls under the heading of 'consolidation', because it is mainly directed against the possibility of Black breaking up White's centre by ...c5.

19...bxa4

Black now threatens to attack the b4-pawn along the half-open file, and White's first priority is to defend it. The pawn on a4 can be recaptured later.

20 ♗b2 ♕b6 21 ♗c3 ♖e7

After 21...c5 White would ignore the hanging piece since 22 dxc5 dxc5 23 ♗xf6 ♕xf6 24 ♕xd7 cxb4 is rather messy. Instead he would continue with the thematic reply 22 bxc5 dxc5 23 d5, when the possible counterplay against f2 is not a serious worry, e.g. 23...c4 24 ♕d2 (24 ♖e2? ♘xe4! draws) 24...♖ab8 25 ♖e2, and White is ready for e5.

After the text-move, White must create his next mini-plan. The centre is secured and Black cannot attack it with ...c5 or ...d5, the latter because the reply e5 would give White an automatic kingside attack.

Black evidently intends to restrain White's centre by doubling rooks on the e-file, which leaves open the question as to how White should make progress. My eye was naturally attracted to Black's kingside; there is only a single knight defending it,

while all the white minor pieces are well placed to create threats on that side of the board. I decided simply to move my pieces towards Black's king by ♘g3 and ♕f3. At this point White could think about a breakthrough by d5 or e5, or simply play ♘f5, gaining the two bishops.

22 ♘g3 ♖ae8 23 ♕f3 ♘h7

Black could have tried the tricky 23...a3, hoping for 24 ♖xa3 ♘d5!, but White would just play 24 ♘f5.

The text-move takes the sting out of d5 or e5, so White goes for ♘f5.

24 ♘f5 ♗xf5 25 ♕xf5 (D)

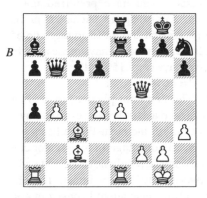

Black's next move anticipates e5 by White.

25...♘f8

White now has the two bishops to show for his efforts, but the knight on f8 is an effective defender of the kingside and direct attacking attempts do not appear promising. White must take care, or else Black's latent pressure along the lines a7-g1 and e8-e1 might be unleashed.

I therefore decided to switch to the queenside, and build up against the a6-pawn. Note that this plan would not have been effective before as Black could simply have played ...♗c8.

26 ♖xa4 ♘e6 27 ♖d1 ♘c7?!

Black decides to pre-empt White's attack on the a-pawn and hopes to occupy a good square at b5, but now the knight is dangerously far away from the kingside. It would have been better to leave the knight on e6, ready to move to c7 or f8 as necessary.

28 ♗b2

The immediate 28 e5 g6 is ineffective as 29 ♕f4 is met by 29...♘d5. Now, however, 29 e5 is a threat. Note how White has again changed his plan to utilize the circumstance that Black's knight has gone to the queenside.

28...♕b5

Black does not want to be mated and, now that a6 is defended by the knight, he switches his queen to the kingside.

29 ♕f3 ♕g5

While in positional terms Black's plan is quite reasonable, it has a concrete defect: the queen is short of squares.

30 ♖a5! *(D)*

Now Black is obliged to make a further concession. Note that the greedy 30 ♕c3 d5 31 ♕xc6 dxe4 32 ♗xe4 would be disastrous for White, since 32...♖xe4 33 ♕xc7 ♗b8, followed by ...♖e2, would give Black a crushing attack.

30...d5

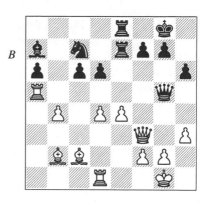

After 30...♕g6 31 ♕c3 ♗b6 32 ♖aa1 Black would not have a good answer to the threats of 33 ♕xc6 and 33 e5.

31 e5

Now White has more advantages to point to: the e-pawn is no longer under pressure, and White can create threats along the b1-h7 diagonal. The immediate threat is 32 ♗c1 ♕h4 33 g3 ♕xh3 34 ♗f5.

31...♘e6?

Alarmed by the growing danger to his king, Hort, who was in severe time-trouble, decides to jettison his a-pawn in order to bring the knight over to the kingside. In many cases, if your pieces are tied down to defending a weak pawn, then letting the pawn go is a way to activate the pieces and develop counterplay (see page 136). In this case, however, it makes little difference: the position remains more or less the same except that Black is a pawn down.

31...g6 would have been a more resilient defence; after 32 g3 ♖e6 33

♕d3 ♕h5 34 ♔g2 ♖b8 35 ♗c3, threatening f4-f5, White would be much better but not yet winning.

32 ♖xa6 ♖c8 33 g3 ♖b7 34 ♕d3 g6 35 ♗c3 ♗b6

White has taken the pawn and met Black's attack on the b-pawn. Now he must turn to a mini-plan for exploiting his advantage. The natural plan is the one which has been in the position ever since White played e4-e5, viz. the advance of the f-pawn.

36 ♔h2 ♗d8 *(D)*

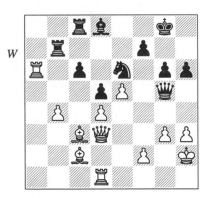

37 ♖f1

Ultra-cautious in time-trouble. 37 f4 ♘xf4 38 gxf4 ♕xf4+ is of course unsound after 39 ♔h1, but I wanted to make really sure there were no complications!

37...♕e7 38 ♕e3 ♕f8 39 f4 ♘g7 40 f5 ♗g5 41 ♕e2 ♘xf5 42 ♗xf5 gxf5 43 h4 ♗e7 44 ♖xf5 ♕g7

Black is quite lost. In addition to the minus pawn, three of his four remaining pawns are weak and his king is exposed. The rest is easy and consists of making one threat after another until Black collapses.

45 ♖f4 ♔h8 46 ♕f3 ♗f8 47 ♖f6 ♖bc7 48 ♖a2

After ♖af2 followed by e6 there will be no defence.

48...♕h7 49 e6 ♗g7 50 ♖xf7 ♖xf7 51 exf7 ♕g6 52 ♖f2 ♗f8 53 ♗d2 ♔h7 54 b5 cxb5 55 ♕xd5 ♕d3 56 ♔h3 ♗g7 57 ♗b4 1-0

The method of comparison

Sometimes it is possible to avoid precisely evaluating the consequences of the various options available. The reason is that you are really interested in relative assessments and not absolute ones. If, for example, you know that move A is '0.2 pawns' better than move B, then you would prefer A to B – it doesn't matter whether A is 0.3 pawns better for you or 0.1 pawns worse for you, it is only the relative evaluation which matters.

In practice, of course, this type of logic is hard to apply if there are many different continuations. If you have alternatives A, B, C, D and E then comparing A with B, C with E, D with A and so on is going to lead to a logical conundrum rather than a decision. It is much simpler to make an absolute assessment that A is a bit better for White, B is equal, and so on, and then pick the move with highest value.

It follows that the method of comparison, as we call it, works best when there are very few options (three at most) and the types of position resulting from these options are rather similar, and so are more easily compared with each other than evaluated absolutely.

The most common case arises when you have the possibility of an intermediary check which forces some kind of concession.

A. Meszaros – Y. Zimmerman
Balatonbereny 1994
Nimzowitsch-Larsen Attack

1 b3 e5 2 ♗b2 ♘c6 3 e3 d5 4 ♗b5 ♗d6 5 f4 *(D)*

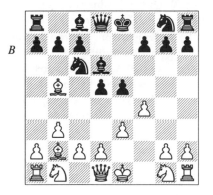

This is a known theoretical position. White's opening is designed to exert pressure on the e5-square. Black cannot play 5...exf4 owing to 6 ♗xg7, and defending the pawn with 5...f6 is rather ugly – after 6 ♕h5+ g6 7 ♕h4 Black's kingside is weakened and his development is impeded.

Therefore Black should defend the e5-pawn by ...♕e7, but he has the

option of playing ...♕h4+ first. The only difference between these two lines is that in one White's g-pawn is on g2 and in the other on g3. There is no question that the additional move g3 helps Black. If White exchanges his b5-bishop on c6, then he will have less control of the light squares in any case; the weaknesses created by playing g3 would then be quite serious. It may well happen that White will change his mind and play the bishop back from b5, but in this case Black has gained time.

5...♕h4+ 6 g3 ♕e7 7 fxe5 ♗xe5 8 ♘c3 ♘f6

8...d4!? 9 ♘d5 ♕c5 is an interesting alternative.

9 ♘f3 ♗g4 10 ♗e2 ♗d6 11 ♘b5 0-0 12 ♘xd6 ♕xd6

White has the two bishops, but Black's development is very comfortable. The position is equal.

13 ♘d4 ♘xd4 14 ♗xd4 ♗h3

Black starts to take advantage of the weakened light squares on the kingside.

15 ♗f1 ♗d7 16 ♗g2 c5 17 ♗xf6?

Too ambitious. White plays to win a pawn, but his lack of development and weakened kingside make it a risky endeavour. 17 ♗b2 would have maintained the balance.

17...♕xf6 18 ♗xd5 ♗g4! 19 ♕c1 ♖ad8 20 ♗xb7 *(D)*

20...♖xd2! 21 ♔xd2?

Now Black gains a clear advantage. White could still have held on by 21 ♕xd2 ♕xa1+ 22 ♔f2 ♕f6+ 23 ♔g2

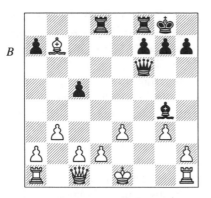

B

♖d8 24 ♕a5! (24 ♕c1 ♕c3!) 24...♕e7 (after 24...♕b6 25 ♕xb6 ♖d2+ 26 ♔f1 axb6 Black will regain his pawn, but in the meantime White can extract his rook and the result should be a draw) 25 ♗f3 ♗xf3+ 26 ♔xf3 ♖e8 27 ♖e1 ♕e4+ 28 ♔f2 ♕xc2+ 29 ♖e2 with a near-certain draw.

21...♖d8+ 22 ♔e1 ♕c3+ 23 ♔f1 ♖d2 *(D)*

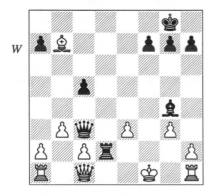

W

24 ♕e1?
Losing by force. The last chance was 24 ♕xd2 ♕xd2 25 h3 ♗e2+ 26 ♔g1 ♕xc2 27 ♗g2 (27 ♖h2 ♕c3!)

27...♕b2 28 ♖e1 ♕xa2 29 ♔h2 ♗f3 30 ♖hg1 ♗xg2 31 ♖xg2 ♕xb3, when Black has the advantage, but White might be able to draw since Black's queenside pawns are disconnected.
24...♗h3+ 25 ♔g1 ♕xc2
A vivid exploitation of the weakness induced by 5...♕h4+.
26 ♕c1 0-1
White resigned without waiting for 26...♖g2+.

Whilst occasions in which one can consciously use the method of comparison are not all that common, in some sense it is being used all the time. When one is thinking 'does that knight belong on c4 or g3?', this is really a comparison. There is no attempt to evaluate the consequences of these two alternatives in absolute terms; one is simply asking which is better. In this wider sense comparison is an important part of chess thinking.

Making your opponent think

Sometimes it is better to pass the responsibility for a difficult decision on to your opponent. You may be contemplating, for example, the move ...h6 which allows a piece sacrifice ♗xh6!?. You look at the sacrifice a little; it is a complete mess, extremely hard to evaluate. However, the alternatives to ...h6 are about equal. You may decide to play ...h6 without further thought, and put the responsibility of evaluating the sacrifice onto your opponent – he will have to spend time coming to a definite conclusion instead of you. There is nothing more frustrating than thinking for half an hour, deciding that the sacrifice is not sound, playing ....h6 and meeting with the reply ♖ad1 within 30 seconds. Indeed, there are many opponents who would use the logic that if you thought about the sacrifice for so long and still allowed it, then it must be unsound. Playing your move fairly quickly short-circuits this logic. Indeed, your opponent may wonder if you have even seen the sacrifice. Obviously, this type of logic can be overdone; it would be ridiculous to allow a sacrifice leading to a clear-cut win. Moreover, if you were playing a dangerous attacking player, then provoking him to make a sacrifice is probably not a good idea.

A 'making your opponent think' move usually works best if you are in a slightly inferior position. Then your opponent will be undecided about whether to continue positionally, in which case his advantage might prove insufficient for a win, or to enter the tactics, when, at the cost of some risk, he might end up with a larger advantage. If your opponent has a large advantage to start with, then he will probably avoid tactics since he has good winning chances in any case.

Here is an example (D).

Black stands badly, mainly because of the miserable position of his bishop on g6. White intends to swap bishops on d6 and then play ♘f4. This will

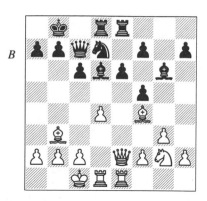

B

J. Nunn – S. Conquest
Hastings 1996/7

increase the pressure on e6 to such as extent that ...f6 will never be possible, and it also removes any possibility of Black playing ...♘f6 and ...♗h5. He might, of course, play ...♘f6-e4, but the knight could be pushed away again by f3 and he would be left with the same problems.

The only way Black can improve his position is to play ...f6, intending ...♗f7, or, if White is careless enough to allow it, ...e5.

17...f6

Conquest played this very quickly, which is a good practical 'make your opponent think' decision. White can take the pawn by 18 ♗xe6, but this involves pinning the bishop, which might have dire consequences. He can also take the pawn by 18 ♗xd6 ♕xd6 19 ♘f4 ♗f7 20 ♘xe6, which is similarly complicated. Finally, White might decide to ignore the offered pawn and continue positionally, although in that case Black can play ...♗f7 and his prospects will have improved as a result of releasing the bishop from the trap on g6.

I was faced with a difficult decision and it took me just over twenty minutes to make up my mind to go for the immediate capture of the pawn. I also considered continuing positionally, but it seemed to me that although White would hold an undoubted advantage, making progress would be far from straightforward. I had plenty of time on the clock, and so I decided to analyse the pawn capture thoroughly. Finally I concluded that White would emerge with a clear advantage, but I still felt a little nervous as I took the pawn!

18 ♗xe6!

The other capture, 18 ♗xd6 ♕xd6 19 ♘f4 ♗f7 20 ♘xe6, is less accurate in view of 20...♘b6 (20...♗xe6 21 ♗xe6 ♘f8 22 d5 cxd5 23 ♖xd5 ♕xd5 24 ♗xd5 ♖xe2 25 ♖xe2 ♖xd5 26 ♖e8+ ♔c7 27 ♖xf8 wins for White) 21 ♖d3 ♘d5 22 ♗xd5 ♕xd5 23 ♖e3 ♖xe6 24 ♖xe6 ♗xe6 25 ♕xe6 ♕xd4 26 ♕e3 with only a slight advantage for White.

18...♘f8

After 18...♗f7 19 ♕c4 ♘b6 20 ♕b3 White keeps his material more easily.

19 ♕c4 ♗h5

The main alternative is 19...♘xe6 20 ♖xe6 ♗xf4+ (20...♕f7 21 ♖xd6 and 20...♗f7 21 ♖xd6 ♖xd6 22 ♕b4 win for White) 21 ♘xf4 ♗f7 22 d5 ♗xe6 23 ♘xe6 ♕d6 24 ♘xd8 ♖xd8

25 ♕d3 ♕xd5 26 ♕xd5 cxd5 27 ♖d4 and the weak black pawns give White a winning rook and pawn ending.

20 ♖d3! *(D)*

Not 20 ♗xd6 ♕xd6 21 ♗f7 ♖xe1 22 ♖xe1 ♗xf7 23 ♕xf7 ♕xd4 and Black even has the advantage.

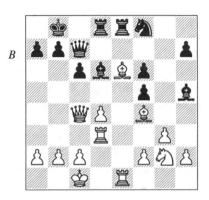

20...♘xe6

There is nothing better, e.g.:

1) 20...b5 21 ♕b3 ♘xe6 22 ♖xe6 ♖xe6 23 ♕xe6 ♗xf4+ 24 ♘xf4 ♖e8 25 ♕b3 ♖e1+ 26 ♔d2 ♖d1+ 27 ♔c3 ♗f7 28 ♕b4 and White consolidates his extra pawn, while retaining a positional advantage.

2) 20...♘xe6 21 ♖xe6 ♗xf4+ 22 ♘xf4 ♗f7 23 d5 ♗xe6 24 ♘xe6 ♕e5 25 ♘xd8 ♖xd8 26 d6 ♕e1+ 27 ♖d1 ♕xf2 28 ♕e6 and the powerful passed pawn is decisive.

21 ♖xe6 ♖xe6 22 ♕xe6 ♗xf4+ 23 ♘xf4 ♖e8 24 ♕xf5

There is no reason why White should not take a second pawn. Black gets a couple of checks, but his counterplay is soon quashed.

24...罩e1+ 25 含d2 罩d1+ 26 含c3
桌g4 27 嚠c5

Applying DAUT. 27 嚠xg4 嚠a5+
28 b4 嚠a3+ 29 含c4 嚠xa2+ 30 含c5
嚠xc2+ 31 含d6 may also win, but there
is no point in analysing such a line
when a safe alternative exists.

27...罩a1 28 罩e3 *(D)*

Black's counterplay has dried up,
and it is White's turn to go on the of-
fensive.

28...桌c8 29 罩e7 嚠d8 30 ②e6

Doubtless there were other ways to
win, but forcing exchanges is a risk-
free approach.

30...桌xe6 31 罩xe6 罩xa2 32 嚠d6+
1-0

While Black is retrieving his rook
from a2, White will make a meal of his
kingside pawns.

Oversights and blunders

Oversights and blunders are merely
two aspects of the same thing. If you
miss something, and by good fortune

the consequences are not too serious,
then you have an oversight; if the upshot is catastrophic, then you have a
blunder.

Why do chess players blunder? Human fallibility is obviously one reason, but the majority of blunders are
not purely the result of chance. There
are several factors that can greatly increase the probability of a blunder and
if one is aware of these factors, then
one can take particular care during
these 'high-risk' periods.

The most common cause of blundering is a previous oversight. Let us
suppose that your opponent suddenly
sacrifices a piece and that this sacrifice comes as a complete surprise to
you. A typical train of thought starts:
"Oh, ****! I completely overlooked
that. It looks strong; perhaps I will
even have to resign. How could I have
overlooked such a simple idea? How
stupid. And I had such a winning position." Not very constructive. Making a
serious oversight is a huge blow to
one's self-confidence, it sends the
mind into a whirl and turns the stom-
ach upside down. Nobody's brain can
function properly in such a state. The
only real solution is to take the time
necessary until one's mind and stom-
ach have quietened down. The length
of time this takes depends on one's
personality and will-power, and of
course how strong the opponent's
move actually is! What is quite useless
is to have a major bout of self-
recrimination at the board – if your

personality tends towards this, try to save it until the end of the game (by which time, hopefully, it may not be necessary). This is another reason why running short of time is a bad idea. If something unexpected happens, you do not have the possibility of a short 'time-out' to recover your composure.

Here is an example of precisely the wrong reaction, taken from one of my own games.

J. Nunn – D. Cox
Norwich Junior International 1974
Sicilian, Pelikan

1 e4 c5 2 ♘f3 e6 3 d4 cxd4 4 ♘xd4 ♘f6 5 ♘c3 ♘c6 6 ♘db5 d6 7 ♗f4 e5 8 ♗g5 a6 9 ♘a3 ♗e6 10 ♘c4 ♗e7? 11 ♗xf6 gxf6 12 ♘e3 ♖c8 13 ♘cd5 f5?! 14 exf5 ♗xd5 15 ♕xd5 *(D)*

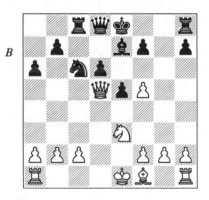

Black's handling of the opening has left a great deal to be desired and White has a large advantage. One more tempo and White would play c3, leaving Black with no compensation for

his minus pawn and crippling light-squared weaknesses.

15...♘b4

Black not surprisingly tries to force through ...d5 before White tightens his grip.

16 ♕e4?

16 ♕b3 was much simpler. After 16...d5 17 a3 d4 18 axb4 dxe3 19 fxe3 Black has very little to show for his two pawns.

16...d5!

I hadn't realized that this move was possible, although in retrospect it is hard to imagine any other follow-up to Black's previous move. At once I saw that the position had become rather more murky than was really necessary and the knowledge that I had made a bit of a mess of it was the trigger for what followed.

17 ♕xe5 f6 18 ♕d4 *(D)*

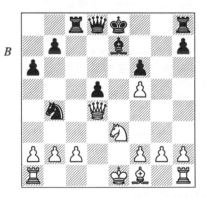

At this point I was getting slightly worried, not about 18...♘xc2+ 19 ♘xc2 ♖xc2 20 ♕a4+ ♖c6 21 ♗xa6! 0-0 22 ♗b5, followed by 23 0-0, with a clear two-pawn advantage, but about 18...♗c5. After 19 ♕d2 ♕e7 Black has some nasty threats, while White has fallen somewhat behind in development. In fact White should be able to retain the better position by 20 0-0-0!, but of course White no longer has the same clear-cut advantage as at move 15.

18...♖xc2!?

This is not a particularly good move, but it had a devastating effect on me because I had completely missed it. Having now overlooked two of my opponent's moves, I went into a panic. I saw horrible threats such as 19...♕a5 or 19...♘c6 followed by ...♗b4+ and quickly decided that I had to get my kingside pieces out as rapidly as possible. I saw that after 19 ♗d3 ♘xd3+ 20 ♕xd3 ♕a5+ (or 20...♗b4+) I would have to play ♔f1, but the resulting position did not look too bad. My king could find safety after g3 and ♔g2, freeing the other rook; in addition Black's d-pawn would be very weak. Unfortunately my brain had stopped functioning.

19 ♗d3?? ♗c5 0-1

I am sure almost all players have had this experience at one time or another – disorientation caused by one mistake immediately leading to a second, much more serious, error. A calm look at the position after 18...♖xc2 would have shown that White is still clearly better after 19 ♗e2 (threatening 20 ♗h5+ followed by 0-0), for example 19...♖g8 20 ♗h5+ ♔f8 21 0-0

♗c5 22 ♕h4 or 19...♗c5 20 ♕g4 ♕a5 21 0-0.

Warning signals

One of the most common reasons for blundering is failure to take warning signs into account. Tactics very rarely strike out of a blue sky. There is normally some underlying weakness, visible beforehand, which the tactic seeks to exploit. When you see such a potential vulnerability, it pays to look very carefully for a possible tactic by the opponent exploiting this weakness.

Once I played 100 games against Mike Cook at 10 minutes (for him) vs 5 minutes (for me). At that time Mike was about 2300 strength. About half-way through the series (which I eventually won 88-12) he explained his disappointment:

"I thought that I would see lots of advanced strategic concepts in these games but actually all I have learnt is LPDO."

"LPDO?"

"Loose Pieces Drop Off."

During the remaining games I saw what he meant. Most of the games were decided by relatively simple tactics involving undefended pieces, when the LP would duly DO.

Now, whenever I see such a combination (they occur quite often), I think 'LPDO'.

Looking at the diagram overleaf, the LP on h8 should have been a

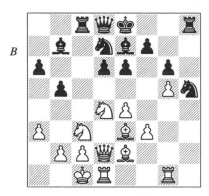

M. Chandler – W. Beckemeyer
Bundesliga 1987

warning sign to Black that he should
look for tactics especially carefully.
16...♘b6?
Walking right into it.
17 ♘dxb5! axb5 18 ♕d4
and White won easily.

What is surprising about this example is that the initial move of the combination is one of the most familiar
tactical blows in the Sicilian. It seems
that the idea of it being followed up by
anything other than ♗xb5+ or ♘xb5
just didn't occur to Black.

Even ex-world champions (or current ones, depending on your perspec-
tive) can fall victim to LPDO *(D)*:
Black already has an LP on h5. He
added a second one by ...
11...♗d6
Christiansen looked amazed.
12 ♕d1 1-0
LPDO!

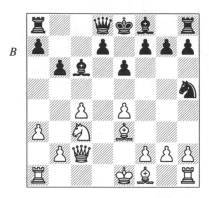

L. Christiansen – A. Karpov
Wijk aan Zee 1993

White's queen had earlier moved
from d1 to c2, so this is also an example of overlooking a switchback (see
page 57).

We will consider two other warning
signals, but virtually any tactical weakness can give the opponent a chance
for a combination. Note that by 'tactical weakness' I do not mean isolated
pawns, bad bishops and other such
long-term weaknesses; these are 'strategic weaknesses'. A tactical weakness is a short-term vulnerability such
as an undefended piece, a potential pin
or fork, or a trapped piece. Tactical
weaknesses may exist only for a single
move, so if your opponent creates one,
you should look for a way to exploit it
straight away.

One of the most common errors
amongst beginners is to allow an e-file
pin of the queen, but even GMs can
underestimate the significance of a
queen + king line-up.

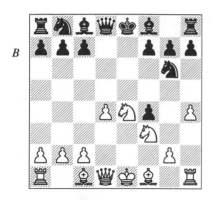

B. Spassky – Y. Seirawan
Montpellier Candidates 1985

The diagram position arose after **1 e4 e5 2 f4 exf4 3 ♘f3 ♘e7 4 d4 d5 5 ♘c3 dxe4 6 ♘xe4 ♘g6 7 h4** *(D)*, when Seirawan faced the problem of dealing with the threat 8 h5, which would regain the sacrificed pawn on f4. Since Black had based his whole strategy on maintaining this pawn, it would be a bitter blow to be forced simply to give it up.

7...♕e7?

This is an example of a major commitment. Black's aim is to inconvenience White's knight; indeed, one's instant reaction is that White must play 8 ♕e2 to avoid losing the knight to ...f5. However, if it turns out that White is not seriously inconvenienced by the pin, then Black has done quite a lot of damage to his own position: the queen obstructs the development of Black's kingside, takes away the last flight square from the knight on g6 and sets Black up for an e-file pin.

Indeed, these defects are so serious that this move falls into the 'has to work' category (see page 28). The potential e-file line-up and the fact that Black has committed himself so heavily are clear warning signals to which Seirawan did not pay sufficient attention.

8 ♔f2!

It suddenly turns out that 8...♕xe4 is impossible because of 9 ♗b5+ ♔d8 10 ♖e1 and the black queen is pinned against a mate on e8. Black is forced to change his plan completely, and all the defects of the move ...♕e7 are exposed.

8...♗g4 9 h5 ♘h4 10 ♗xf4 ♘c6 11 ♗b5 0-0-0 12 ♗xc6 bxc6 13 ♕d3 ♘xf3 14 gxf3 ♗f5 15 ♕a6+ ♔b8 16 ♘c5 ♗c8 17 ♕xc6 ♖xd4 18 ♖ae1 ♖xf4 (18...♕xc5? 19 ♗xc7#) 19 ♕b5+ ♔a8 20 ♕c6+ ♔b8 21 ♖xe7 ♗xe7 and White won easily.

Of course 8 ♔f2 is a very unusual move and one can easily imagine how Seirawan came to overlook it. In Open Games, White does not normally voluntarily deprive himself of the right to castle, and in most positions it would be a waste of time for Black to start analysing king moves to the second rank. How, then, can one expect to spot moves such as ♔f2 in advance? This really is the point of the warning signs – they tell you when to take time out to look for unusual tactical motifs, which might only be justified because you have a potential vulnerability in your position.

Our final warning sign is the weak diagonal. Here is a vivid example:

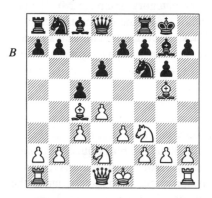

Ye Rongguang – L. van Wely
Antwerp Crown Group 1997

The diagram position arose after **1 d4 ♘f6 2 ♘f3 g6 3 ♗g5 ♗g7 4 ♘bd2 0-0 5 e3 d6 6 ♗c4 c5 7 c3** *(D)*. Now Van Wely decided to develop his c8-bishop at b7, and played **7...b6??**. The weakness along the h1-a8 diagonal is quite apparent, but Van Wely had overlooked the simple continuation **8 ♗xf6 ♗xf6 9 ♗d5**, winning a piece. The game ended **9...♗a6 10 ♗xa8 d5 11 c4 dxc4 12 0-0 cxd4 13 exd4 ♗xd4 14 ♘xc4 1-0**. This horrible disaster was the direct result of not taking account of the danger sign 'trapped rook on a8'. Had he looked a little longer, Van Wely would surely have seen **♗xf6**. The problem here is psychological: White would never normally play an anti-positional move such as **♗xf6**, giving up the two bishops for no good reason, so Van Wely did not

consider it a possibility for his opponent. However, an extra piece provides pretty good compensation for the two bishops!

Curiously, a similar 'diagonal disaster' occurred in another game from the Open Group of the same event.

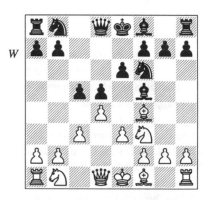

A. Stefanova – S. Giddins
Antwerp Open 1997

After **1 d4 d5 2 ♘f3 ♘f6 3 ♗f4 c5 4 e3 ♗f5 5 c3** Black decided to continue his development with the natural move **5...e6?** *(D)*. This ignored the danger of leaving the light squares on the queenside exposed by developing the c8-bishop to f5, and then preventing it from returning by ...e6. Black doubtless took into account lines such as **6 ♗b5+ ♘c6 7 ♘e5 ♖c8 8 ♕a4 ♕b6**, when there are no more pieces White can bring to bear on c6. However, he failed to take into account that the b8-knight is really the only piece that can interpose on the b5-e8 diagonal. Therefore **6 ♗xb8!** put him in an awkward situation. After the check on b5 Black will have to move his king, as 7...♘d7 loses to 8 ♘e5. In the game Black chose 6...♖xb8 7 ♗b5+ ♔e7 8 dxc5 and soon lost. Perhaps 6...♕xb8 7 ♗b5+ ♔d8 was slightly better, but in any case Black's position is hardly enviable. Here there were three factors that led to Black's oversight: failure to take into account the warning sign 'weakness along the b5-e8 diagonal', the anti-positional nature of ♗xb8 and the soporific effect of White's unambitious opening.

A similar motif occurred in the following diagram after the moves 1 d4 ♘f6 2 ♗g5 ♘e4 3 ♗f4 d5 4 e3 ♗f5 5 f3 ♘f6 6 c4 c5?! 7 cxd5 ♘xd5 (D).

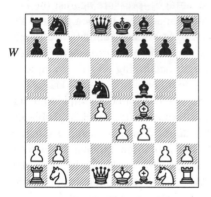

M. Adams – L. Van Wely
Tilburg 1996

8 ♗xb8!

Black is obliged to surrender a piece, as e3-e4 is coming. The consequences were less catastrophic this time as after 8...♘xe3 9 ♗b5+ ♗d7 10 ♗xd7+

♕xd7 11 ♕e2 ♘xg2+ 12 ♕xg2 ♖xb8 13 dxc5 g6 14 ♘c3 ♗g7 Black had some compensation for the piece and managed to draw in the end.

We deal with the question of how to continue after you have made an oversight under 'Defence' (see page 97).

'Hard-to-see' moves

Another type of oversight is the simple 'blind spot'. In this case it is not a question of a misjudgement, but of a move, either for oneself or for the opponent, simply not entering one's mind at all. This is usually because there is something odd about the move, so that it doesn't fit into any of the standard patterns. Here is a clear example.

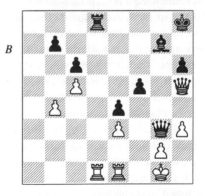

U. Andersson – A. J. Mestel
London (Philips & Drew) 1982

It is Black to play; Mestel continued 29...♖d5 and White's material advantage eventually proved sufficient to win. However, Black could have forced instant resignation by 29...Rd2!, which either wins a rook or mates. Admittedly, Mestel was somewhat short of time, but even so it is not hard to calculate this simple combination, *provided that the idea crosses one's mind in the first place.*

When two line-moving pieces are facing each other, the options are usually limited to exchanging, allowing the opponent to exchange, or moving the attacked piece away. It is very unusual for the piece to move part of the way towards the enemy piece. The exception is when there is a very juicy outpost somewhere on an open file, practically begging a piece to land on it. That was not the case here, so the winning move was a little hard to see. Nevertheless, it is surprising that Mestel did in fact play a move along the file, so he must have noticed that it was impossible for White to take the rook after such a move. Evidently the fact that the rook was undefended on d2 formed just enough of a mental block to cause the oversight.

I call such moves along the line of attack (without capturing the attacking piece) *collinear moves*. They are even more difficult to spot when the attacked piece moves away from the attacking piece. Here is one example from opening theory: **1 e4 c5 2 ♘f3 d6 3 d4 cxd4 4 ♘xd4 ♘f6 5 ♘c3 a6 6 ♗e2 e5 7 ♘b3 ♗e6 8 0-0 ♘bd7 9 f4 ♕c7 10 f5 ♗c4 11 a4 ♗e7 12 ♗e3 0-0 13 a5 b5 14 axb6 ♘xb6 15 ♗xb6 ♕xb6+ 16 ♔h1** *(D)*

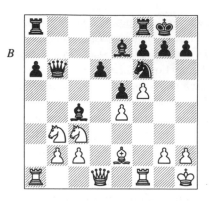

M. Tal – R. Fischer
Curaçao Candidates 1962

In this position White is aiming for the exchange of light-squared bishops. Then he will have certain potential advantages: pressure against the isolated a-pawn on an open file and the possibility of an eventual good knight vs bad bishop position with White's knight occupying d5 (for example, if White plays ♖a2, then ♘d2-c4-e3-d5). Fischer found a simple and elegant solution to Black's problems: **16...♗b5!**. This collinear move leaves White with three options: to leave the bishop on b5, to play ♘xb5, or to play ♗xb5. If White ignores the bishop, then Black's next move will be ...♗c6, both attacking the weak e4-pawn and supporting the thrust ...d5. To meet these threats White will be forced to play ♗f3, but this is hardly the most active square for the bishop; Black would obtain good counterplay by ...a5-a4, when the b2-pawn is vulnerable. The second option, 17 ♘xb5, swaps off the knight which White was hoping to put on d5 later, and moves the weak a-pawn off the open file. The result would be a near-certain draw in view of the opposite-coloured bishops, but this might be White's best option.

Fischer played 16...♗b5 in two games; both opponents chose the third option and the games continued **17 ♗xb5 axb5 18 ♘d5 ♘xd5 19 ♕xd5 ♖a4!** (a second collinear move, putting pressure on e4; if White takes, then his b-pawn will be in trouble) **20 c3 ♕a6** (D).

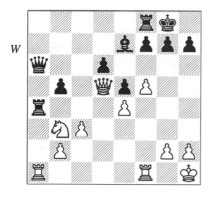

Not only does White have no advantage, but he is even slightly worse. His queen looks impressive on d5, but actually it is the knight which should be there instead. The knight has no route to reach d5, and indeed after ...♗g5 it will be virtually immobilized. Black can improve his position by ...h6 and ...♖c8-c4, for example.

The Tal game continued **21 ♖ad1 ♖c8 22 ♘c1 b4 23 ♘d3 bxc3 24 bxc3**,

and now 24...♖xc3 would have left Black a pawn up with a good position. In the later game Unzicker-Fischer, Varna Olympiad 1962, the German grandmaster chose **21 h3** but lost in only five more moves: **21...♖c8 22 ♖fe1 h6 23 ♔h2 ♗g5 24 g3? ♕a7 25 ♔g2 ♖a2 26 ♔f1 ♖xc3 0-1**.

Fischer's handling of this game was very impressive.

Switchbacks are another potential blind spot. If you have just moved a piece from A to B, the idea of moving it back from B to A can be hard to spot.

The third type of move which is hard to spot is the 'hesitation move'. This arises when a piece can move from A to either B or C. You decide that it is bad to move it to C and play it to B instead. Next move it would be good to play it from B to C, but you don't consider it because this is precisely the move that you rejected a few moments ago.

Here is an example *(D)*:

Black has a fairly miserable position. He is a pawn down, his king is somewhat exposed and White has a passed d-pawn which bears constant observation. However, the opposite-coloured bishops make it very hard for White to win, and in addition Black came up with an excellent defensive idea:

1...h4!

Now 2 ♗xh4 ♕f4+ 3 ♗g3 ♕h6+ leads to perpetual check, so I tried ...

2 d7 ♗xd7

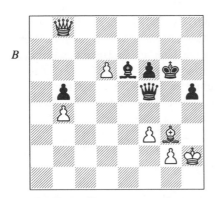

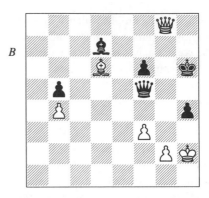

J. Nunn – R. Filguth
*World Student Team Championship,
Mexico City 1977*

Not, of course, 2...hxg3+ 3 ♕xg3+
followed by 4 d8♕.

3 ♕g8+ ♔h6

Black's best move. After 3...♔h5 4
♗xh4! Black is more or less forced to
play 4...♔h6, but then White has an
extra tempo. In fact, even this would
only offer White marginal winning
chances because he has nothing forced
and the exchange of White's dangerous d-pawn for the enemy h-pawn has
clearly favoured Black.

After the text-move, 4 ♗xh4 ♗e6
allows Black to defend comfortably.

4 ♗d6 (D)

My opponent appeared surprised by
this move, which has the nasty threat
of 5 ♗f8+ ♔h5 6 ♕h8+ ♔g6 7 ♕g7+
♔h5 8 ♕h6#. It is quite hard to stop
this threat, for example 4...♕g6 5
♗f4+ ♔h5 6 ♕h8+, 4...♕g5 5 ♗f8+
♔h5 6 ♕h7+ and 4...♕h7 5 ♗f4+ are
no help.

Based on these lines, Black concluded that there was no defence and
so...

1-0

Filguth had overlooked the simple
4...♔h5!, after which White has no
winning chances at all. The reason: he
had rejected playing the king to h5 the
previous move, but under the changed
circumstances it had become the only
saving possibility.

As an aside, I am one of those players who gets up from the board after
almost every move (but even when
walking around, I am still thinking
hard about the position). However, after playing ♗d6 I stayed at the board.
When players are completely winning, they often remain at the board in
order to accept their opponent's resignation, and I suspect that Filguth thus
interpreted my unusual immobility. In
fact, of course, I was frantically trying
to find a good reply to ...♔h5.

I seem to be especially prone to
overlooking 'hesitation' moves.

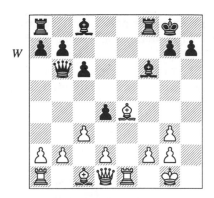

J. Nunn – J. de la Villa
Szirak Interzonal 1987

In this position White is a pawn up but has yet to develop his queenside pieces. Here I rejected 18 ♕b3+ because after 18...♔h8 19 ♕xb6 axb6 it is quite hard for White to continue his development. 20 d3 is impossible because of the pressure on c3, and 20 c4 is met by 20...d3! 21 ♗xd3 ♗d4 22 ♖f1 ♗g4, which leaves White totally paralysed. Black could just continue with ...♖ae8 and ...♗e2, eventually winning the pawn on f2 and setting up possible mating threats along the h-file.

I therefore played **18 ♕c2!** which, in addition to the attack on h7, threatens to bring the queenside pieces out by 19 d3 and 20 ♗f4. Black responded with **18...d3!?**, based on the tactical point 19 ♗xd3? ♕xf2+!! 20 ♔xf2 ♗d4++ 21 ♔e2 ♗g4#. I actually played 19 ♕xd3 ♗xc3 20 bxc3 ♕xf2+ 21 ♔h2 ♕xe1 22 ♗a3! and won after immense complications. However, the

simple 19 ♕b3+ would have been enormously strong. After 19...♕xb3 (or else White swaps queens and takes on d3) 20 axb3 ♖d8 21 ♖e3 White wins the pawn, after which Black doesn't have much to show for his two-pawn deficit.

I didn't even consider 19 ♕b3+ for the simple reason that I had rejected it the previous move. It didn't occur to me that the 'extra' tempo ...d3 is actually very helpful to White, because it severely weakens Black's d-pawn and, unlike the line after 18 ♕b3+, White has not weakened the d4-square by playing c3-c4.

It is worth trying to pinpoint repetitive errors in one's own play. These days, with the availability of strong computer programs, finding tactical errors is quite easy. I always quickly run my games past *Fritz* – it is often quite shocking what turns up!

Time-trouble

The advice here is quite simple: don't get into time-trouble in the first place. This immediately raises the question: what constitutes time-trouble? Some people panic when they have ten minutes left for ten moves, while others appear quite calm even when down to their last thirty seconds.

I will propose a definition: time-trouble arises if you have less than one minute left per move. In my opinion this is the lower limit for guaranteeing an acceptable standard of play. It is of course possible to play well even with less time than this, but you are really putting yourself in the hands of fate. If no unexpected problems arise, no shocks, no really tricky decisions, then you will probably survive more or less unscathed, but how can you be sure this is going to happen? Those who are addicted to time-trouble will show you the remarkable games they won despite extreme time shortage; they probably won't show you the much larger number which they lost because of the same time shortage.

If you regularly run into time-trouble, according to this definition, then you are doing something wrong and it is almost certainly costing you points.

The reasons for running short of time are many. Here is a selection of the most common:

1) Indecision. Probably the most common reason. If you spend a long time agonizing over decisions, then you will inevitably run short of time. The pragmatic approach I recommend in this book should help. If you find that, after lengthy thought, you usually end up playing the move that you wanted to play straight away, then learn to trust your intuition more.

2) Worrying too much about very minor matters. There is no point thinking for half an hour about a possible advantage or disadvantage of what a computer would call '0.1 of a pawn'. This almost certainly is not going to

cost you a half-point. The piece you hang later during time-trouble probably is.

3) Providing yourself with an excuse. To those who do not suffer from this particular ailment, it probably sounds ridiculous, but it is surprisingly common. In these cases there is a (possibly subconscious) reluctance to admit that a loss is due to bad play; problems with the clock provide an alternative explanation. If you find yourself saying to people after a game 'I had a perfectly reasonable position until I ran into time-trouble' then you probably have this disease to some extent. It really is an absurd attitude. The clock is just as much a part of the game as the board and pieces, and losing because of time-trouble is no different to losing because of weak play – it's still a zero on the score-sheet. The only difference is that if you run very short of time you will almost certainly lose; if you play more quickly, you may lose because of weak play, but then again you may not. The best way to improve is to gain over-the-board experience and if your games just become a time-trouble mess, then you are probably not learning very much from them.

If you have time-trouble problems, then in addition to the points mentioned above, bear in mind the following tips:

1) Arrive for the game on time. The most obvious and simplest way of saving time!

2) Don't spend a long time considering which opening to play. If you have the luxury of knowing more than one opening, then you should think about this before the game.

3) Don't think about theoretical moves. Some players spend an inordinate length of time reaching a position with which they are already familiar. An extreme case was a game I played as White against Stohl in the Poisoned Pawn, an opening with which we were both very familiar. I played a line which was believed to lead to equality. He was so worried about the improvement he felt sure was coming that he thought carefully about each move, trying to spot the 'improvement' in advance. By the time the improvement arrived, well into the ending, he had used 90 of his 120 minutes reaching a position he knew perfectly well. The 'improvement', when it finally came, was actually a rather modest affair, but thanks to Stohl's lack of time I won the game.

4) Don't use up time thinking about obviously forced moves. Your opponent takes a piece; you suddenly notice that after your recapture he has a possibility that you hadn't noticed before. Don't think – just take back. Thinking not only wastes time, it also alerts your opponent to the fact that there is something you are worried about. It he hasn't noticed it before, he probably will now! Of course, you should be sure that the recapture really is the only possibility, otherwise you might overlook a powerful *zwischenzug*.

5) Chess is all about making decisions. Postponing a decision doesn't necessarily improve it. Try to get into the habit of asking yourself: is further thought actually going to beneficial?

I won't give any advice about what to do if you are in time-trouble, since this situation shouldn't arise.

If your opponent is in time-trouble, the main piece of advice is to stay calm. It is quite easy to become so excited that you start bashing out moves as quickly as your opponent and thus make no use of your time advantage. You should also avoid thinking "I *must* try to win the game during his time-trouble" and then embark on some risky venture which you would never play under normal circumstances. This is only justified if you have a very bad or losing position, and the time-trouble really is your only hope. Given a choice between a quiet continuation and an equally good sharp continuation, then by all means choose the sharp continuation, but an opponent in time-trouble is no justification for knowingly playing an inferior move.

Players in time-trouble tend to spend most of their time analysing forcing, tactical continuations, so be especially careful not to allow a tactical trick. Where strategy is concerned, they will probably decide on a 'default move' to play if your move carries no special threat. Very often this 'default move' will be part of a plan for transferring a badly-placed piece to a better square. If they are deprived of any such obvious plan, then the result is usually confusion or a 'nothing' move. With any luck, you can use the moves before the time-control to gain a positional advantage which will set you up nicely for next phase of the game.

Laziness

Laziness at the chessboard manifests itself in two ways. The first is when you have a complicated possibility, but decide not to analyse it on the grounds that it would be too much work. Note that is not the same as the 'DAUT' principle mentioned on page 21. That represents a conscious weighing of the balance between the time spent and the possibility of finding a better move. It comes into play most often when there is a perfectly adequate alternative which can be played with little calculation. Laziness, on the other hand, is a deliberate turning away from a move which may turn out to be very strong indeed. Losing a game because you have overlooked a move is one thing, but losing because you have spotted the correct move and could not be bothered to analyse it is quite another!

A second, more understandable, form of laziness is when your opponent has an irritating possibility. You have to consider this same possibility

every move until you become fed up with it and spend a tempo ruling it out completely. The most common manifestation of this form of laziness is preventing a possible check by the opponent. You have to calculate the check in every single line, and in the end you just pre-empt the check by moving your king. There are, of course, many situations in which such a move is perfectly reasonable, but there are also many in which the loss of time is important. Playing ♔h1 after 0-0 (or ♔b1 after 0-0-0) may be just such a waste of time. When such a move is justifiable, it is normally because of a concrete reason rather than because it is annoying to have to do a bit more calculation.

Here is an unusual example of laziness:

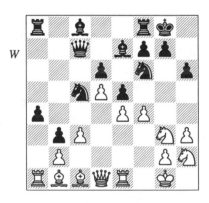

J. Nunn – Xie Jun
Hastings 1996/7

In this position, it suddenly occurred to me that Black might play

...a3 as a pawn sacrifice at some stage. I started to calculate lines such as 21 ♘f3 exf4 22 ♗xf4 a3 23 ♖xa3 ♖xa3 24 bxa3 and wondered if Black has enough compensation for the pawn. I decided that she does not, because White's ♘d4 is annoying for Black, aiming at both c6 and f5. I started calculating more and more lines and in each I had to take into account the possibility of ...a3. In the end I just became fed up with this, and decided to rule it out.

21 ♖a3?

My reasoning was that since the rook is blocked in by both bishops and unlikely to move along the first rank, it might as well perform a useful task (preventing ...a3). Deep down I was aware that this move looks highly artificial; my 'logic' was really just a rationalization for an outbreak of laziness.

A more sensible piece of reasoning would have been to note that Black's queenside pawn majority will be very good in an ending, and so White must play for a decision in the middlegame. For the moment White need not worry about ...a3, since the b1-bishop will prevent the b-pawn promoting for several moves.

Thus 21 f5 is correct, aiming to play ♘g4 or ♘h5 to eliminate the defensive knight. Since White's position in the diagram is not especially good, he should probably be happy with a sacrifice on h6 leading to perpetual check.

21...♗d7 22 ♗d3 ♕b6 23 ♔h1 exf4 24 ♗xf4 ♘xd3 25 ♕xd3 ♕f2 26 ♕d2 ♕xd3 27 ♗xd2 ♖fe8

Things have not gone very well for White. His rook is still on the ridiculous square a3, Black has the two bishops and White's e-pawn is weak. All this adds up to a clear plus for Black and the main cause was the lazy move 21 ♖a3.

Determination

Of all the personal qualities which are important at the board, determination is probably the most significant. Some players, when confronted with an onerous defensive task, such as defending an inferior and long-drawn-out ending, suffer a crisis of will-power. They see the gloom ahead of them, with only the distant prospect of at most half a point, and become despondent. The result is either a feeble resistance, or a decision to stake everything on a half-hearted swindle. When this is brushed aside, they feel that they can resign with good grace. Not surprisingly, this behaviour no recipe for success.

Even very strong players can become so resigned to the prospect of inevitable defeat that they do not notice when a saving opportunity is presented to them.

Here are a couple of notable recent examples.

The position overleaf is a simple technical win for White, and it is hard

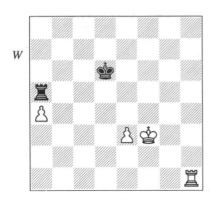

G. Kasparov – N. Short
*London PCA World
Championship (9) 1993*

to imagine Kasparov going so far
wrong as to reach a drawn position,
yet that is what happened.

45 ♖a1

Not a particularly accurate move,
although it does not throw away the
win. White should simply put his rook
on the fourth rank and march his king
to b4. Thus 45 ♖d1+ ♔e5 46 ♖d4 or
45 ♖h6+ ♔c7 46 ♖h4 would have won
easily.

45...♔e5 46 e4??

An amazing blunder. One way to
win is by 46 ♔e2 ♔e4 47 ♖a3 (47 ♖f1
and 48 ♖f4 is also good) and Black
must either allow the king to reach d3,
or permit the advance of the pawn. In
either case White wins easily.

46...♔e6??

An equally serious error. Black can
draw by 46...♖c5! 47 a5 (after 47 ♖a3
♖c4 48 a5 ♖xe4 49 a6 ♖f4+ and
50...♖f8 Black's rook makes it back)

47...♖c3+ 48 ♔g4 ♔xe4 49 a6 ♖c8 50
a7 ♖g8+ 51 ♔h5 ♖a8 and Black simply marches his king over and takes
the pawn.

**47 ♔e3 ♔d6 48 ♔d4 ♔d7 49 ♔c4
♔c6 50 ♔b4 ♖e5 51 ♖c1+ ♔b6 52
♖c4 1-0**

In order to understand this double
blunder, you have to take into account
the course of the game. Short had been
losing from an early stage, and Kasparov had been exchanging down to a
simplified endgame. Both sides were
simply acting out the final stages of a
drama which had been decided in the
opening, and they knew full well what
the result of the game would be. In this
frame of mind it is possible to let one's
attention wander away from the position on the board. Nevertheless, it is an
astonishing error to occur at such a
high level.

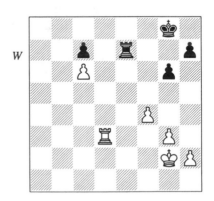

A. Shirov – J. Timman
Wijk aan Zee 1996

Black had been under pressure for some time and ended up in this rook ending a clear pawn down.

45 g4?!

Both players seemed to believe that this position should be a clear-cut win for White, but in fact it is not so simple. The move played is probably already an inaccuracy. After 45 ♔f3 ♖e6 46 ♖d8+ (Shirov comments that 46 ♖c3 should win, but White's rook is tied to the defence of c6 more or less permanently and the win does not look at all simple to me) 46...♔f7 47 ♖d7+ ♖e7 48 ♖xe7+ ♔xe7 White can force a winning queen and pawn ending by 49 ♔g4 ♔d6 50 ♔g5 ♔xc6 51 ♔h6 ♔b7 52 ♔xh7 c5 53 ♔xg6 c4 54 f5 c3 55 f6 c2 56 f7 c1♕ 57 f8♕ ♕c2+ 58 ♕f5 ♕xh2 (after 58...♕c6+ 59 ♔h5 ♕e8+ 60 ♔g4 ♕g8+ 61 ♔f4 White remains two pawns up) 59 g4. The evaluation of endings with ♕+♙ vs ♕ is a simple matter at home, because one only has to consult a computer-generated database. The oracle informs us that this one is indeed winning, but of course it is not so easy at the board. The general feeling amongst GMs is that endings with ♕+g♙ vs ♕ (and the defending king cut off from the pawn) are almost impossible to defend in practice, even if some of them are drawn with perfect play (see page 150 for more details). Thus even without consulting the database, Shirov would have been aware that this ending offers White excellent winning prospects. In the specific position

above it is quite easy to see that Black only has a few checks and then White can advance his pawn to the fifth rank (59...♕d6+ 60 ♔g7 ♕d4+ 61 ♔f7 ♕c4+ 62 ♔f8 ♕b4+ 63 ♔g8), which would provide further evidence in favour of assessing it as winning for White.

45...♖e6

Black must try to force White's rook into a defensive position.

46 ♖d8+

White could still play 46 ♖c3.

46...♔f7 47 ♖d7+ ♖e7 48 ♖xe7+??

This move throws away the win. White could still have retreated his rook and defended the c-pawn along the c-file.

46...♔xe7 49 g5 1-0??

Resigning is an even more astonishing blunder than Shirov's mistaken rook exchange. After 49...♔d6 Black draws without undue difficulty:

1) 50 f5 gxf5 51 h4 ♔e5 52 ♔f3 f4 53 h5 ♔f5 54 g6 hxg6 55 h6 ♔f6 56 ♔xf4 g5+ draws.

2) 50 h4 ♔xc6 51 f5 ♔d6 52 f6 ♔d7 53 ♔f3 ♔e6 54 ♔f4 ♔f7 55 ♔e5 ♔e8 56 ♔d5 ♔d7 57 ♔c5 ♔e8 and White cannot make progress, provided Black meets ♔c6 with ...♔d8. If the white king is on c5 or d5, then Black can play either ...♔e8 or ...♔d7. The fact that Black has this choice of moves means that these is no chance of White winning by somehow losing a move, because only after ♔c6 is Black restricted to a unique square for his king.

What makes Timman's decision to resign so surprising is that he could have quite easily taken the pawn on c6 and waited to see Shirov's intention. Giving up so early is an indication of defeatism – he felt that the rook ending was dead lost and, since the king and pawn ending was a natural consequence of the rook ending, then that too must be lost.

In these examples, both Short and Timman were paying scant attention to the position on the board and were heavily influenced by the preceding play.

The lesson to be learnt from this is that while the game is in progress, you should be concentrating on the current position, regardless of what has happened before. There are very few players who have the technical skill to convert advantageous positions into a win without at some stage allowing the opponent a chance for counterplay. The defender's task is to maintain his concentration, so that when a possible saving opportunity arises, he does not overlook it. There is no point in playing on if all you are doing is going through the motions, waiting for the right moment at which to resign.

2 The Opening

Building a repertoire

It would be nice to start the construction of an opening repertoire from scratch, so that everything fits together neatly, and all transpositions are taken care of. However, most players don't have an elegant opening repertoire. They play a motley collection of openings which they have accumulated, more or less by chance, over the years. However, we will take the idealized situation of someone starting from square one (a1, presumably).

The first step is to think about your personal style. Do you prefer open, tactical positions or closed, strategic positions? Does an attack on your king make you nervous, or are you happy so long as you have a counter-attack? Do you prefer main lines, or something slightly offbeat? Next, look at the various openings available, and see which ones fit in with your personal style. For example, when choosing an opening with Black against 1 e4, you might make some notes along the following lines:

1...c5: Open positions, tactical, attack and counter-attack. Scheveningen and Taimanov systems safer and less tactical than the Dragon, Najdorf and Pelikan.

1...c6: Solid positions, strategic, safe king.

1...e6: Closed positions, strategic.

1...e5: Fairly solid, but can lead to almost any type of position, depending on the follow-up. Petroff the most solid option.

1...d6: Sharp positions. Attack and counter-attack. However, White does have solid options.

1...d5: Slightly off-beat, fairly solid but a little passive.

1...♘f6: Sharp positions. These days considered slightly off-beat.

1...♘c6: Slightly off-beat. Need to consider what to play after 2 ♘f3.

Do the same with openings against 1 d4, flank openings and with White. Then you have to consider how all these fit together. If you choose the Pirc against 1 e4, it makes sense to consider the King's Indian against 1 d4. This is more flexible and will give you additional options later. For example, you may decide later that you would prefer not to allow the Sämisch against the King's Indian. To this end you decide to meet 1 d4 with 1...d6, and against 2 c4 you will play 2...e5. Many players who would quite like to play this system with Black are put off by two things: firstly, White can play 2 e4 and secondly White can play 2 ♘f3 (it is true that Black can meet 2 ♘f3 by 2...♗g4, but many regard this as somewhat better for White). However, because your openings have been chosen to fit together, neither of these problems will bother you. The Pirc is already in your repertoire, and after 2 ♘f3 you can play 2...♘f6 and enter a King's Indian, but with the Sämisch having been ruled out.

Likewise, the Caro-Kann and the Slav fit together, and then you can answer 1 c4 by 1...c6, without having to undertake any additional learning to cope with 2 e4.

There is a temptation to choose some really unusual openings, because the amount of study required is much less. However, I would advise against this. Rarely played openings are usually rare precisely because they have some defect. Sooner or later your opponents will start to exploit this defect and then you will have to switch openings. If you choose another very unusual opening, the process will repeat itself. After a few years, you will have spent just as much effort as if you had chosen a mainstream opening in the first place, and you will have little to show for your efforts.

This problem doesn't arise with a repertoire based on main lines. First of all, such lines, which have been tried and tested in thousands of grandmaster games, are unlikely to be 'busted' in the first place. The worst that usually happens is that a small finesse leads to a minor reassessment of one

line. Secondly, even if the worst happens and a blockbuster novelty finishes off a line, it is usually relatively easy to switch to another line within the same opening. Mainstream openings such as the Ruy Lopez or the Orthodox Queen's Gambit are not merely single lines; they are massive complexes of different systems for both colours. Suppose, for example, you play the following line of the Chigorin Defence in the Closed Ruy Lopez: 1 e4 e5 2 ♘f3 ♘c6 3 ♗b5 a6 4 ♗a4 ♘f6 5 0-0 ♗e7 6 ♖e1 b5 7 ♗b3 d6 8 c3 0-0 9 h3 ♘a5 10 ♗c2 c5 11 d4 ♕c7 12 ♘bd2 cxd4 13 cxd4 ♗d7 14 ♘f1 ♖ac8 15 ♘e3 ♘c6 16 d5 ♘b4 17 ♗b1 a5 18 a3 ♘a6. Suddenly you see a game in this line which seems to cast doubt on Black's play. You need a replacement line, quickly. There is a wide range of possibilities to choose from; you could try 15...♖fe8 or, slightly earlier, 13...♘c6. Perhaps delaying the exchange on d4 and playing 12...♗d7 or 12...♘c6 might be an idea. All these are viable lines, so there is no need to panic. They all lead to the same general type of position, so that the experience you have gained with your former line will not be wasted The general principles governing play with these Chigorin Defence pawn structures will be still be valid in your new line. Moreover, all the effort you have put into learning how to combat earlier deviations by White (Exchange Spanish, Lines with ♕e2, etc.) will remain valid. Instead of facing a major overhaul, only a minor modification will be necessary.

Once you have chosen your openings, how best to study them? There is nothing better than a good book, which brings us on to our next topic.

Using opening books

These days there are books on virtually every opening under the sun. Some are good, some are competent and some are bad. Unfortunately, it is often not easy to decide which is which. In choosing a good book, reviews are an obvious guide, but these are often not very helpful in the chess world. This is not necessarily the fault of the reviewers; I can testify from personal experience that reviewing openings books is a difficult and thankless task. In order to assess an opening book properly, you really have to be an expert in that particular opening. Of course, you can check to see if it is up-to-date and well-written, but a really good openings book will contain all those finesses which only a practitioner of the opening will know. Cunning move-orders designed to avoid particular lines, moves which caused a particular variation to be abandoned, but which were never actually played in a game – only a specialist will know whether such things are in the book or not. If one adds that chess book reviewers are normally unpaid (apart from receiving a free copy of the book), it is scarcely surprising that reviews of opening books tend towards a certain blandness. Major publishers are perhaps slightly safer than smaller operations, since they normally have some sort of quality control; having said that, they are also under far more commercial pressure to bring a book out on time, which can lead to a rushed job. The saying 'Don't judge a book by its cover' is especially valid for chess books. The covers are normally made by designers rather than chess-players; of course they should be checked, but even so howlers occasionally slip through. In the end, the reputation of the author is probably the best guide to the quality of a book.

Having chosen a book, it is best first of all to gain an overview of the opening. Look first at just the main lines to create a mental picture of the general structure of the opening. If the book contains illustrative games, it is worth playing these over first; you will probably already notice certain typical themes repeating themselves. In most major openings you will have a choice against each of the opponent's possibilities. As with the choice of the main openings, make a list of the various options and see which ones suit your style. Keep transpositional possibilities and move-orders in mind, to make sure that your opponent cannot circumvent your proposed repertoire by a simple variation in move-order. Suppose, for example, that you are going to play a line of the Sicilian with 1 e4 c5 2 ♘f3 e6, and are thinking about how to meet the 2 c3 Sicilian. You notice that the defence 1 e4 c5 2 c3 d5 3 exd5 ♕xd5 4 d4 ♘f6 5 ♘f3 ♗g4 is currently popular, and decide to play that. It would be easy to overlook the fact that White can play 1 e4 c5 2 ♘f3 e6 3 c3 instead. Of course you can still play 3...d5, but now the line with ...♗g4 is impossible. There are ways round this particular problem, but it is important to have something ready in advance, and not to be caught out over the board.

Notice that so far there has been no detailed study. Everything has been careful planning – good groundwork and thoroughness is the secret of successful opening preparation. Once you have your repertoire mapped out, then you can study each line in detail. To begin with, only study the main lines – that will cope with 90% of your games, and you can easily fill in the unusual lines later.

One important question is whether it is better to study an opening book that offers a pre-selected repertoire (often called 'Winning With ...', or a similar title), or one that offers a complete coverage of an opening. Certainly both books have their place and the ideal situation is to have one of each type for a given opening. It is certainly useful to have someone do much of the above-mentioned work for you, but nevertheless some lines in the proposed repertoire may not suit you, or developments since the book

was published may throw doubt on some recommendations. In this case it is essential to have a source of alternative possibilities.

More serious players who have a chess database (see also page 166) may like to check this for recent developments before playing a particular line. A database is also useful for seeing which lines are currently popular, and therefore where one should be focusing one's efforts.

At first you may find that your results with a new opening are disappointing. This is more likely with strategic openings than ones based on precise analysis. When I started playing the Sicilian Najdorf, my results were very good. This is an opening in which concrete knowledge of specific lines is very important. I had just studied the opening in great detail, and so my knowledge was often better and more up-to-date than that of my opponents. On the other hand, playing a strategic opening requires a positional understanding which is better learnt by experience than from books. It may be several games before you get up to speed with such an opening, but be persistent – your efforts will be rewarded in the end.

Books on offbeat openings

A particular genre of books which deserves special attention is that dealing with dubious and rarely-played openings. As in all categories of opening books, there are good and bad examples. Typically, such a book will claim that opening X is unjustly neglected, that recent games have shown X to be playable after all and that all sorts of hidden resources and novelties are revealed for the first time in the book.

Unfortunately, 99% of the time the reasons X is rarely played are entirely justified, the 'recent games' turn out to be encounters of little value between unknown players, and the resources and novelties will only stand a few seconds' close examination. The tricks which authors can use to make openings such as X appear playable are many and varied, and are, of course, revealed for the first time in this book!

It is hard to give details without concrete examples, so that means I will have to choose a couple of victims. In this particular genre there is a depressingly high proportion of poor books, and it would be easy to choose one of the really bad ones and have some fun. In fact I have chosen one of the better examples, Tony Kosten's *The Latvian Gambit* (B.T. Batsford, 1995). This book is unusual in that a strong grandmaster has taken a look at a rarely played opening with a poor reputation. Tony was certainly taking on a real challenge with this title! When it arrived, I was quite baffled as to how the author had managed to fill up 144 pages; I had thought a detailed refutation would take 10 pages at most.

I decided to use the book as a basis for a couple of hours' analysis on the Latvian (pages 72-76 are based on this analysis). It is, of course, very rarely played and I would not expect a GM to dare it, but this enhances its surprise value. It would certainly be embarrassing to face it and plunge into deep thought on move three! Moreover, when a new book appears on an opening, it always encourages a few people to take it up, so the chances of meeting it were high enough to warrant devoting a little time to it.

When I was a teenager, there were a couple of junior players who used the Latvian which, if you don't know already, is characterized by the moves 1 e4 e5 2 ♘f3 f5. For many players this opening offers a huge advantage: it provides a more or less complete defence to 1 e4. If you play a line of the Spanish, then you have to worry about various white systems in the Spanish, such as the Exchange Variation and early d3 lines, plus the Scotch and 3 ♗c4 – quite a body of theory to study. Adopting the Latvian short-circuits all that; apart from the King's Gambit and a few other openings, you don't have to study anything else to meet 1 e4. The question is: can the Latvian be considered playable?

The move 2...f5 has a dubious appearance; it doesn't develop a piece and it weakens the diagonals h5-e8 and c4-g8, the latter being important if Black intends to castle kingside later. I always viewed 3 ♘xe5 as the most logical reply – Black should be punished for not defending his e-pawn with 2...♘c6. I had scored well with this reply in my youth, so I decided to concentrate on it.

My first surprise came when I examined the list of contents. Chapter 6 dealt with (after 3 ♘xe5) "3...♘c6 and other third move alternatives for Black". I was stunned – I hadn't realized that 3...♘c6 was even vaguely possible. In fact Tony justifiably dismisses the "other third move alternatives" but devotes over nine pages to 3...♘c6 *(D)*. My first reaction on seeing an unfamiliar move in a book is not to look at the author's analysis, but to set the position up on a board and decide what would be the most natural response.

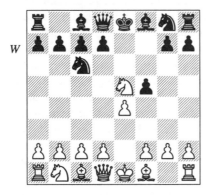

I noticed that White could win the exchange by 4 ♕h5+ g6 5 ♘xg6 ♘f6 6 ♕h4 hxg6 (6...♖g8!?) 7 ♕xh8 ♕e7. In return Black has a substantial lead in development. An assessment of this relatively complicated position would take some time, so bearing in mind DAUT I decided to look for something simpler.

4 ♘xc6 is another obvious move, but after 4...dxc6 I felt that this was rather playing into Black's hands. All Black's minor pieces can immediately come into play, while White still has to move his d-pawn to bring his c1-bishop out. Moreover, White has no minor pieces on the kingside, and if White intends to castle on that side the deficiency might allow Black to work up an attack. Neither of these lines is particularly clear, but the point of this initial evaluation is not to assess each possibility rigorously, but simply to decide which move looks best based on general principles. If I had not found a possibility that really struck me as the most promising, then I would have gone round again for a second look at 4 ♕h5+ and 4 ♘xc6.

However, at this moment I noticed a very tempting move: 4 d4!. This seemed to me to fit in best with the principle of rapid piece development in the opening. White creates a 'two-abreast' pawn centre and allows the c1-bishop to be developed without making any concession. The most obvious reply is 4...fxe4, but this just loses after 5 ♘xc6 dxc6 6 ♕h5+ and 6...g6 costs a rook, so Black must move his king. Nor is 4...♘f6 possible, as 5 ♘xc6 followed by 6 e5 gives White an extra pawn and a good position. Black can, of course, play 4...♘xe5 but after 5 dxe5 the pawn on e5 prevents ...♘f6 and Black's development is correspondingly awkward. If he tries to get the pawn back by 5...♕e7, then 6 ♕d4 looks very unpleasant, threatening ♘c3-d5. After five minutes I was still unable to see any playable line for Black against 4 d4, so I decided see what Kosten gave. His main lines are 4 ♘xc6 and 4 ♕h5+, with 4 d4 being relegated to a small note, which continues "4...♕h4! 5 ♗d3 fxe4 6 g3 ♕h3 7 ♗xe4 ♘f6" and ends up as "fine" for Black. Well, 4...♕h4 was certainly a surprise! However, I remained unconvinced. Black has violated virtually every principle of opening play, making weakening pawn moves, giving up a pawn and now developing his queen before the other pieces – surely there had to be a way to gain a clear advantage at the very least? Suddenly, I had an idea. How about 5 ♘f3 ♕xe4+ 6 ♗e2 *(D)*?

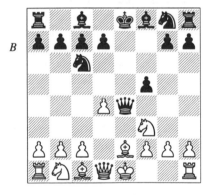

B

The more I looked at this the more it appealed to me. White threatens simply 0-0 and ♖e1. Black has insufficient time to develop his kingside minor pieces and get castled, for example 6...♘f6 7 0-0 ♗e7 8 ♖e1 and

8...0-0 loses to 9 ♗c4+. At the very least Black will have to make several more moves with his queen and fall hopelessly behind in development. In addition one must also take into account:

a) the dreadful positioning of the pawn on f5, which has no positive features at all and only weakens Black's position;

b) the possibility of d5, forcing the c6-knight to retreat; and

c) the plan of attacking c7 by ♘c3-d5 (or b5), possibly coupled with ♗f4.

Summing up, Black's position is probably just lost. There remained only one more point to be checked, viz. that Black could not exploit the temporarily active position of his queen by 6...♘b4. However, it would be a miracle if Black could get away with breaking the one remaining unbroken rule of opening play, that one should not repeatedly move the same pieces while leaving the rest of the army at home.

The analysis, however, is fairly simple: 6...♘b4 7 0-0 ♕xc2 8 ♕e1 ♗e7 (8...♕e4 9 ♘c3 ♕e7 10 ♕d1 ♘f6 11 ♖e1 ♘e4 12 a3 ♘c6 13 ♗d3 wins) 9 ♘c3 ♘f6 10 ♘e5 (threatening 11 ♗d1) 10...f4 11 a3 ♘c6 (11...d6 12 axb4 dxe5 13 dxe5 ♘g4 14 ♘d5 ♗d8 15 e6 ♘f6 16 ♘xf4 0-0 17 ♗d3 wins) 12 ♗d3 ♕b3 13 ♘b5 ♘xe5 14 dxe5 and Black's position collapses. Even this is presented in rather unnecessary detail; Black's development is so dreadful that it would not be amiss to condemn his position without concrete analysis.

Having done away with 3...♘c6, I turned my attention to the main line, 3...♕f6, again focusing my efforts on the line I had played decades earlier, namely 4 ♘c4 fxe4 5 ♘c3. In those far-off days the main continuation was 5...♕g6, after which I racked up quite a few wins with 6 d3 ♗b4 7 dxe4 ♕xe4+ 8 ♘e3. Kosten considers this very good for White, and his main line is 5...♕f7, a move which was practically unknown in 1970. I was aware of this move, and indeed had faced it once quite recently against *Fritz* in a man vs computer tournament. I won that game, but my handling of the opening was rather cautious due to lack of knowledge.

Kosten's main line is 6 ♘e3 c6! *(D)* (his exclamation mark).

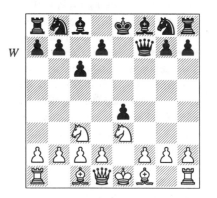

His principal variation runs 7 d3 exd3 8 ♗xd3 d5. Of course, White has a substantial lead in development, but Black has some strategic assets. He

has an extra central pawn, and the position of his queen will turn out to be quite useful if he castles kingside, as he will have instant pressure along the f-file. Indeed, it quickly becomes apparent that Black will have a fine game if he has a few tempi to complete his development. After ...♗d6, ...♘e7 and ...0-0 his king is safe, and the white knights are poorly placed. Black's central pawns prevent the knights from moving forwards and the knight on e3 blocks in the c1-bishop. A quick look at Kosten's analysis bears this out; in most lines White feels obliged to sacrifice a piece by ♘exd5 or ♘c4 to disturb Black before he can castle. All these lines are very complicated so, invoking DAUT again, I decided to return to the diagram position. I immediately wondered why White should not take the pawn on e4. After 7 ♘xe4 d5 8 ♘g5 ♕f6 9 ♘f3 I was again feeling confident about White's position. White has admittedly moved his knights several times, but Black cannot really boast about this, as so far the only piece he has moved is his queen. In terms of development, the two sides are roughly equal and White's position is without weaknesses – in fact, Black's compensation for the pawn is simply invisible. Kosten gives two lines: 9...♗e6, aiming to castle queenside, and 9...♗d6. Taking 9...♗e6 first, Kosten's continuation is "10 d4 ♘d7 11 ♗d3 0-0-0 *(D)* 12 c3 g5 13 0-0 h5, not fearing 14 ♘xd5?! ♗xd5 15 ♗xg5 ♕g7."

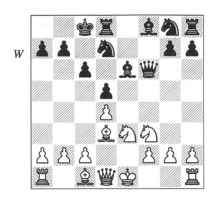

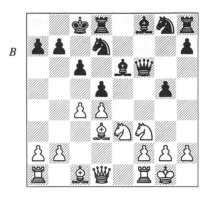

This line shows a typical ploy used by those attempting to make a very dubious line playable: the totally irrelevant move. Nobody could criticize the natural developing moves 10 d4 and 11 ♗d3, but what on earth is 12 c3 for? The d4-pawn isn't attacked, it isn't likely to be attacked and White isn't freeing his f3-knight to move anywhere. If White does nothing, then of course Black will eventually work up a serious attack on the kingside, but in opposite-side castling positions speed is of the essence. The correct plan for White is to play c2-c4 to develop counterplay in the centre and on the queenside.

Suppose White starts with the most obvious move, 12 0-0, and Black plays as in Kosten's line with 12...g5. White plays 13 c4 (D) and Black is already in a very bad way:

1) 13...♗d6 14 ♕a4 ♔b8 15 c5 ♗c7 16 b4 with an extra pawn and a very strong attack. If Black plays 16...a6, White can either sacrifice on a6 immediately or prepare it by 17 ♖b1.

2) 13...g4 14 cxd5 cxd5 15 ♘e5.

3) 13...dxc4 (relatively the best) 14 ♘xc4 h6 (14...g4 15 ♘fe5 ♗xc4 16 ♘xd7 ♖xd7 17 ♗xc4 is also very bad, for example 17...♖xd4 18 ♕b3 ♘e7 19 ♗e3) 15 ♗e3, to be followed by some combination of ♕a4, ♖c1 and ♘fe5. Black is a pawn down for nothing.

If Black plays some other 12th move, for example 12...♗d6, White again plays 13 c4 and in this case matters are even worse as ♘xc4 comes with gain of tempo.

Kosten's other line is 9...♗d6, and here he gives 10 d4 ♘e7 11 c4!, which is indeed White's strongest line. The continuation is 11...0-0 12 ♕b3 ♔h8!? (D) 13 ♗d2!? dxc4 14 ♗xc4 ♘d7 15 0-0, which he assesses as favouring White (and therefore recommends 9...♗e6 as above).

The point of 13 ♗d2 is to prevent a check on b4, and therefore to threaten to win a pawn on d5. It is also possible to play 13 ♗e2 followed by 0-0, when White would also threaten the

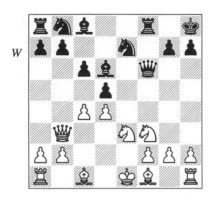

d5-pawn, and would have achieved this purpose using only natural developing moves. Therefore this line may be slightly more accurate. Once again, Black's compensation cannot be detected. The position resembles one from a normal opening such as the Petroff, except that Black's f-pawn has unaccountably dropped off the board.

When looking through 'dubious opening' analysis, look out for the following:

1) 'Nothing moves' by the opponent (i.e. the one facing the dubious opening), which only waste time.

2) Lines in which the opponent pretends he is in the nineteenth century, co-operatively grabs all the material on offer and allows a brilliant finish.

3) Lines which are given without any assessment.

4) Secret code words.

The fourth point perhaps requires some explanation. An author who is

both honest and a strong player will have some doubts about the lines he is giving, and this often manifests itself in phrases which are the chess equivalent of a disclaimer in a contract.

After "6...c6!" in the above line Kosten writes "Calmly leaving the e4-pawn to its fate; what exactly does Black obtain in return? Objectively, very little: just a slight lead in development and a lot of fun." Not exactly confidence-inspiring for Black, but of course having taken on the book he can hardly admit that the whole opening is just unsound. The publisher would doubtless not be amused by a manuscript consisting of a ten-page refutation! Similar key phrases are 'might appeal to a tactically-minded player', 'offers practical chances' and 'Black's position is no worse than in main-line openings such as the Ruy Lopez'. Depends which variation, I suppose!

Less honest authors are entirely shameless about such matters. They recommend the most outrageously unsound lines without blushing even slightly. They would never play such lines themselves, of course.

My second example is also a relatively high-quality product from a reliable GM author, *Winning With the Giuoco Piano and the Max Lange Attack* by Andrew Soltis (Chess Digest, 1992).

Books with 'Winning With' in the title confer an extra responsibility on the author, in that the result of the author's research is pre-determined. If the author reaches page 100 and discovers that the opening he is recommending is unsound, then he is unlikely to abandon the whole project. Of course, this probably won't happen if the opening chosen is a popular, main-line system. 'Winning With the Ruy Lopez' is an uncontroversial title; many top GMs regularly play the Ruy Lopez hoping to win. The problems start to arise when 'Winning With...' is combined with an offbeat and unpopular opening, such as the Giuoco Piano. You can be sure that if the established theory of the Giuoco Piano favoured White, then lots of GMs would play it, but of course it does not. The author is therefore undertaking to discover something new which overturns the prevailing opinion. Then the crucial question is how convincing these new ideas are.

The line of the Giuoco Piano recommended in the above book runs 1 e4 e5 2 ♘f3 ♘c6 3 ♗c4 ♗c5 4 c3 ♘f6 5 d4 exd4 6 cxd4 ♗b4+ 7 ♘c3 ♘xe4 8 0-0 ♗xc3 9 d5 (this is called the Møller Attack) 9...♗f6 10 ♖e1 ♘e7 11 ♖xe4 d6 12 ♗g5 ♗xg5 13 ♘xg5 and now there are basically two variations. The old continuation is 13...0-0, when White replies 14 ♘xh7. The more modern option, and the one which has really put people off the Møller Attack, is 13...h6!, which leapt to prominence following Barczay-Portisch, Hungarian Ch 1968/9. Let's take these two lines in turn.

After 13...0-0 14 ♘xh7 (D) Black can, of course, accept the sacrifice.

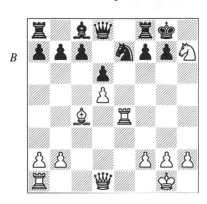

Traditional theory has it that this is a forced draw. Soltis offers some new ideas in the extremely complex positions which result but, taking DAUT into account, we will not look at these. In any case, I think many players would prefer to avoid 14...♔xh7 if at all possible; it has the defect that White can force perpetual check virtually at will, and of course a difficult defence in which a slight slip might be fatal is not to the taste of many players. The reasonable alternative to taking the knight is 14...♗f5, when the following moves are virtually forced: 15 ♖h4 (15 ♖xe7 ♕xe7 16 ♘xf8 ♖xf8 is entirely comfortable for Black) 15...♖e8 16 ♕h5 ♘g6 17 ♖d4 (D).

Now Soltis gives 17...♖e5 18 f4 ♘xf4! 19 ♖xf4 ♗g6 20 ♕f3 ♗xh7 21 ♗d3 "which is described as unclear by Harding and Botterill – a judgement that apparently has yet to be tested. However, it is not easy for Black to

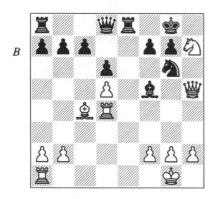

defend against the threat of doubling on the h-file, e.g. 21...♗xd3 22 ♕h3+! ♔g8 23 ♖h4 or 21...♕e7 22 ♕h3+ (not 22 ♖xf7? ♖e1+ 23 ♔f2 ♕h4+). Black's best appears to be 21...♔g8 22 ♗xg6 fxg6 but 23 ♖f1 retains an edge."

The Harding and Botterill book quoted is *The Italian Game* (B.T. Batsford, 1977). However, in the later book *Open Gambits* (B.T. Batsford, 1986), Botterill gives "20 ♕f3 ♔xh7 21 ♗d3 ♗xd3 22 ♕xd3+ ♔g8 ... it is questionable whether White has enough for the pawn. However White can hold the balance with 20 ♕h3 ♕c8 (Vuković) 21 ♘f6+ gxf6 and now:

"a) 22 ♕h4 f5 (intending ...♕d8) retains tension, though I think Black is better.

"b) Simply 22 ♕xc8+ ♖xc8 23 ♖xf6 is equal."

What is the poor reader to make of all this? Soltis and Botterill give completely different lines and offer different evaluations. I will try to clarify the

situation. The first important point is that Soltis notices, as Botterill does not, that 21...♗xd3 loses Black's queen after 22 ♕h3+ ♔g8 23 ♖h4. However, Soltis does not add that the position after 23...♕xh4 24 ♕xh4 ♖xd5 offers White essentially zero winning prospects. Soltis in fact mentions Black's best move, 21...♕e7, but then gives 22 ♕h3+ and stops (see point 3 above).

After 22...♔g8 (D) it is quite impossible to see how White can even equalize.

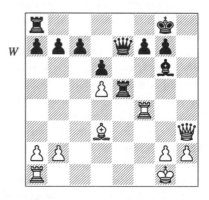

23 ♖h4 is met by the simple tactical point 23...♖h5! 24 ♖xh5 ♗xh5 25 ♕xh5 ♕e3+, while after 23 ♗xg6 fxg6 Black will force exchanges by either ...♖e1+ or ...♖f8, leaving White a pawn down. This brings us to another warning:

5) 'Winning With' authors display great ingenuity in finding resources for 'their' side, but often overlook even quite simple tactical defences for the 'other' side.

Botterill's other line for White, 20 ♕h3, can be met by 20...♕c8, although I would feel a bit queasy about allowing my kingside pawns to be broken up by ♘f6+ and then blocking in my bishop by ...f5. I would prefer to play 20...♖h5!, which again depends on a small tactical point: 21 ♘f6+ ♕xf6! (avoiding any damage to the kingside pawns) 22 ♖xf6 ♖xh3 23 ♖xg6 ♖h4! and Black reaches a four-rook ending with a clear extra pawn. White should prefer 21 ♕b3 ♔xh7 22 ♕xb7, when 22...♕b8 reaches a more or less equal ending, while 22...♖b8 23 ♕xa7 ♖xb2 is unclear, Black's more active pieces balancing the long-term danger posed by the passed a-pawn.

The above analysis shows that after 17...♖e5 18 f4 White has a draw at most, but I will be fair and point out an improvement for White: by 18 ♘g5! ♕f6 19 ♕h7+ ♔f8 20 ♕h5 he can more or less force Black to accede to a repetition of moves by 20...♔g8. However, going back one move, there is an interesting possibility for Black to play for an advantage: 17...♗c2! *(D)*.

The point of this is quite simple. Black clears the fifth rank for his rook and threatens (amongst other things) 18...♖e5 19 ♕h3 ♕e7, followed by ...♖e8, with a winning position since White is completely hamstrung by the trapped knight on h7 and can hardly move a piece.

The alternatives are:

1) 18 ♖d2 loses to 18...♘f4 19 ♕g4 ♗xh7 20 ♕xf4 ♖e4.

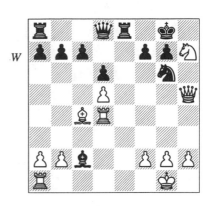

W

2) 18 ♖g4 ♘e5 19 ♖h4 f6 20 ♗b5 ♗g6 wins material.

3) 18 ♖c1 ♖e5 19 ♕h3 ♗f5 20 g4 ♕h4! and again White loses material.

4) 18 f4 ♕e7 with a nasty check on e3 to come.

5) 18 ♘g5 (relatively the best move) 18...♕f6 19 ♕h7+ ♔f8 20 ♘f3 ♗e4 with advantage to Black.

Now we return to 13...h6!, which most players cite as the reason for rejecting the Møller Attack.

Soltis recognizes the importance of the line by devoting 16 pages of analysis to the position after 13...h6. The critical position arises after 14 ♕e2 hxg5 15 ♖e1 ♗e6 16 dxe6 f6 17 ♖e3 *(D)*.

Soltis boldly states "This move, attributed to the Finnish correspondence player Juhani Sorri, rehabilitates the new Møller." We will take a look at two possibilities for Black, 17...c6 and 17...♔f8.

After 17...c6 play proceeds 18 ♖h3 ♖xh3 19 gxh3 g6. Soltis surveys the

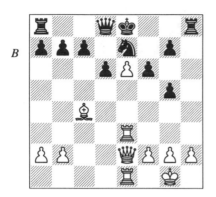

moves which have been tried in practice and concludes that they favour Black. His suggestion is 20 ♕d2 *(D)*.

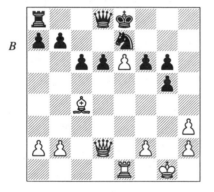

White prevents ...♕a5, and threatens 21 ♕c3. Soltis analyses 20...d5, but he doesn't consider the reply 20...♔f8, intending ...♔g7 followed by gradual consolidation with ...d5 and ...♕d6, when White will be a pawn down in a bad position. White's only active move is 21 h4, but after 21...gxh4 22 ♕h6+ ♔g8 23 ♕xh4 (23 ♖e4 fails to 23...♕f8 24 ♕xh4 d5, while 23 ♕xg6+ ♘xg6 24 e7+ d5 25 exd8♕+ ♖xd8 26 ♗f1

♔f7 wins for Black) 23...♔g7 Black cannot be prevented from consolidating with ...♕a5 followed by ...♖h8, or ...d5 followed by ...♕d6 and ...♖h8 (note that 24 ♖e3 loses to 24...♘f5). It seems to me that Black is virtually winning.

After 17...♔f8, Soltis's main line runs 18 ♗d3 ♔g8 19 ♕c2 ♖h6 20 ♖g3, and ends with the rather weak comment that "White will now follow with either ♖ee3 and ♖h3, or by preparations for f2-f4". However, after 20...d5 it is hard to see either of these plans being effective, for example 21 ♖ee3 ♕d6 22 ♖h3 ♖xh3 23 gxh3 (23 ♖xh3 ♕xe6 24 ♕xc7 ♖c8) 23...♖e8 or 21 ♖f1 ♕d6 preventing White's f4. Again there are no practical examples.

This brings us to our next warning:

6) Do not trust lines which are not based on practical examples. The more examples there are, and the higher the standard of the players, the more trust you can place in the line.

The above analysis shows up the weakness of the 'Winning With' approach applied to offbeat openings. Theory in the Giuoco Piano gives a unanimous thumbs up to Black; an author claims to have discovered something new which rehabilitates one line. You build your entire repertoire on the basis of this claim. With the Soltis book, this involves learning something against the Two Knights

Defence and against the various other systems Black might employ in the Giuoco Piano. In fact your whole repertoire is founded on one move, 20 ♕d2, which has never been tested in practice and which is analysed for just over half a page. Then it suddenly turns out that there is something wrong with 20 ♕d2. What do you do? It is no good switching to another line in the Giuoco Piano, as these have long been dismissed as offering White nothing. In fact, you may as well dust off your books on the Ruy Lopez.

3 The Middlegame

This is the part of the game in which it is hardest to set down rules and give good advice. For every rule one proposes, there will be so many exceptions that the rule may be more misleading than helpful. Accordingly, we are going to deal more with the psychological side of the middlegame than with technical issues.

Good positions

Congratulations, you have the advantage! But what do you do next? The first step is to judge whether your advantage is of a short-term or long-term nature. If it consists of better development or attacking chances, then it is probably short-term; if it is based on better pawn structure or superior minor pieces, then it is probably long-term. Many advantages, such as control of an open file, may be either short- or long-term depending on whether the opponent has a means of challenging the asset. This step will provide you with a clue as to whether you should be thinking of quick action to exploit your advantage before it disappears, or whether you can afford to manoeuvre slowly, tidying up your position ready for further action.

It is also important to take into account your opponent's possibilities for counterplay. It is no good starting some leisurely manoeuvres if your opponent has a passed pawn thundering down the board. Only if both conditions are satisfied – a long-term advantage and a lack of counterplay – can you afford to indulge in luxuries such as improving your king position. However, in this case you not only *can* take your time, you *should* do so. You may not be able to see a concrete reason why a particular 'tidying-up' move might be useful, but you lose nothing by playing it.

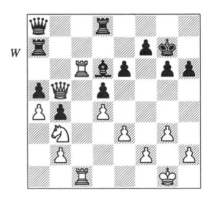

T. Petrosian – W. Unzicker
USSR – West Germany match,
Hamburg 1960

White's absolute domination of the c-file and pressure against the vulnerable a5-pawn give him a long-term advantage, and Black is so tied up as to have no realistic prospects of counterplay. Nevertheless, White still has to come up with a plan for improving his position. He decides that a kingside pawn advance is the best way to proceed, but if played immediately this would expose his king. Petrosian therefore decides to play his king to the secure refuge on a2 before proceeding with his kingside plan. Only a complete lack of counterplay could justify such an extravagant manoeuvre, but in this particular position White has absolutely no need to hurry.

29 ♔f1 ♔g8

After 29...♖b8, White would make progress by 30 ♖b6 ♖d8 31 ♖cc6 ♗c7 32 ♖a6.

30 h4 h5

A very unpleasant decision. This gives White the chance of eventually opening up the kingside with g4, but meeting h4-h5 with ...g5 would have a similar effect, since White could later play f4.

31 ♖1c2 ♔h7 32 ♔e1 ♔g8 33 ♔d1 ♔h7 34 ♔c1 ♔g8 35 ♔b1 ♔h7 36 ♕e2 ♕b7 37 ♖c1 ♔g7 38 ♕b5!

Petrosian observes that 38 g4 hxg4 39 ♕xg4 ♖a6 40 ♖xa6 ♕xa6 41 h5 ♕d3+ allows Black to develop some activity, so he arranges to play f4 before starting his kingside play with g4.

38...♕a8

Or 38...♕xb5 39 axb5 a4 40 b6 ♖ad7 41 ♘a5 ♖a8 42 ♖xd6! ♖xd6 43 b7 ♖b8 44 ♖c8 ♖d8 45 ♖xd8 ♖xd8 46 ♘c6 and White wins.

39 f4 ♔h7 40 ♕e2 ♕b7 41 g4! hxg4 42 ♕xg4 ♕e7 (D)

Now 42...♖a6 may be met by 43 ♖6c2! and, thanks to f4, White can swing both rooks to the kingside, giving a winning attack.

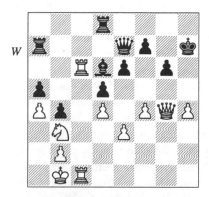

43 h5 ♕f6 44 ♔a2 ♔g7 45 hxg6 ♕xg6 46 ♕h4

The open files on the kingside, coupled with all Black's other problems, prove too much.

46...♗e7 47 ♕f2 ♔f8 48 ♘d2 ♖b7 49 ♘b3 ♖a7 50 ♕h2 ♗f6

After 50...♗d6 White wins by 51 ♖xd6! ♖xd6 52 f5 exf5 53 ♖c8+ ♔e7 54 ♕h8.

51 ♖c8 ♖ad7 52 ♘c5! b3+ 53 ♔xb3 ♖d6 54 f5! ♖b6+ 55 ♔a2 1-0

One common error in prosecuting an advantage is to indulge in tactics for the sake of it. There is a general feeling that the ideal game is one in which you positionally outplay your opponent and then finish with a burst of scintillating tactics. In fact, the ideal game is one in which you win without allowing any unnecessary counter-chances. If you can win with a clear-cut combination, then that is the best way to eliminate counterplay, because the game is over! However, you should be really sure that your combination does work; it is quite easy to miscalculate complex tactics, and if there is an element of doubt then a purely strategic approach is probably better. Even if your combination 'works' (i.e. is not tactically unsound) then you should also be sure that your advantage in the resulting position is greater than it is in the position beforehand. A common error is to play an elaborate tactical line gaining, for example, the exchange for a pawn, only to discover that there are fewer winning chances after the combination than before.

In the following example White, with a strategically winning position, spotted a seductively beautiful combination *(D)*:

This position is a Benoni gone horribly wrong for Black. White's pieces are all actively placed and he has the two bishops, while Black's a8-rook is useless and his knights poorly placed.

19 e5!

This is the thematic Benoni breakthrough, so it came as no surprise.

19...dxe5 20 d6

But this was unexpected. I had anticipated the natural 20 f5 when Black is probably just lost. White threatens to complete his blockade by ♘e4,

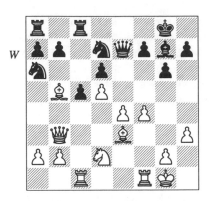

J. Bellon – J. Nunn
Zurich 1984

when a list of the threats shows just how awful Black's position is: d6, fxg6, ♗g5, ♗c4, ♘g5. Consequently, Black would have to try 20...♘f6 (20...e4 21 fxg6 hxg6 22 d6 and 23 ♗c4 wins), but 21 fxg6 hxg6 22 ♗g5 e4 23 ♖ce1 is crushing. One possible continuation would be 23...c4 24 ♗xc4 ♘c5 25 ♕g3 ♘h5 26 ♕e3 ♗f6 27 ♗xf6 ♘xf6 28 ♕d4 ♘cd7 29 ♘xe4 ♘xe4 30 d6! and Black's position is torn to shreds.

Bellon's move gave me a momentary glimmer of hope, but then I realized he intended 20...♕xd6 21 ♘e4 ♕e7 22 f5 with the same type of position as after 20 f5. White, it is true, has given up a second pawn, but his knight has arrived on e4 with gain of tempo. A quick look convinced me that there was no real answer to the threats to f7 arising after fxg6, ♗c4 and, if necessary, ♘g5. However, there was obviously nothing better than to take the pawn.

20...♕xd6 21 ♕xf7+? *(D)*

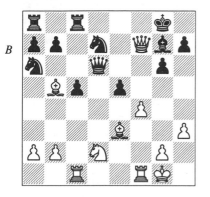

I hadn't seen this queen sacrifice at all, and when he touched his queen I couldn't imagine where it was going. A second later I found out! It is of course desirable to avoid revealing to your opponent that you have overlooked something, but in this case my body language must have broadcast the message far and wide.

The question mark attached to this move is perhaps a little harsh, because White retains a winning position even after it. Yet from the practical point of view it is undoubtedly a mistake. 21 ♘e4 would have led to a position in which White's win would require only straightforward, obvious moves – he just has to take aim at f7 and Black will soon collapse. The move played alters the character of the position completely and presents both players with new problems to solve.

White had noticed an attractive combination without tactical flaws and leading to a won position. He then made the mistake of not asking the question 'Is my advantage after the combination greater or smaller than my current advantage?'

21...♔xf7 22 fxe5+ ♔g8

I would have preferred to approach the passed d-pawn that is about to be created, but after 22...♔e6 23 exd6 ♗xb2 (23...♔xd6 24 ♘c4+ ♔e6 25 ♗xd7+ ♔xd7 26 ♖f7+) 24 ♖cd1 the threats against Black's exposed king are too strong, e.g. 24...♗d4 25 ♗xd4 cxd4 26 ♘f3 ♘e5 27 ♖fe1 ♖c5 28 ♗xa6 bxa6 29 ♖xd4 and Black cannot both save his pinned knight and stop the d-pawn.

23 exd6 ♘e5 24 ♘e4

White's two active bishops, better development and dangerous d-pawn are undoubtedly enough to win, but although there are many very promising continuations, there is no way to finish Black off instantly. After 24 ♗xa6 bxa6 25 ♖xc5 (25 ♗xc5 ♘d3) 25...♖xc5 26 ♗xc5 ♘d3, for example, Black regains the pawn on b2 (White should avoid 27 b4? ♘xc5 28 bxc5 ♗d4+). In view of the doubled a-pawns, White would be effectively almost a pawn up, but the win would not be guaranteed.

24...c4

Keeping the pawn for the moment.

25 ♗g5 *(D)*

25 ♗f4 is also very strong.

25...♘b8

When you are desperate, it is sometimes necessary to play ugly moves. The threat of 26 d7 can only be met by

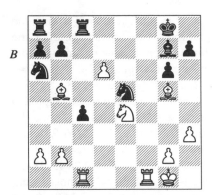

B

moving the a6-knight, but 25...♘c5 loses to 26 ♗xc4+ ♘xc4 27 ♖xc4 ♗xb2 28 ♘xc5 ♖xc5 29 ♖xc5 ♗d4+ 30 ♔h1 ♗xc5 31 d7 ♗b6 32 ♖c1 and 32 ♖c8, so the move played was the result of a process of elimination.

If your position is objectively lost, the most important rule is 'Keep the game going'. This doesn't mean that you should play on for a long time in a resignable position; it means 'do not allow your opponent a simple forced win'. The longer you can force your opponent to work, the greater the chances he will eventually go wrong. In the diagram position, White would be looking for a knock-out blow and would probably reject lines in which he is 'only' a pawn up. Denying him a quick win will eventually cause frustration, a loss of objectivity and a possible error.

26 ♘f6+?!

Once again this does not throw away the win, but a pragmatic player would have contented himself with the gain of a pawn by 26 b3. After

26...♘bd7 27 bxc4 a6 28 ♗xd7 ♘xd7 29 c5! ♗d4+ 30 ♔h1 ♗xc5 31 ♘xc5 ♖xc5 (31...♘xc5 32 ♖fd1) 32 ♖xc5 ♘xc5 Black can regain the pawn, but White wins by 33 ♖c1 ♘d7 (33...b6 34 ♖xc5) 34 ♖c7.

It is clear from this variation that White's queen sacrifice made the win considerably more difficult; instead of a clear-cut and straightforward positional win, White now needs to calculate quite lengthy lines.

26...♗xf6 27 ♗xf6 a6!

Again presenting White with the maximum difficulty. After 27...♘bd7 28 ♖ce1 a6 29 ♗xd7 ♘xd7 30 ♖e7 ♘xf6 31 ♖xf6 the passed pawn and threat to double rooks on the seventh rank would give Black no chance.

28 ♗a4 ♘bd7

At last Black has managed to set up some sort of blockade for the d-pawn, but it is not permanent because the knights lack any pawn support.

29 ♖ce1 ♘c6 (D)

Possible thanks to the interpolation of ...a6 and ♗a4.

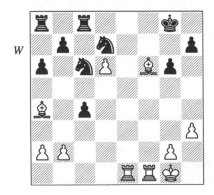

W

30 ♗c3

White decides to keep his bishops. Once again there was a tempting alternative in 30 ♗xc6 ♖xc6 31 ♖e7 ♘xf6 32 ♖xf6 ♖d8 33 ♖ff7 ♖cxd6 34 ♖g7+ ♔f8 35 ♖xb7 (35 ♖ef7+ ♔e8 36 ♖xb7 ♖8d7 offers Black fair drawing prospects), but after 35...h5 it is hard to say whether White's advantage will necessarily lead to a win.

30...b5

The queenside pawn majority is Black's only hope of counterplay.

31 ♗d1!

The correct plan; if the bishop can reach the b3-g8 diagonal (via f3 or g4) then Black will be mated.

31...b4 32 ♗g4

The simple move 32 ♗d2 would also have been very awkward. Black's queenside pawns aren't going anywhere because pushing them would open the diagonals leading to Black's king. Thus White has time to play ♗f3-d5 or ♗a4 and exploit his great piece activity.

32...bxc3 33 ♗xd7 cxb2 *(D)*

Black's first real glimmer of counterplay, and the decisive moment of the game.

34 ♗e6+?

The earlier complications, coupled with White's fruitless search for a knock-out, had left him short of time. Just at the moment when he could have really used a few extra minutes, he was forced to move quickly and threw the win away. The complexity of the position is such that in my

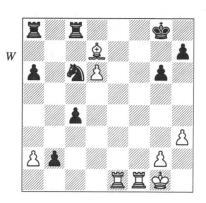

original notes (published, for example, in *Informator*) I gave two possible wins for White, only one of which works. I suppose I should be thankful that I got 50% correct!

The first 'win' was 34 ♗xc6 ♖xc6 35 d7 and now 35...♖cc8 36 dxc8♕+ ♖xc8 37 ♖f2 c3 38 ♖c2, followed by ♖b1. However, 35...♔g7! draws after 36 ♖e8 (36 ♖e7+ ♔h6 37 ♖e8 doesn't make any difference – Black can still play 37...♖f6) 36...♖f6 37 ♖b1 c3 38 ♖c8! (White is slightly lucky even to draw!) 38...♖d6 39 ♖xc3 ♖d8 40 ♖xb2 ♖8xd7 drawing.

My second line does indeed lead to a win: 34 ♗xc8! ♖xc8 35 d7 ♖d8 (35...♖c7 36 ♖e8+ ♔g7 37 ♖e7+ ♔h6 38 d8♕ ♘xd8 39 ♖xc7) 36 ♖e6! (this is the tricky move to see) and there is no defence to the threat of ♖xc6.

34...♔g7 35 ♗xc4

It is now too late to take on c8: 35 ♗xc8 ♖xc8 36 d7 ♖b8 37 ♖e8 b1♕ 38 ♖xb1 ♖xb1+ 39 ♔f2 ♖b2+ 40 ♔g3 ♖xa2 41 ♖c8 ♖d2 42 ♖xc6 ♖xd7 43 ♖xc4 a5, followed by ...♖a7, gives

Black a rook ending with excellent winning chances. Besides, having refused to take on c8 the move before, it would be surprising if White changed his mind now.

35...♘d4

Suddenly everything starts to go wrong for White. The bishop has to retreat along the a6-f1 diagonal, since 36 ♗d5 (36 ♗d3 loses at once after 36...♖c1) 36...♖ab8, threatening to play 37...♖c1, is very bad for White.

36 ♗d3 ♖c3 37 ♗b1 ♖d8

Black can force a draw by 37...♖c1 (intending 38...♖d8) 38 ♗d3 (covering e2 and so threatening 39 ♖xc1) 38...♖c3, but now that things are turning his way he decides to play for a win. If Black can take the d-pawn, then his own passed b-pawn will decide the game.

38 ♖e7+?

There are very few players who defend well when they have slipped from a winning position into an inferior one. It requires exceptional self-control to forget about what has gone before and just to concentrate on the current situation. White could still have held the game by 38 ♖f2! ♖c1 39 ♖ef1 with a dead draw after the exchange of b- and d-pawns. The move played is a reflex action to preserve the d-pawn, but White should never have abandoned the first rank, except to attack the pawn on b2.

38...♔h6 39 d7

In my *Informator* notes I gave 39 ♖b7 as drawing, but in fact Black wins

by 39...♘b5! 40 a4 ♖c1! 41 axb5 ♖f8 and the f1-rook is caught in a pincer-movement.

39...♖c1 *(D)*

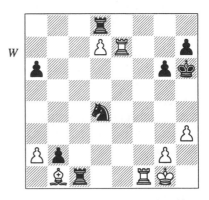

40 ♗d3

White is almost without a reasonable move, for example 40 h4 ♖f8 (this is Black's main threat) 41 ♖ee1 (41 ♖fe1 ♘c6 42 ♖e8 ♖f7 wins the d-pawn) 41...♘e2+ 42 ♔h2 ♖d8 43 ♗d3 ♖xd7 44 ♗xe2 ♖xe1 45 ♖xe1 ♖e7, followed by ...♖xe2, with a winning rook and pawn ending.

40...♘c2 41 ♗xc2 0-1

After 41...♖xc2 42 ♖b1 ♖c1+ 43 ♖e1 ♖xe1+ 44 ♖xe1 ♖xd7, followed by ...♖b7, White's rook becomes immobilized on b1 and Black has an easy win.

Bad positions

The first piece of advice is simple: don't give up hope. The history of chess is littered with won positions thrown away. Even world champions have been known to do this, and it is much more common at lower levels. However, you should not just hope that your opponent is going to make a mistake – you have to help him to do so. Being determined to make the win as difficult as possible is the first step in the right direction. A stiff resistance is almost always unnerving for the side with the advantage – he may well have over-estimated the strength of his own position and be anticipating a quick finish.

There are two basic strategies when confronted with a bad position. The first is to find some way to hang on, often by liquidating to an endgame. The attacker may not fancy winning a long endgame a pawn up and so may unwisely continue to seek a middlegame win. Even if he does go for the endgame, a sudden switch from tactical middlegame play to technical endgame play can often prove disorientating. We call this the 'grim defence' response.

The second strategy is to seek to gain the initiative, even at material cost, hoping to stir up complications and cause the opponent to go wrong. We call this the 'create confusion' response.

The choice between these alternatives depends mainly on the position on the board, but other factors can enter the calculation. For example, if your opponent is short of time he may welcome simplification to an endgame, so in this case the 'create confusion' approach may be better. If you are aware of your opponent's style, then this might also affect your decision. One important point is that you should not change plans in midstream. If you have decided on 'grim defence' then you should not lose patience and switch plans later unless your opponent carelessly allows you a chance to break out. 'Grim defences' most often fail because the defender creates unnecessary additional weaknesses, opening the door to the opponent's pieces. The whole point of 'grim defence' is to set up a solid position which your opponent has to work hard to break down; such positions do not lend themselves to the creation of active counterplay.

If you decide to go for 'create confusion' then you should press the panic button sufficiently early to give yourself a reasonable chance of success. However, you should be sure that your position is really bad enough to warrant such drastic measures. In my experience, it is far more common to panic too early than too late.

Here is an example of each type of strategy, in both cases in response to a stunning opening novelty.

J. Nunn – W. Browne
Gjøvik 1983
Sicilian, Najdorf

1 e4 c5 2 ♘f3 d6 3 d4 cxd4 4 ♘xd4 ♘f6 5 ♘c3 a6 6 ♗g5 e6 7 f4 ♗e7 8 ♕f3 ♕c7 9 0-0-0 ♘bd7 10 g4 b5 11

♗xf6 ♘xf6 12 g5 ♘d7 13 f5 ♘c5 14
h4 b4 15 ♘ce2

In retrospect, one can say that White
should choose something else round
about here, for example the sacrifice
15 fxe6!?.

15...e5 16 ♘b3 (D)

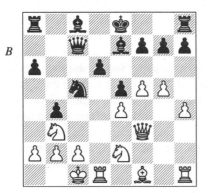

I was feeling quite happy with the
opening. In previous games Black
had invariably continued 16...♗b7,
and I had analysed the resulting positions and concluded that they favoured
White.

16...♘xe4!!

I was dumbfounded when this move
appeared on the board and for several
minutes I just couldn't see the point of
it. After 17 ♕xe4 ♗b7 18 ♖d5, followed by ♗g2 if necessary, everything
seemed to be fine for White. Sooner or
later Black would have to take on d5
when White would have complete
domination of the light squares. Then
I suddenly saw the idea (which will be
revealed in the game continuation)
and realized I was in trouble. Even

though Browne failed to win the game,
his novelty was voted the most important of the second half of 1983. As the
similar vote in the first half of 1983
gave a lower score to the winner, it
would be fair to say that the most stunning novelty played anywhere in the
world during 1983 had just landed on
my board.

After I had recovered from the
shock, I settled down to decide on the
best reply. I saw that I could take the
knight, which leads ultimately to a
better ending for Black, or I could try
17 ♗g2, which sacrifices a pawn for
not very impressive compensation.
My choice was determined largely by
practical factors. I realized that Browne
would have analysed both these lines
carefully at home, so this was certainly a crucial decision. I had spent a
great deal of time sitting at the board,
calculating these alternatives and so,
unusually when facing Browne, I was
far behind on the clock. In view of the
time situation, I doubted my ability to
find my way through continuing complications which Browne would have
analysed at home. I therefore decided
to go for the 'grim defence' option,
when the many possibilities for both
sides would inevitably mean leaving
Browne's analysis within a few moves
of entering the ending. Moreover, my
lack of time would be a less relevant
factor as the complications would be
less intense.

As an aside, there is very little you
can do to prevent the occasional

shocking opening novelty – if you play sharp openings then it is an occupational hazard.

17 ♕xe4

In a later game Wedberg-de Firmian, Oslo 1984, White did indeed try 17 ♗g2 ♗b7 18 ♕e3 d5 19 ♗xe4 dxe4 20 ♘g3 a5, but lost after great complications.

17...♗b7 18 ♖d5 ♖c8 19 c3!

The only move, since 19 ♔b1 ♗xd5 20 ♕xd5 ♕xc2+ 21 ♔a1 0-0! leaves White completely tangled up. He can try 22 f6 gxf6 23 gxf6 ♗xf6 24 ♖g1+ ♔h8 25 ♕xd6, but after the simple 25...♗g7 White has not solved any of his problems.

19...♕c4 20 ♕xc4

Not 20 ♗g2 ♗xd5 21 ♕xd5 ♕xe2 and Black wins.

20...♖xc4 21 ♗g2 ♗xd5!

Black must take straight away, because 21...♖xh4? 22 ♖xh4 ♗xd5 (or 22...♗xg5+ 23 ♖d2!) 23 ♖g4 gives White an extra piece.

22 ♗xd5 ♖xh4! *(D)*

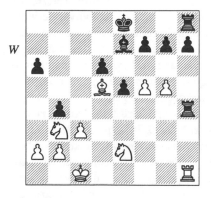

This move is the key point which it took me several minutes to see at move 16. The upshot is that Black gains a rook and two pawns for two knights. In an ending, a rook and two pawns is worth more than two minor pieces at least 90% of the time. Two bishops may sometimes hold the balance, but two knights have almost no chance.

23 ♖g1!

White must try to keep Black's bishop passive. The material situation would be the same after 23 ♖xh4 ♗xg5+ 24 ♔c2 ♗xh4 25 cxb4, but Black would have a far easier time. His bishop can emerge via f2, his h-pawn is already passed and his king can obstruct White's queenside pawns by ...♔d7-c7.

23...bxc3

After 23...♖h2? 24 ♗c4! White gains time by attacking the a-pawn.

24 ♘xc3 ♖f4!

Black fastens onto the weak kingside pawns.

25 ♗c6+!

An important finesse. After 25 ♗e4 ♔d7 Black develops his h8-rook easily, while on 25 g6 fxg6! 26 fxg6 h5 Black has no need to develop his h8-rook – it is already ideally placed behind the passed h-pawn.

25...♔f8

After 25...♔d8? 26 ♘a5! Black's king becomes exposed, for example 26...♖xf5 27 ♘b7+ ♔c8 28 ♘d5 ♗xg5+ 29 ♔b1 and Black is obliged to play 29...♖d8 in order to avoid a worse fate. Therefore Black has to move his king the other way, but this blocks in the rook on h8.

26 ♗e4 h5!

After 26...d5 27 ♗d3! Black has rather a lot of pawns attacked. The move played is best; White cannot afford to let the pawn race down the board, so he has to exchange on h6, but then Black has activated the h8-rook.

27 gxh6 ♖xh6 28 ♘d2! ♖h2 29 ♘d5!

Utilizing a tactical point to occupy the key d5-square. If now 29...♖xd2, then 30 ♖h1! (30 ♘xf4? ♖d4 31 ♖h1 ♗g5 wins for Black) 30...g6 (30...♔e8? 31 ♘xf4 ♖d4 32 ♗c6+ and White wins) 31 ♘xf4 ♖d4 32 ♘d5 ♖xe4 33 f6 ♗xf6 and Black has only a slight advantage.

'Grim defence' doesn't necessarily mean that you should ignore tactics completely. Tactics are not the sole preserve of the attacker.

29...♖ff2 30 ♘f3! ♖h3 31 ♘d2 ♖hh2 (D)

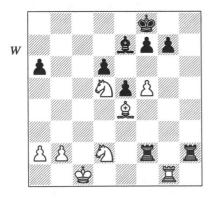

White has made considerable progress since the last diagram in setting up a light-squared blockade; of course, he is quite happy to repeat moves. His main problem is the insecure position of the bishop on e4.

32 ♘f3 ♖h3 33 ♘d2 ♖h4!

Black finds a way to play on. He both prevents 34 ♘f3 and threatens 34...♖xd2.

34 ♘c3!

This only apparently allows the black bishop to emerge via d8 and b6. In fact, 34...♗d8 could be met by 35 ♘c4.

34...d5!

A combination liquidating to a rook ending favourable for Black. However, there is saying that 'all rook endings are drawn'. While this is clearly not intended literally, it contains a large element of truth. Rook endings are often tricky to judge, because in one position an extra pawn may be insufficient to win, while in another, one player may have a decisive advantage despite material equality. The reason for this is that piece activity is very important in rook endings and can often prevent the exploitation of a material advantage. Likewise, if material is equal a difference in piece activity may decide the game.

35 ♘xd5 ♖xd2 36 ♔xd2 ♖xe4 37 ♘xe7 ♔xe7 38 ♖xg7 ♖f4?

This wins a pawn, but allows White to activate his king and rook. By now Browne had become short of time himself, and so missed the stronger continuation 38...♔f6 39 ♖h7 a5, aiming to push the pawn to a4 before going after the f-pawn with ...♖f4. In this case Black would have preserved good winning chances.

39 ♖g8!

White's first chance to play actively since the opening!

39...♖xf5 40 ♖a8 ♖f2+ 41 ♔c3 ♖f6

The only way to keep the extra pawn, but now Black's king is driven back.

42 ♖a7+ ♔f8 43 ♔d3 ♖e6 44 ♔e4 ♔g7 45 ♔f5 *(D)*

Countering Black's threat of ...♔f6, ...♖d6, ...♔e6 and finally ...f5+.

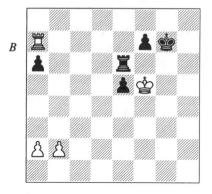

B

45...e4

The only chance is to push the e-pawn, but White can round it up once it has become disconnected from the rest of Black's forces.

46 ♖c7 e3 47 ♖c1 ♖d6

The only try, since after 47...e2 48 ♖e1, followed by ♔f4-f3, White draws easily.

48 ♖g1+!

A counterpart to the check on move 25. White seizes his chance to force the black king into a more passive position.

48...♔f8 49 ♖e1 ♖d2 50 ♖xe3 ♖f2+ 51 ♔e5 ♖xb2 52 ♖a3 ♖b6 53 ♔f5 *(D)*

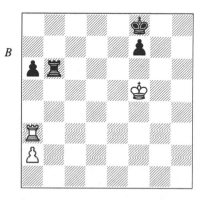

B

The exchange of another pair of pawns brings White closer to the draw. In view of the active position of White's king and rook, Black's winning prospects are minimal, and now it only requires moderate care to steer the game safely home.

53...♔g7 54 ♖g3+ ♖g6 55 ♖a3 ♖f6+ 56 ♔e5 ♖b6 57 ♖g3+ ♖g6 58 ♖a3 ♖e6+ 59 ♔f5 ♖f6+ 60 ♔e5 ♖h6 61 ♔f5 ♖c6 62 ♖g3+ ♔f8 63 ♖b3 ♖c2 64 ♖a3 ♖c5+ 65 ♔f6 ♖c6+ 66 ♔f5 ♔e7 67 ♖e3+ ♔d7 68 ♖d3+ ♔c7 69 ♖f3 ♔d7 70 ♖d3+ ♔e7 71 ♖e3+ ♖e6 72 ♖b3 ♔d6 73 ♖b7 ♖e5+ 74 ♔f4 ♖a5 75 ♖xf7 ♖xa2 76 ♔e4 ♔c5 ½-½

This was a good example of 'grim defence'. Faced with a choice of evils,

White decided to go for the inferior ending. After placing as many difficulties as possible in Black's way, he was eventually rewarded with a slip allowing the half-point to be saved. The next game provides a real contrast.

J. Plaskett – J. Nunn
Lambeth Open 1979
Sicilian, Najdorf

1 e4 c5 2 ♘f3 d6 3 d4 ♘f6 4 ♘c3 cxd4 5 ♘xd4 a6 6 ♗e2 ♘bd7 7 ♗e3 ♘c5

After the present game I gave up this line. The idea of playing the knight to c5 is to exert pressure on e4, but once White has played f3 this pressure is irrelevant, and then it is hard to see what the knight is doing on c5.

8 f3 e6 9 ♕d2 ♕c7 10 0-0 ♗e7 11 a4 0-0 12 a5 d5 *(D)*

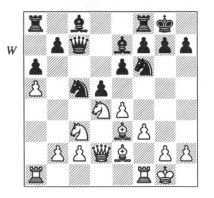

At this stage I was feeling quite confident, because in an earlier game Jansa-Nunn, Budapest 1978 White

had continued 13 exd5 exd5 14 ♗f4 ♕d8 15 ♘a4 and here a draw was agreed. After 15...♘xa4 16 ♖xa4 ♖e8 Black's pieces are quite active and the rook on a4 is misplaced, factors that balance the slight weakness of the isolated d-pawn.

13 e5!!

A complete shock for me. Objectively speaking, this move simply refutes Black's opening strategy. I saw at once that after 13...♕xe5 14 ♗f4 my queen would be in trouble, so I looked to see where I could move my knight. Unfortunately, Black's natural retreat 13...♘fd7 loses a piece after 14 b4, so Black would have to play 13...♘e8. However, then 14 f4 f5 15 exf6 (best; if White tries to play on the kingside with h3 and g4, then the knight on e8 might actually become useful with ...g6 and ...♘g7) 15...♘xf6 16 ♗f3 gives White a clear positional advantage – the e6-pawn is weak and it is hard for Black to bring his c8-bishop into play. However, Black is by no means lost and this would be a reasonable attempt at a 'grim defence' strategy.

In the late 1970s Plaskett was prone to time-trouble, and he had already thought a long time before playing 13 e5. Given the choice between a messy, complicated position and one in which he could increase the positional pressure by straightforward moves, I would certainly have preferred the former. I therefore decided to look again at the capture on e5 and in the end I found the continuation played in the game.

13...♕xe5 14 ♗f4 ♕h5 15 g4 ♕g6

I didn't spend long on the moves 15...♕h4 and 15...♕h3. It is quite easy to refute the former: 15...♕h4 16 ♗g3 ♕h3 17 ♖fe1 ♘e8 (17...♕h6 18 g5) 18 ♗f1 ♕h6 19 ♕xh6 gxh6 20 ♘xd5 and Black's position is disgusting. Although it is quite hard to find a clearcut refutation of 15...♕h3, there is little point in thinking about such moves. White can regain his pawn immediately, and there is almost no chance that Black can survive with his queen stuck on h3 and none of his other pieces co-operating with it. Home analysis shows that 15...♕h3 16 ♖f2 ♘e8 17 b4 ♘d7 18 ♘xd5 ♗d8 19 ♘e3! is very strong; e.g. 19...♗f6 loses to 20 ♗f1 ♕h4 21 ♗g3 ♕g5 22 f4.

16 b4

This was the point of White's pawn sacrifice. The knight has to move, and then ♗d3 traps the queen.

16...♘ce4!

Except, of course, if it moves to e4! Black can avoid immediate material loss by 16...e5 17 ♗xe5 ♘e6, but after 18 ♗d3 ♕g5 19 ♕xg5 ♘xg5 20 h4 ♘e6 21 ♘f5 he has a very bad ending, for example 21...♗xb4 22 ♗xf6 gxf6 23 ♘xd5 ♗c5+ 24 ♔h1. This doesn't even qualify as a 'grim defence' – it is just very bad without any redeeming features.

17 fxe4 dxe4 *(D)*

This continuation is Black's best practical chance, once he has decided

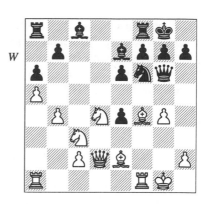

on the 'create confusion' method. He has two pawns for the piece and, owing to the attacks on b4 and g4, he is sure to gain a third pawn. This is not a coincidence, but results from the fact that White's tactical operation depended on the weakening pawn stabs b4 and g4. Given that Black obtains a material equivalent for the piece, you may wonder why he is worse. The answer is simply development. All the white pieces are in active play, while Black's queenside is still sitting at home.

18 ♔h1

White decides to jettison the b4-pawn, preferring to keep the pawn on g4 which shields his king. After 18 ♗g5 ♖d8 (18...♗xb4 is also possible) Black has sufficient play.

18...♗xb4

Not 18...♘xg4 19 ♗xg4 ♕xg4 20 ♖g1 ♕h4 21 ♘xe4 b5 (the only hope is to get the bishop to the long diagonal) 22 ♕g2 g6 23 ♘c6 and White wins.

19 ♗e5!

An excellent move. The bishop serves several useful functions on e5; it supports the knights on d4 and c3, threatens ♗xf6 in some lines and rules out any possibility of Black activating the c8-bishop by ...e5. At first sight Black can reply 19...e3 20 ♕xe3 ♗xc3 21 ♕xc3 ♕e4+ regaining the piece, but White continues 22 ♘f3 ♕xe2 23 ♖fe1 ♕b5 (23...♕f2 24 ♗d4 loses the queen) 24 ♗xf6 gxf6 25 ♕xf6 ♕c6 26 ♖e5 h6 27 g5 with a decisive attack.

Up to here, White has handled the game well. He has not simply been content to keep his material, which might have allowed Black to complete his development and create strong counterplay. Instead, he has kept his pieces active and not been afraid to calculate tactical lines.

19...b6!?

Following the confusion policy. White's last move demolished Black's hopes of activating his light-squared bishop on the c8-g4 diagonal, so now the idea is to develop it on the long diagonal. The choice of ...b6 rather than ...b5 was based on two factors: firstly, in some lines Black plays ...♗c5 and then it is useful to have the bishop defended (see the game); secondly, the possibilities of axb6 and ...bxa5 give White more to think about.

20 ♕e3

Both unpinning the c3-knight and preventing the e4-pawn's advance.

20...♗b7 21 ♘f5?

An incredibly ingenious idea, which aims once more to exploit the poor position of Black's queen. However, the resulting complications are not in White's favour.

This was the moment to switch from tactics to calmer play. After 21 ♗xf6 gxf6 22 axb6 ♖ac8 23 ♘a4 ♗d2 24 ♕g3 ♖fd8 25 c3 White's pieces may appear scattered and poorly co-ordinated, but Black does not seem able to exploit this. One possible line is 25...♗xc3 (25...e3+ 26 ♗f3) 26 ♘xc3 ♖xd4 27 ♗xa6 and now 27...♗xa6 28 ♖xa6 ♖d3 fails to 29 b7.

A common error in wild games is to overlook a positional continuation. With the adrenaline pumping, and mates all around, it is easy to develop 'tunnel vision' that only sees tactical possibilities; then a calm liquidating line can easily be missed.

21...exf5 22 gxf5 ♗c5! *(D)*

Black makes use of the protection of c5. After 22...♘g4 23 ♗xg4 ♕xg4 24 ♖g1 ♕f3+ 25 ♕xf3 exf3 White forces mate by 26 ♖xg7+ ♔h8 27 ♖g8+ ♔xg8 28 ♖g1#.

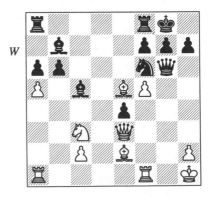

23 ♕xc5
Forced, as after 23 fxg6 ♗xe3 Black
is material up.
23...e3+! 24 ♗f3
Black wins after 24 ♖f3 ♗xf3+ 25
♗xf3 ♕xf5 26 ♕xe3 ♖ae8.
24...♗xf3+ 25 ♖xf3 ♕h5 26 ♕xe3
After 26 ♕c6 ♖ac8 27 ♕b7 ♘g4 28
♗c7 Black has the pleasant choice between 28...♘xh2 29 ♗xh2 ♖xc3 30
♖g3 ♖xc2 31 ♖g2 ♖xg2 32 ♕xg2
bxa5 and 28...♖xc7 29 ♕xc7 ♘xh2 30
♕xh2 ♕xf3+ 31 ♕g2 ♕xf5 32 axb6
♕f6. In both cases Black ends up with
four pawns for the piece.
26...♘g4 (D)
The unexpected point of Black's
play. After the queen moves, Black
takes on c5, regaining his piece.

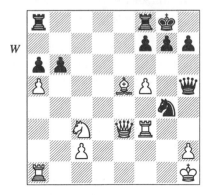

27 ♘d5??
A horrible blunder in extreme time-
trouble – White plays for a mate which
does not exist. Despite the downturn
in his fortunes, if White had kept a
clear head then he would probably
have saved the game. The correct

continuation was 27 ♖g1! ♘xe5 (not
27...♘xe3? allowing mate in five) 28
♖fg3 (28 ♖f4 f6 29 axb6 is unclear; the
passed b-pawn is an asset, but White's
king is exposed and the e5-knight is
impossible to dislodge) 28...♕xf5! 29
♖xg7+ ♔h8 30 ♕h6 (30 axb6 ♘g6 31
♕h6 ♕f3+ 32 ♖g2 is also a draw)
30...♕f3+ with perpetual check.
**27...♘xe3 28 ♘f6+ gxf6 29 ♖g3+
♘g4 0-1**

Defending well after having made
an oversight requires especially cool
nerves. We have previously discussed
the possible causes of oversights and
the warning signs which can indicate
when danger is near. Suppose, despite
this advice, you nevertheless overlook
a surprising and strong move by your
opponent. The first piece of advice is
to stay calm. It is all too easy to bash
out an instinctive response, either
through uncontrollable nervous agita-
tion or in an attempt to persuade your
opponent that you had foreseen his
move and had a reply ready. This is a
mistake. The correct approach is to
spend a few minutes just calming your
nerves. Don't get caught up a mental
loop of self-recrimination – you don't
have time for this while you are at the
board. Try to forget about the history
of the position, and just consider the
current state of affairs on the board. A
calm look will very often show that
your opponent's move is not nearly as
strong as you feared at first and that
there are still fighting chances. Then

you can choose one of the defensive techniques outlined above and continue the struggle.

Attack

'Inviting everyone to the party'

Most books dealing with attacks on the king discuss the various typical methods of breakthrough; sacrifice on h7, sacrifice on g7, double bishop sacrifice, and so on. I will not deal with these, partly because they are discussed at length in many other places, but also because they represent only the final stages of an attack. Most players can manage a double bishop sacrifice, provided that they first arrive at a position in which such a sacrifice is possible.

The main factor governing the success of an attack on the enemy king is whether you can bring more attacking pieces to bear on his king position than he can muster for the defence. If you have a large local superiority of force, then a sacrificial breakthrough will often arise as a matter of course. You still have to calculate that the sacrifice works, but the odds will be heavily in your favour if you have enough wood in the vicinity.

This title of this section is Yasser Seirawan's catchy phrase for an important attacking principle. Incorporating every possible piece into an attack greatly increases its chance of success. If you have staked everything

on your attack, there is no point holding pieces in reserve, since the game will be decided before reserve pieces will be of any use.

The following position is a classic example:

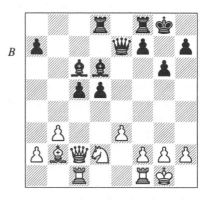

A. Nimzowitsch – S. Tarrasch
St Petersburg 1914

Black already has a local superiority on the kingside, because White has no defensive pieces there at all. However, 18...♕h4 is ineffective owing to 19 ♘f3 and the kingside is shored up. Tarrasch's next move brings the c6-bishop into the attack as well.

18...d4!

Not only unveiling the bishop, but also ruling out both the defensive ♘f3 and counterplay by ♕c3.

19 exd4

There is nothing better as White is unable to feed any pieces across for the defence. Now, however, 19...♕h4 20 g3 ♕h3 gets nowhere after 21 ♘e4.

19...♗xh2+!

The moment is ripe for the double bishop sacrifice.

20 ♗xh2 ♕h4+ 21 ♔g1 ♗xg2 22 f3

Forced. After 22 ♔xg2 ♕g4+ 23 ♔h2 ♖d5 24 ♕xc5 ♖h5+ 25 ♕xh5 ♕xh5+ 26 ♔g2 ♕g5+ Black picks up the knight on d2, while 22 f4 ♕g3 is deadly.

22...♖fe8

With the pawn on f3, 22...♕g3 may be met by 23 ♘e4.

23 ♘e4

A desperate bid for counterplay based on the long diagonal and weakness of f6. After 23 ♖fe1 ♖xe1+ 24 ♖xe1 ♕xe1+ 25 ♔xg2 ♕e2+ 26 ♔g3 ♖d5 Black wins easily, for example 27 f4 ♖h5 (threatening 28...♖h2) 28 ♕c1 ♕h2+ 29 ♔f3 ♖h3+ 30 ♔e4 ♕g2+ 31 ♔e5 ♖e3+ 32 ♔d6 ♖e6+ 33 ♔xc5 ♖c6+ picking up the queen.

23...♕h1+ 24 ♔f2 ♗xf1 25 d5

25 ♖xf1 ♕h2+ wins the queen.

25...f5 26 ♕c3 ♕g2+ 27 ♔e3 ♖xe4+ 28 fxe4 f4+

Overlooking a quicker mate after 28...♕g3+ 29 ♔d2 ♕f2+ 30 ♔d1 ♕e2#, but Black wins easily anyway.

29 ♔xf4 ♖f8+ 30 ♔e5 ♕h2+ 31 ♔e6 ♖e8+ 32 ♔d7 ♗b5# (0-1)

Many familiar attacking manoeuvres are designed to gain the local superiority which is usually necessary for a successful attack. When you play ♖e1-e3-g3 or ♕d1-e1-h4, you are creating the preconditions for the attack to break through. The opponent must counter these manoeuvres either defensively or by generating counterplay in another part of the board.

In addition to bringing your own pieces to bear on the enemy king, it is also important to block the passage of enemy pieces to the threatened area. Sometimes a sacrifice is necessary.

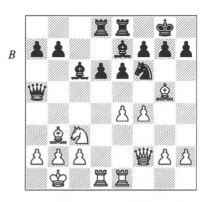

S. Dvoiris – A. Khalifman
Russian Championship, Elista 1997

15...h6 16 h4!?

A brave decision, but it was probably made easier by the fact that 16 ♗h4 ♕h5 is rather bad for White, who cannot play 17 ♗g3 on account of 17...♘xe4 and the d1-rook hangs.

16...♕c5

Black can accept the piece at virtually any stage over the next few moves; in each case the verdict would be unclear.

17 ♕g3 ♘h5

Svidler suggests 17...♔f8!?, intending to take on g5 and then retreat the knight to g8.

18 ♕h2 hxg5?!

Khalifman finally decides to grab the bishop, but it turns out to be the wrong moment to do so. Having said this, it would be a far-sighted player who anticipated White's 21st move. The safest continuation was 18...♕f2 19 ♗xe7 ♖xe7 20 ♖f1 ♕g3, heading for the exchange of queens and a roughly equal position.

19 hxg5 g6 20 g4 ♘xf4 (D)

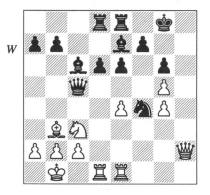

Now Black appears to have everything under control. After 21 ♖h1 Black can play 21...♕e5, using his queen like a Dragon bishop. 21 ♕xf4 is also inferior after 21...♗xg5, followed by ...♕e5, when Black has an extra pawn and a large positional advantage.

21 ♘d5!!

An amazing move. Black's defence is based almost entirely on switching his queen to the kingside. White is prepared to offer another piece to prevent this. The result is that White is able to operate with his queen and two rooks on the kingside, whereas Black

is defending with very limited material.

21...exd5

Other moves are hopeless, for example 21...♘xd5 22 ♖h1 ♘c3+ 23 bxc3 ♕xc3 24 ♕h7+ ♔f8 25 ♖df1 ♕g7 26 ♖xf7+ ♕xf7 27 ♕h8+ ♕g8 28 ♖f1+ ♗f6 29 ♕xf6+ and mate, or 21...♗xg5 22 ♖h1 ♘h5 23 gxh5 ♔g7 24 hxg6 ♖h8 25 ♕g3 exd5 26 ♕xg5 dxe4 27 ♕g4 ♗d7 28 ♕xe4 ♗f5 29 ♕xb7 ♗xg6 30 ♖hg1, followed by ♖df1, with equal material and a crushing attack for White.

22 ♖h1 ♘h5

Again a forced move; 22...f6 allows 23 ♕h7+ ♔f8 24 exd5 ♗xd5 25 ♖xd5 ♘xd5 26 ♕xg6, while after 22...f5 23 ♕h7+ ♔f8 24 exf5 the kingside pawn-mass is immediately decisive.

23 gxh5 ♔g7 24 exd5

The key feature of the rest of the game is the way White's blockade on d5 prevents Black's queen from taking part in the defence.

24...♗d7

24...♖h8 loses to 25 dxc6 ♖xh5 26 ♕f4, but perhaps Black could have put up slightly more resistance with 24...♗b5. However, even in this case I think White should win by 25 hxg6 ♖h8 26 ♕f4 fxg6 (26...f6 27 ♕e4 ♕c7 28 ♕e6 wins) 27 ♖he1 ♕c7 28 ♖e6 (intending ♕e4) 28...♖h7 (28...♖h5 29 ♕e4 ♔f8 30 c4 gains access to f1, while after 28...♖dg8 29 ♖de1 ♗d8 30 ♕d4+ ♔f8 31 ♗a4! a rook will land on either e8 or f1) 29 ♖de1 and now Black can try:

1) 29...♔g8 30 ♖xg6+ ♖g7 31
♖xg7+ ♔xg7 32 ♕d4+ ♔f7 (32...♔g8
33 ♖h1) 33 g6+ ♔xg6 34 ♖g1+ ♗g5
35 ♕e4+ winning for White.

2) 29...♖e8 30 c4 ♗a6 31 ♕d4+
wins.

3) 29...♗f8 30 c4 ♗a6 (30...♗d7
31 ♖xg6+ ♔h8 32 ♗c2 ♗g7 33 ♖h6!
♗xh6 34 gxh6 is lost for Black) 31
♗c2 ♔g8 (31...♗xc4 32 ♗xg6 ♖h3
33 ♗f5 ♖h5 34 ♖h6 ♗xa2+ 35 ♔a1!
wins, or 32...♔g8 transposing) 32 ♗xg6
♖h3 (32...♗xc4 33 ♗xh7+ ♕xh7+ 34
g6 ♗d3+ 35 ♔a1 ♕d7 36 ♖e7) 33 b3
b5 (Black has nothing else) 34 ♖e7!
♗xe7 35 ♕f7+ ♔h8 36 ♖xe7 ♖h1+
37 ♔b2 ♖h2+ 38 ♗c2 and wins.

25 hxg6 ♖h8 26 ♕f4 f5
26...fxg6 27 ♖he1 is dead lost.
27 ♖h6!
A nice collinear move (see page
56). The threat is simply ♕h2 and
♖h1, and thanks to Black's inability to
feed pieces to the threatened sector,
there is not much he can do to stop it.
27...♖de8
Alternatively, 27...♖xh6 28 gxh6+
♔h8 (28...♔xg6 29 ♕g3+ ♗g5 30
♖g1) 29 c3 ♗f6 (29...♖g8 30 g7+ ♔h7
31 ♗c2 ♕c8 32 ♖e1 ♗f6 33 ♖e6!
wins neatly) 30 ♗c2 ♕b6 31 g7+ ♔g8
32 ♕g3! (threatening 33 h7+ ♔xh7 34
g8♕+) 32...♔f7 33 ♖g1 ♗xc3 34
g8♕+ ♖xg8 35 ♕xg8+ ♔e7 36 ♖g7+
♗xg7 37 ♕xg7+ ♔d8 38 h7.
28 ♕h2
Decisive.
**28...♗xg5 29 ♖h7+ ♖xh7 30
♕xh7+ ♔f6 31 ♕f7+ ♔e5 32 ♕xd7**

♖e7 33 ♖e1+ ♔f4 34 ♖f1+ ♔g3 35
♕xf5 ♕e3 36 a3 ♖e5 37 ♕f8 1-0

A common method of excluding
defensive pieces from the critical sector is the pawn-wedge. A chain of
pawns extending deep into enemy territory has the effect of cutting his position in half, and may in itself prove
sufficient to prevent any pieces coming to the rescue of the beleaguered
king. Then it is a matter of whittling
away the defensive pieces on the side
of the wedge near the king, by sacrificial means if necessary. It is important
to watch out for a counter-sacrifice
breaking up the wedge, but otherwise
such attacks are usually plain sailing.

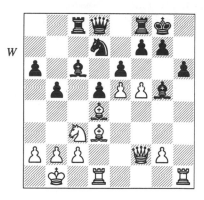

J. Nunn – A. Vydeslaver
Leeuwarden Open 1995

I had earlier sacrificed my h-pawn
in order to gain time for my attack.
This had the positive effect of opening
the h-file and allowing the f-pawn to
advance, but on the other hand Black's

bishop has occupied a post on g5 that is invulnerable to pawn attack.

20 f6!

White establishes his pawn-wedge.

20...b4

The tactical justification for White's last move lies in the line 20...gxf6 21 exf6 e5 (21...♘xf6 22 ♖xh6 ♗xh6 23 ♗xf6 ♕c7 24 ♖h1 wins) 22 ♖xh6!! ♗xh6 23 ♕g3+ ♔h8 24 ♕h4 ♕xf6 25 ♗xe5 and wins.

Since Black cannot remove the intruding pawn, he decides to continue on the queenside. Now White's task is to remove the only piece left defending Black's kingside, the g5-bishop.

21 ♖h5!

Getting rid of the bishop by the most direct method possible. The material loss involved is irrelevant. Not 21 ♘e2? ♗b5!, when the exchange of the d3-bishop greatly weakens White's attack.

21...♘xf6

After 21...bxc3 22 ♖xg5 hxg5 23 ♕g3 mate is inevitable within a few moves, and is only delayed by one move after 23...♖b8 24 b3. 21...gxf6 22 exf6 bxc3 23 ♖xg5+ hxg5 24 ♕g3 and 21...♗xf6 22 exf6 ♘xf6 23 ♖xh6 bxc3 24 ♗xf6 are no better, so Black decides to offer a piece to break up the deadly pawn-wedge.

22 exf6 ♗xf6 23 ♖xh6!

White should win in the end after 23 ♗xf6 ♕xf6 24 ♕xf6 gxf6 25 ♘e2 ♔g7 26 ♗xa6, but I decided to calculate a tactical kill out to the end. The next few moves are all forced.

23...♗xd4 24 ♗h7+ ♔h8 25 ♕xd4 e5

Or 25...bxc3 (25...f6 26 ♖h3) 26 ♗f5+ ♔g8 27 ♖dh1 gxh6 28 ♖xh6 f6 29 ♕g4+ ♔f7 30 ♖h7+ mating.

26 ♕xe5 f6 27 ♕h2 gxh6 28 ♕xh6

Black is helpless against the many threats.

28...♕e7 29 ♗f5+ ♔g8 30 ♗e6+! ♖f7 31 ♖h1 1-0

In the following example, all the above three elements (inviting everyone to the party, excluding defensive pieces and the pawn-wedge) come together.

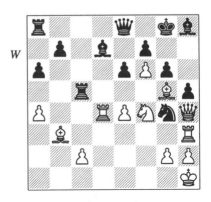

N. Short – A. Chernin
European Team Championship,
Pula 1997

In this position White clearly has a very strong attack, but Black has certain counterchances based on White's weak back rank and the possibility of ...♘f2+. Chernin thought that he had prevented the sacrifice on h5, but ...

29 ♘xh5!

... Short played it in any case. The point is that after 29...gxh5 White does not continue 30 ♕xh5, which allows 30...♘f2+, but 30 e5!. This includes the d4-rook in the attack, excludes the c5-rook from the defence and cements the e5-f6 pawn-wedge. White would then threaten the devastating 31 ♖xg4, and Black wouldn't be able to do much: 30...♖d5 (30...♖xe5 31 ♖xg4 ♖e1+ 32 ♕xe1 hxg4 33 ♖xh8+ ♔xh8 34 ♕h4+ ♔g8 35 ♗h6 mates) 31 ♗e3! (the simplest, covering f2 and so threatening to take on h5; after 31 ♗xd5? exd5 Black would defend g4, when the attack would be stopped) 31...♘xe5 (31...♘xe3 32 ♕g5+ ♔f8 33 ♖xh5 mates) 32 ♕xh5 ♗xf6 33 ♖xd5 exd5 34 ♕h7+ ♔f8 35 ♗c5+ winning Black's queen.

29...♖xg5 30 ♕xg5

White could have won instantly by 30 ♘g7! ♖h5 (30...♘f2+ 31 ♕xf2 ♗xg7 32 fxg7 ♔xg7 33 ♕d2 wins a piece) 31 ♘xh5 gxh5 32 ♕g5+ ♔f8 33 e5 ♘f2+ 34 ♔g1 ♘xh3+ 35 gxh3 and Black has no defence to the threats of 36 ♕xh4 and 36 ♖h4 followed by ♖xh5.

However, even after the move actually played White retains a clear advantage.

30...♘f2+ 31 ♔g1 ♘xh3+ 32 gxh3 ♗c6?

Black collapses. This move fatally weakens e6.

33 ♘f4 ♔h7 34 e5 ♗f3 35 ♔f2 ♕c6 36 ♖c4 1-0

Over-sacrificing

Most chess players love to attack. Pressing home an assault against the enemy king, sacrificing a couple of pieces and finally delivering mate is a great thrill ... provided it works.

One of the great dangers of even a correct sacrificial attack is over-sacrificing. It very often happens that the first sacrifice is sound, but then the player gets overwhelmed with the desire to finish 'brilliantly' and instead of just bringing up all his pieces and mating his opponent, he goes on a quite unnecessary sacrificial spree, endangering the win. As the material deficit increases, the opponent gains more and more chances to return some or all of the material in order to fend off the attack. Sometimes some quite unlikely-looking moves become possible if there is enough spare wood to jettison.

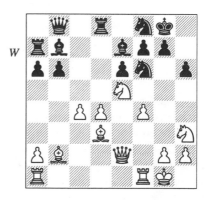

M. Botvinnik – V. Chekhover
Moscow 1935

White's minor pieces are ideally placed to attack Black's king, except for the knight on h3. The ugly cluster of black pieces on the queenside is not doing much and is certainly of little help in defending the kingside. White therefore decides, quite correctly, to sacrifice his one poorly placed piece in the interests of opening up Black's king position.

22 ♘g5! hxg5

Black must accept, since otherwise he cannot defend f7.

23 fxg5 ♘8d7 *(D)*

After 23...♘6d7 24 ♘xf7, followed by ♕h5, White has a crushing attack, so Black offers to return the piece.

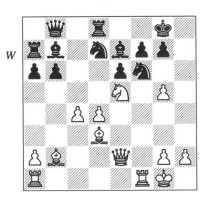

24 ♘xf7?

This second sacrifice is not only unnecessary, it even endangers the win. After 24 ♘xd7 ♖xd7 (or 24...♘xd7 25 ♖xf7 ♔xf7 26 ♕h5+ and White forces mate) 25 gxf6 ♗xf6 26 ♖xf6 gxf6 27 ♕g4+ ♔f8 28 ♗a3+ ♖d6 29 ♕g3 ♔e7 30 c5! White's attack breaks through without any difficulty. This

winning line is mundane, but it is efficient.

24...♔xf7 25 g6+ ♔g8?? *(D)*

After this Black gets mated. He should have played 25...♔f8 26 ♕xe6 ♘e5! (Black's two extra pieces justify this odd-looking move) 27 ♖xf6+ gxf6 28 ♕h3 (thus far given by Botvinnik) and now either 28...♗c5! or 28...♗b4 29 ♖e1 ♗xg2! 30 ♔xg2 ♗xe1 31 dxe5 fxe5. The position is still very complicated, but Black, a rook and a piece up, has plenty of possibilities to return some of the material. My own view is that White would be struggling to draw in these lines.

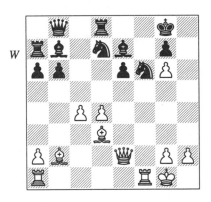

After the move played, White finished nicely:

26 ♕xe6+ ♔h8 27 ♕h3+ ♔g8 28 ♗f5 ♘f8 29 ♗e6+ ♘xe6 30 ♕xe6+ ♔h8 31 ♕h3+ ♔g8 32 ♖xf6 ♗xf6 33 ♕h7+ ♔f8 34 ♖e1 ♗e5 35 ♕h8+ ♔e7 36 ♕xg7+ ♔d6 37 ♕xe5+ ♔d7 38 ♕f5+ ♔c6 39 d5+ ♔c5 40 ♗a3+ ♔xc4 41 ♕e4+ ♔c3 42 ♗b4+ ♔b2 43 ♕b1# (1-0)

Defence

The principles for defending against an attack on the king are to some extent the converse of those given above in the section on attack. The defender should try to move his own pieces across to help the endangered king while, if possible, obstructing the free passage of the opposing pieces to the critical sector.

One particular motif which often arises in practice is that of the defensive sacrifice. The idea of the attacker sacrificing material is a familiar one, but it happens almost as often that the defender gives up material. Here I am not talking about the situation in which the attacker has sacrificed, and the defender is returning material, but about cases in which the defender is prepared to accept a genuine material deficit.

The basis for such sacrifices very often lies in the positional concessions made by the attacker. In a Sicilian, it may be very useful for attacking purposes if White pushes his kingside pawns to g5 and f6, but if the attack collapses the white king may not appreciate having had his defensive pawn wall sent into the other half of the board. Launching an attack usually involves a concession of some sort; it may be the creation of weaknesses, as in the case of a pawn advance, or it may be sending pieces offside. If White plays his rook to h3 and queen to h4, then mate on h7 will end

the game, but if there is no mate then queen and rook may have to grovel back to the centre, with great loss of time.

The defender can often exploit the negative side of an attack by a suitable sacrifice to take the sting out of the onslaught.

G. Sax – M. Stean
*European Team Championship
Final, Moscow 1977*
Sicilian, Scheveningen

1 e4 c5 2 ♘f3 e6 3 d4 cxd4 4 ♘xd4 ♘f6 5 ♘c3 d6 6 ♗e2 a6 7 0-0 ♗e7 8 ♗e3 ♕c7 9 f4 0-0 10 g4 ♘c6 11 g5 ♘d7 12 f5 ♘de5 13 f6 ♗d8 *(D)*

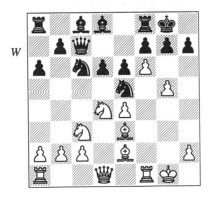

A typical Sicilian position. The white kingside pawns have launched themselves forward, but in return Black has undisputed control of the square e5.

14 fxg7?!

This looks like a mistake as there is no need for White to commit himself to this capture so early. Recently this intuitive feeling was backed up by a practical test; Sutovsky-J.Polgar, Tilburg 1996 continued 14 ♗d3 (enabling the white queen to reach h5) 14...♘xd4 15 ♗xd4 ♕a5?! 16 fxg7 ♔xg7 17 ♔h1 ♗b6?! 18 ♗xe5+ ♕xe5 19 ♕h5 ♗e3 20 ♖f3 ♗xg5 21 ♖g1 f6 22 h4 1-0. Subsequent analysis of this game suggests that although Black need not have lost so quickly, White retains some advantage after any defence.

14...♔xg7!

Bravely eliminating one of the dangerous white pawns. After 14...♖e8?! 15 ♕d2 b5 16 ♗h5 ♘e7 17 b3! ♘7g6 18 a4! bxa4 19 ♖xa4 ♗b7 20 ♘f3 White had a slight advantage in Kholmov-Spassky, Moscow Zonal 1964.

Stean's move may appear suicidal, but it turns out that White has problems continuing his attack because his development is rather poor (all those pawn moves on the kingside). He really needs his queen on the kingside in order to create genuine threats, but both 15 ♗d3 (intending ♕h5) and 15 ♕e1 drop a pawn after ...♘xd4 and ...♗xg5. Note that in the latter case Black justifies his play with a tactical point: 15 ♕e1 ♘xd4 16 ♗xd4 ♗xg5 17 ♕g3 ♔h8! and the bishop is invulnerable.

Thus White has to proceed with his attack much more slowly, but Black only needs to play ...b5 and ...♗b7 to set up a further awkward threat against the e4-pawn.

15 ♕d2 b5! 16 g6?!

White decides to grab the exchange, but Black obtains tremendous compensation. It would have been better to try 16 a3 followed by, for example, doubling rooks on the f-file. However, I do not believe that Black has any problems as a major threat from White is still several moves away.

16...hxg6 17 ♗h6+ ♔g8 18 ♗xf8 ♔xf8 19 ♘xc6 ♕xc6 *(D)*

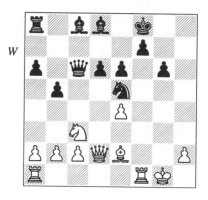

The transformation since the previous diagram is remarkable. There is no trace left of White's advanced kingside pawns. Now Black only needs to play ...♔g7 to secure his kingside completely. He has a monster knight on e5, and tremendous pressure on the dark squares. Finally, once he has played ...♔g7, ...♗b6 and ...♗b7, his rook can swing across to h8 and White's king will be the one subject to attack. In return for these many positional advantages all White has to show is the very small material advantage of rook for bishop and pawn.

20 ♗d3

After 20 ♕h6+ ♔g8 21 ♖xf7 ♔xf7 22 ♖f1+ ♔e8 23 ♕g7 ♗e7 Black defends easily.

20...♔g7 21 ♘e2 ♗b7 22 ♘f4 ♗b6+ 23 ♔h1 ♖h8

All Black's pieces are in attacking positions; White is obviously in trouble.

24 ♕g2 ♕d7 25 ♖ae1 ♕e7 26 ♕g3 ♕h4 27 ♔g2 (D)

The exchange of queens would be no help to White. One line is 27 ♕xh4 ♖xh4 28 ♖e2 ♘g4 29 ♖f3 ♗d4 30 b3 g5 31 ♘h3 f6 32 ♖g3 b4 33 ♖d2 ♔h6, and now that Black has everything prepared, he is ready for the deadly breakthrough ...f5.

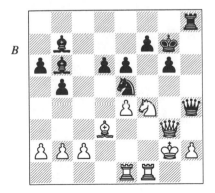

27...g5 28 ♘h3 f6

White has no active play at all, so Black has plenty of time to tidy up his position before making further progress.

29 ♖e2 ♘g6 30 ♖ee1 ♗d4

The changing of the guard. Now the bishop comes to occupy e5.

31 c3 ♗e5 32 ♕xh4 ♖xh4

Material loss is inevitable.

33 ♖h1 ♖xh3 34 ♔xh3 ♘f4+ 35 ♔g4 ♘xd3 36 ♖e2 f5+ 0-1

A defensive sacrifice can also prove effective for psychological reasons. The attacker is mentally geared up for a possible sacrificial assault on the enemy king, and then suddenly he is defending and trying to nurse his material advantage to an ending. This requires a complete shift of mental gears which can prove difficult to achieve.

L. Ljubojević – A. Miles
European Team Championship Final, Skara 1980
Sicilian, Dragon

1 e4 c5 2 ♘f3 d6 3 d4 cxd4 4 ♘xd4 ♘f6 5 ♘c3 g6 6 f4 ♘bd7 7 ♘f3 ♕c7 8 ♗d3 ♗g7 9 0-0 0-0 10 ♔h1 a6 11 a4 b6 12 ♕e1 ♗b7 13 ♕h4 e5 14 ♗d2 ♘c5 15 ♖ae1 ♖ae8 16 fxe5 dxe5 (D)

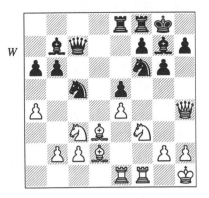

A fairly typical position for the 6 f4 Najdorf (the game started as a Dragon, but later transposed into a Najdorf). White has attacking chances on the kingside, while Black can organize counterplay against the isolated e4-pawn. The long-term chances are with Black, because of his superior pawn structure, so the burden of proof lies with White.

The normal plan of attack is based on ♗h6 and ♘g5, but this is not very effective here because White would be losing a tempo with his bishop and so Black would be able to meet 17 ♗h6 by 17...♘h5.

17 ♘g5

This appears very dangerous, since 18 ♖xf6 is threatened, and 17...h6 18 ♖xf6! ♗xf6 19 ♕xh6 ♗xg5 20 ♗xg5 ♖e6 21 ♗c4 ♖d6 22 ♘d5 ♗xd5 23 ♗xd5 gives White a crushing attack.

17...♘cd7

Therefore this move is forced. If White's bishop were on h6 instead of e3, then he would have a standard attacking plan of g4 (preventing ...♘h5), followed by doubling rooks on the f-file, but as it is White always has to take ...h6 into account.

18 ♖f3 h6 19 ♘h3 ♘h5!

Not 19...g5 20 ♘xg5 hxg5 21 ♗xg5 with a tremendous attack for White. One line is 21...♖e6 22 ♘d5 ♕d6 23 ♖ef1 ♘xd5 24 exd5 ♖g6 25 ♖h3 f5 26 ♕h7+ ♔f7 27 ♗xf5 ♖xg5 28 ♗g6+ ♔e7 29 ♕xg7+ ♔d8 30 ♖xf8+ ♘xf8 31 ♖h8, and wins.

The text-move shields the pawn on h6 and prepares the following pawn sacrifice.

20 g4?!

White was wrong to take the pawn. 20 ♖ef1 would have been better, when 20...f5 21 exf5! ♗xf3 22 ♖xf3 is a very dangerous exchange sacrifice. Therefore Black would have to continue more slowly, for example by 20...♕c5, but White would have an edge.

20...♘f4 21 ♘xf4 exf4 22 ♗xf4 ♘e5 23 ♖h3?!

White will be forced to take on e5 in any case, and it seems odd to put the rook offside. 23 ♖ff1 was better.

23...g5 24 ♗xe5

The rook would only be useful on h3 if White could play 24 ♗xg5 here, but then 24...♘g6 25 ♕h5 ♖e5 wins a piece.

24...♖xe5 25 ♕g3 *(D)*

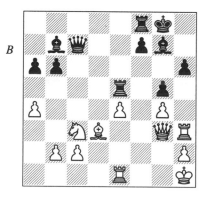

Again, there has been a remarkable transformation in the position. The only trace remaining of White's attack is the misplaced rook on h3. In return for the pawn, Black completely dominates the dark squares, while White's pieces are doing little apart from defending the pawn on e4. Moreover, the advance g4 has seriously weakened White's kingside, and if Black manages to play ...f5 under favourable circumstances then White will be in real trouble.

An additional point is that Ljubojević is an attacking player who does not adapt well to positions requiring careful defence; this game is a case in point.

25...♕c5 26 ♕g1

White should be thinking about how he can draw, and his pieces are so passive that the only realistic chance is to play ♘d5 at some stage, returning the pawn to reach the haven of opposite-coloured bishops. However, the immediate 26 ♘d5 is impossible because of 26...♗xd5 27 exd5 ♕xd5+ 28 ♔g1 ♖xe1+ 29 ♕xe1 ♗d4+ 30 ♔f1 ♕h1+ and Black wins.

26...♕b4 27 ♖b1?

White has failed to adjust to the changed situation. He tries to hang on to his pawn, but putting another piece on a bad square allows Black's initiative to increase decisively. After 27 ♖f3! ♕xb2 28 ♘d5 he would still have had good drawing chances.

27...f5!

An excellent move. Black gets rid of his backward f-pawn and activates the f8-rook without actually moving it!

28 gxf5 ♖exf5

The additional threats which result from the penetration of the black rook

put White's position under intolerable stress.

29 ♕e1 ♕c5 30 ♖e3

The tricky 30 ♗xa6 leads only to self-destruction: 30...♗xa6 31 exf5 ♗b7+ 32 ♘e4 ♕xf5 33 ♖e3 ♗d4.

30...♖f2 31 ♖g3

31 ♖e2 ♗d4 32 ♖xf2 ♖xf2 33 ♘d1 ♖xc2 34 ♗xc2 ♕xc2 wins for Black.

31...♗d4 32 ♘d5 ♕d6

Threatening 33...♖xh2+.

33 ♘e3 ♕g6

Avoiding the trap 33...♗e5? 34 ♘c4 ♖xh2+ 35 ♔xh2 ♗xg3+ 36 ♔g2! and White survives.

34 ♘g2 (D)

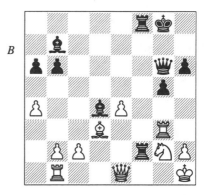

34...♕h5?

A pity. Black could have finished the game immediately with the pretty stroke 34...♗xe4! 35 ♗xe4 ♕xe4, for example 36 h3 ♕xe1+ 37 ♖xe1 ♖f1+ 38 ♔h2 ♖xe1 39 ♘xe1 ♗e5.

35 ♕d1

After 35 ♕g1 ♗e5 36 ♖e3 ♖d2, followed by ...♖ff2, White would be totally paralysed.

35...♕xd1+ 36 ♖xd1 ♗xe4 37 h4?
Loses at once. The only chance was 37 ♗c4+ ♔g7 38 ♖g4 ♗f3 39 ♖gxd4 ♖xg2 40 ♗d5 ♗xd5 41 ♖xd5 ♖xc2 (41...♖ff2 42 ♖d7+ ♔g6 43 ♖1d6+ ♔h5 44 ♖h7 ♖xh2+ 45 ♔g1 may not be a win), but even here Black has excellent winning prospects.
37...♗e5 38 ♗xe4 ♗xg3 39 ♘e3 ♖h2+ 40 ♔g1 ♖xh4 41 ♗d5+ ♔g7 42 ♔g2 ♗f2 0-1

It goes without saying that the attacker should strive to prevent such a defensive sacrifice, although this often involves being quite far-sighted.

1 e4 c5 2 ♘f3 ♘c6 3 d4 cxd4 4 ♘xd4 ♘f6 5 ♘c3 d6 6 ♗c4 e6 7 ♗e3 ♗e7 8 ♕e2 a6 9 0-0-0 ♕c7 10 ♗b3 0-0 11 g4 ♘d7 12 ♖hg1 ♘c5 13 g5 b5 14 ♘xc6 ♘xb3+ 15 axb3 ♕xc6 16 ♕h5 b4 17 ♗d4 ♗b7 (D)

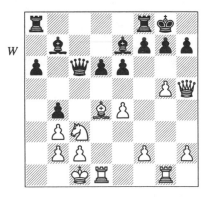

This is a theoretical position from the Velimirović Attack in the Sicilian. White's aim is to transfer a rook to the h-file in order to deliver mate on h7. However, White must be careful because Black threatens to defend h7 by ...bxc3 followed by ...♕xe4. The solution appears simple: White must play his g1-rook to h4, so as to both defend h7 and cover e4.

That is indeed what happened in one of the first games to reach this position, Chandler-Yudasin, Minsk 1982, but after the further moves **18 ♖g4 bxc3 19 ♖h4 cxb2+ 20 ♗xb2** White was shocked by **20...♕xe4! 21 ♖xe4 ♗xe4** (D).

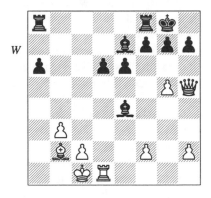

Once again, if we compare the diagrams then we can see the change that has taken place. Black's light-squared bishop is absolutely secure on the c2-g6 diagonal and while it is there White has no attacking chances on the kingside. Indeed, it is now White who has to think about defence, since c2 is very weak and Black can open further lines by advancing his a-pawn. The position is in fact favourable for Black and White was soon in trouble: **22 ♗a3**

♖fc8 23 ♖d2 ♖ab8 24 ♔b2 ♖b5 25 h4 ♗f6+ 26 ♔c1 ♗e5 27 ♕g4 ♖xb3 28 ♕xe4 ♖xa3 29 ♔d1. Now, if Black had played 29...♖ac3, it is doubtful that White could have survived. In the game Black played the less forceful **29...g6** and White eventually escaped with a draw.

However, that is not the end of the story. James Howell realized that the sacrifice on e4 is Black's only method of preventing mate on h7, and so drastic measures to prevent it are justified. Howell-Wahls, World Junior Championship, Gausdal 1986 continued **18 ♘d5!** (to block the queen's path to e4) **18...exd5 19 ♖d3 ♖fc8 20 c3** (D).

Now Black has no reasonable answer to the threat of ♖h3. The finish was **20...dxe4 21 ♖h3 ♔f8 22 g6! fxg6 23 ♕xh7 ♔e8 24 ♖xg6 bxc3 25 ♕g8+ ♔d7 26 ♕e6+ ♔d8 27 bxc3 ♗f8 28 ♕f7 ♗e7 29 ♕xe7+ ♔xe7 30 ♖xg7+ 1-0**.

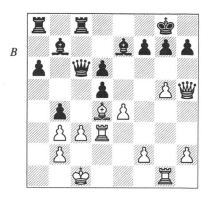

B

Howell's stunning innovation was widely publicized and sent Black hunting for earlier alternatives. These days you can only expect to get one point from a piece of homework, but several years later Howell was the fortunate recipient of a second point – Howell-E.Ragozin, Cannes Open 1993 continued as above up to move 24, and ended **24...♔d7 25 ♖xg7 ♖e8 26 ♗f6 ♕b5 27 c4 ♕c6 28 ♖xe7+ ♖xe7 29 ♕xe7+ ♔c8 30 ♖h7 1-0**.

4 The Endgame

Many games are decided in the endgame, especially between players of comparable strength. Mastery of the endgame is just as important as proficiency in the opening and middlegame. Even though this truth has been repeated over and over again, the endgame still remains a neglected area of chess study, especially amongst club players.

In the past they had some excuse, as many club games were decided by adjudication before the endgame was reached, but quickplay finishes are now the rule rather than the exception. In tournaments, too, the quickplay finish is the most common method of deciding long games. The practical effect is that players can no longer rely on an 'if I get an endgame, I'll work it out over the board' attitude. The fast time-limit implies that you have to know the correct method beforehand. Moreover, familiarity is very important. If you have to ransack your memory for some half-forgotten but vital snippet of information, the chances are that you will have lost on time before your memory cells release the necessary information.

This chapter is therefore designed as a quick guide to what it is absolutely essential to know about the endgame.

King and Pawn endings

King and pawn endings very often represent the final phase of a game. Of course, both sides may promote, in which case the players can look forward to a lot more fun, but the majority of ♔+♙ endings are decided in the pawn ending itself. Unlike most other types of position, the concept of an 'inaccuracy' is almost unknown in ♔+♙ endings. Given sufficient energy and skill, most positions are capable of being analysed to a definite conclusion. This means that errors can only occur in half-point jumps. Also, unlike other types of position, in which you may recover from a mistake and gradually fight your way back into the game, a slip in a ♔+♙ ending usually means the certain loss of half a point.

This means that accuracy is at a special premium in this type of ending, so it is essential to be familiar with the main principles.

There are three fundamental concepts in ♔+♙ endings. Surprisingly, however, not even all GMs are familiar with their correct application.

Opposition

This is the most basic principle and has the widest application. The following position provides us with a clear-cut example.

The two kings face ('oppose') each other with the minimum possible gap of one empty square between them. White has the advantage because his king is one square further advanced. This advantage is sufficient to win if Black is to move, because the black king has to move to one side or the other. This allows White's king to advance to the fifth and run to one or other of the enemy pawns. In this situation we say that 'White has the opposition'.

However, even in this relatively simple case there is still one finesse. After **1...♔c6** White must not run directly to the g-pawn with 2 ♔e5, because after 2...♔c5 3 ♔f5 ♔b4 4 ♔xg5 ♔xa4 5 ♔f5 ♔b4 6 g5 a4 both sides promote at the same time and the position is a draw. Instead, **2 ♔c4!** is correct, again taking the opposition, but under even more favourable circumstances. If Black plays **2...♔b6 3**

♔d5 ♔b7, then White can win in two ways:

1) If White now heads for the g-pawn, he has gained a vital tempo: **4 ♔e5 ♔b6 5 ♔f5 ♔c5 6 ♔xg5 ♔b4 7 ♔f5 ♔xa4 8 g5 ♔b4 9 g6 a4 10 g7 a3 11 g8♕**. It is worthwhile thinking for a moment about why moving one file to the queenside has actually gained a tempo in this line. The point is that after 3 ♔d5 the black king is not only unable to approach the a-pawn, but must actually move one square further away. Thus White loses one tempo but Black loses two.

2) **4 ♔c5** (White mops up the a-pawn before heading for the kingside) **4...♔a6 5 ♔c6 ♔a7 6 ♔b5 ♔b7 7 ♔xa5 ♔c6 8 ♔b4 ♔b6 9 ♔c4** with an easy win.

If the black king heads the other way with **2...♔d6**, then White heads for the a-pawn, having gained an extra tempo because his king is one square nearer the queenside: **3 ♔b5 ♔e5 4 ♔xa5 ♔f4 5 ♔b4 ♔xg4 6 a5 ♔h3 7 a6 g4 8 a7 g3 9 a8♕**. This position is a technical win; if you are unfamiliar with the process, here it is: **9...g2 10 ♕f3+ ♔h2 11 ♕f2 ♔h1 12 ♕h4+ ♔g1 13 ♔c3 ♔f1 14 ♕f4+ ♔e2 15 ♕g3 ♔f1 16 ♕f3+ ♔g1 17 ♕f4 ♔h1 18 ♕h4+ ♔g1 19 ♔d2 ♔f1 20 ♕e1#**.

The situation after **1...♔e6** is virtually symmetrical. Once again White must avoid the immediate dash for the pawn with 2 ♔c5?. The correct method is **2 ♔e4 ♔f6** (2...♔d6 3 ♔f5 and White promotes first; Black's a-pawn does not reach the seventh rank) **3 ♔d5 ♔f7 4 ♔c5** (4 ♔e5 also wins) **4...♔e6 5 ♔b5 ♔e5 6 ♔xa5 ♔f4 7 ♔b5 ♔xg4 8 a5 ♔h3**, transposing to line 2 above.

While the details of this position include one or two subtle points, the basic principle is clear enough: when White has the opposition, Black must give way with his king and permit White's own king to advance. It is worth noting that if White is to move in the diagram, then Black has the opposition, but because of White's initially more favourable king position, he can hold the draw: **1 ♔c4** (1 ♔e4 also draws, but any king retreat to the third rank loses, as Black can transpose into the above analysis with reversed colours) **1...♔c6** (after 1...♔e5 both sides promote simultaneously) **2 ♔d4** and Black has nothing better than to return to d6.

The situation becomes only a little more complicated when the kings are further back:

With White to play, one's first impulse is to rush forward with the king by 1 ♔c3?, but this is a mistake: Black replies 1...♔c7! and after 2 ♔c4 ♔c6 or 2 ♔d4 ♔d6 Black gains the opposition and White cannot make progress. The basic principle governing such cases of what is called the 'distant opposition' is that when the kings face each other with an odd number of squares in between, then the player to move loses the opposition. The situation when there is just one square in between the kings (discussed above) is then just a special case of this rule.

In the above position, it follows that **1 ♔c2!** is the correct move (1 ♔b3? is also bad, since after 1...♔d7! Black can meet 2 ♔c4 by 2...♔c6 and 2 ♔c3 by 2...♔c7). Black replies **1...♔d8**. Now 2 ♔b3? can be met by 2...♔d7, and of course 2 ♔c3? ♔c7 and 2 ♔d3? ♔d7 give Black the opposition. The correct move is **2 ♔d2!**, again in accordance with our 'odd-square' rule. At first sight White is not getting anywhere, since if Black just keeps moving his king up and down the first rank by 2...♔e8, White can apparently only follow suit on his second rank.

However, White can make progress by carrying out what is called a 'by-pass'. This involves moving in the opposite direction to Black's king and at the same time advancing. If it works, then the result will be to regain the opposition, but with the kings two squares closer together. White can repeat the manoeuvre until there is just one square between the kings and then we have the situation discussed in the previous diagram. Here White executes a by-pass with **3 ♔c3!**. Now there is a direct threat to play 4 ♔c4 and 5 ♔b5, so Black has to head for c6 by **3...♔d7**. White continues **4 ♔d3** and he has achieved his objective. Now the situation is simpler. 4...♔c7 and 4...♔e7 lose because White just heads for the g-pawn or the a-pawn respectively, so Black's king must advance to third rank. White just opposes the enemy king and gains the 'close' opposition, winning as in the previous diagram. Had Black played **2...♔c8**, White would have by-passed on the other side by **3 ♔e3**.

When I first saw this idea as a very young player, one point really confused me. On most files White was content simply to maintain the opposition but then, suddenly, on one particular file White would abandon the opposition and perform a by-pass. How do you know on which file to execute the by-pass? Eventually I was able to answer my own question and in doing so gained a deeper understanding of king and pawn endings. In positions dominated by the opposition, the attacker has two targets. In the above diagrams these are the pawns on a5 and g5. This is perfectly natural: the nature of the opposition is that if Black's king goes to the queenside, then White's king slips through to the kingside and vice versa. If there were no kingside target, then Black would

lose nothing by allowing White's king to penetrate in that direction. Similarly there must be a queenside target or Black could safely move his king to the other side of the board. The by-pass manoeuvre is almost always performed on the file which is equidistant between the two targets. In the above case this is the d-file.

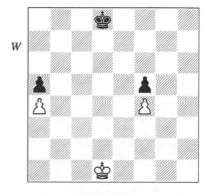

In this position, which is superficially similar to the above, White to play cannot win because there is no by-pass. White does win if he takes the opposition with his king on the fourth rank, but he cannot force this from the diagram. The critical position arises after **1 ♔d2 ♔d7 2 ♔d3** and now Black must take care. 2...♔c6? 3 ♔c4 and 2...♔d6? 3 ♔d4 allow White to gain the 'close' opposition, and in addition Black's king must also be ready to stop White lunging for the a-pawn. It follows that **2...♔c7!** is the only drawing move. This would be the ideal time for a by-pass, except that the e4-square, which White needs for the operation, is controlled by a black pawn.

In the above examples, the 'two-target' situation was quite obvious, because the targets were far apart. Cases in which the targets are closer together are governed by the same principles, even if their nature is less transparent.

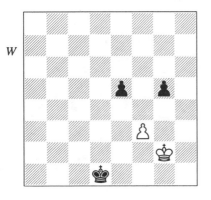

H. Neustadtl, 1890

In this position the target squares for Black are (obviously) f3 and (less obviously) f1. The latter is a target because if Black's king reaches f1 then White is losing no matter where his king is (within reason) or who is to play. For example, if White's king is on g3, then, with White to play, 1 ♔h3 ♔f2 2 ♔g4 ♔g2 wins easily. If Black is to play then 1...♔g1 forces the same line. It follows that the opposition manoeuvres will take place along the ranks (because the ranks are at right angles to the line joining the two targets) and that any by-passing will take place on the second rank.

White to play can draw, but only if he starts with the paradoxical move 1 ♔h1!. Other moves fail, for example 1 ♔f1? (this loses because White cannot maintain the close opposition) 1...♔d2 2 ♔f2 ♔d3 (White would like play 3 ♔f3, but his pawn is in the way) 3 ♔g3 ♔e3 4 ♔g2 ♔e2 5 ♔g3 ♔f1 and Black reaches a target. Other first moves fail similarly: 1 ♔h2 ♔d2! (preparing the by-pass) 2 ♔g1 (2 ♔g2 ♔e2) 2...♔e3 (by-pass executed) 3 ♔g2 ♔e2 and wins, or 1 ♔g3 ♔e1 2 ♔g2 ♔e2.

After 1 ♔h1! Black cannot make progress, as White can always maintain the opposition:

1) 1...♔e2 2 ♔g2 ♔d3 3 ♔h3! ♔e3 4 ♔g3, etc.

2) 1...♔c1 2 ♔g1! (the only move) 2...♔c2 (2...g4 is met by 3 ♔g2!, but not 3 fxg4? e4 4 ♔f2 ♔d2 and Black wins) 3 ♔g2 ♔c3 4 ♔g3 ♔d3 5 ♔h3 and so on.

We end this section on the opposition with the usual warning that while general principles can provide excellent guidance, in the end it is the specific position on the board that matters and a forced win overrides any other considerations.

The following diagram is very similar to the Neustadtl position given above. On this basis one might assume the position to be a draw, because after 1 ♔f6 ♔b6 or 1 ♔g6 ♔a6 Black gains the distant opposition. However, there is a slight difference because the kings are further apart than in the Neustadtl

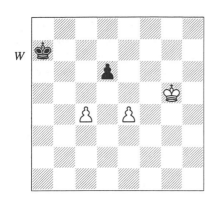

A. Mandler
Prager Presse 1929

point, because a new factor entered the equation.

The Réti manoeuvre

There is no better way to explain this idea than to give Réti's original example, even though it is one of the most famous endgame positions in chess history.

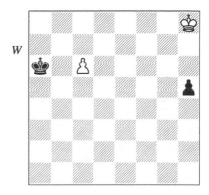

R. Réti
*Kagan's Neueste
Schachnachrichten 1921*

position and this operates in White's favour. After 1 ♔f6? ♔b6 play proceeds exactly as before, but with the kings on the g- and a-files a second factor enters the position: the possibility of a breakthrough by c5. This only works if Black's king is on the back rank, so that White will promote with check. Moreover, Black's king must be on a8, because otherwise c5 can be met by ...♔c7 (we saw this in line 2 of the previous diagram). Thus White can win by 1 ♔g6! ♔a6 (Black must maintain the opposition; if he deviates, then White gains the opposition himself and wins by reaching d6 or d8 with his king) 2 ♔g7! ♔a7 3 ♔g8! (3 ♔f8? ♔b8 4 c5 ♔c7!) 3...♔a8 (Black is dragged to his doom; 3...♔b8 4 ♔f8, 3...♔b7 4 ♔f7 and 3...♔b6 4 ♔f8 all win for White, the last line being a by-pass) 4 c5 dxc5 5 e5 and promotes with check. In this case the logic of the opposition broke down past a certain

White appears to be two tempi short of catching the h-pawn, but he nevertheless manages to overhaul it by simultaneously threatening to promote the c-pawn. The analysis runs 1 ♔g7! h4 (1...♔b6 2 ♔f6 h4 3 ♔e5 transposes to the main line) 2 ♔f6! ♔b6 (2...h3 3 ♔e7 ♔b6 4 ♔d6 and both sides promote at the same time) 3 ♔e5! ♔xc6 (3...h3 4 ♔d6 and again both sides promote) 4 ♔f4 and the impossible has been achieved.

If you have not seen this position before, it is worth playing over the solution several times to see exactly why it works. Once again, the 'two-threat' concept is important, but this time it is not a question of tempo play, but the exploitation of the fact that a diagonal king move, if measured with a ruler, is longer than an equivalent horizontal or vertical one. In terms of catching the h-pawn, the routes ♔h7-h6-h5 and ♔g7-f6-e5 are identical. The advantage of the latter is that it activates a second threat, that of promoting the c-pawn. It takes Black two tempi to deal with this threat, by taking the c-pawn with his king, and this is exactly the time White needs to catch up with the h-pawn.

Despite this coldly logical explanation, it is a remarkable idea and there still seems to be a whiff of magic about the position.

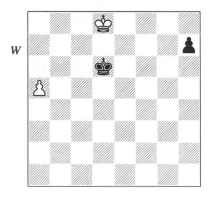

L. Prokeš
Šachové Umĕni 1947

The use of a second threat as a kind of warp-drive for White's king occurs in quite a wide range of situations. The above diagram is a second example in which White's king goes on a lengthy detour before catching the enemy pawn.

In this case the white king is one tempo short of catching the h-pawn, for example 1 a6? ♔c6 2 ♔c8 ♔b6 3 ♔b8 ♔xa6 4 ♔c7 h5 and White is too late. However, by correctly exploiting the threat of promoting the a-pawn White can make up the time: 1 ♔c8! ♔c6 2 ♔b8 ♔b5 3 ♔b7 (this is the key move; the white king just makes it into the square of the pawn) 3...♔xa5 4 ♔c6 and White is in time.

Triangulation

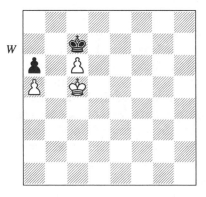

If it were Black to play in the diagram then he would lose immediately, as White's king penetrates to b6 and takes the a-pawn. If it is White to move then his task is considerably harder. The key is a king manoeuvre which, by losing a tempo, transfers the move from White to Black. However, before starting this manoeuvre White has to play what is, in any case, a forced move: **1 ♔d5**. Now 1...♔d8 2 ♔d6 is a win even without the a-pawns, so **1...♔c8** is forced. White cannot then win with the direct 2 ♔d6 ♔d8 3 c7+ ♔c8 because 4 ♔c6 is stalemate – he must be more subtle. While the white king remains adjacent to c5 Black's king cannot occupy c7, and so is restricted to shuffling back and forth along the first rank. If the white king moves around the triangle c4-d4-d5 the effect will be to transfer the move to Black: **2 ♔c4 ♔d8 3 ♔d4 ♔c8 4 ♔d5** and now we have the position after the first move, but with Black to play. White wins after 4...♔d8 5 ♔d6 or 4...♔c7 5 ♔c5.

White's triangulation worked because of Black's lack of space; he could not emulate White's manoeuvre without stepping off the edge of the board.

If you have looked at an advanced book on king and pawn endings, you will probably have noticed something called 'the theory of corresponding squares'. This is normally accompanied by diagrams with lots of little numbers (or letters, or sometimes both) on the squares. While this is an interesting subject from the theoretical point of view, to be quite honest it is of almost no practical value (not to mention that your opponent might object when you start adorning the board

with mystic numbers). The opposition, triangulation and a little bit of brain-power are all that are needed for the types of position that arise in over-the-board play. Of course there a few esoteric positions which cannot be solved by such straightforward techniques, but in all my career I have never seen such a position arise in practical play. The following position represents about the limit of complexity that one can anticipate over the board.

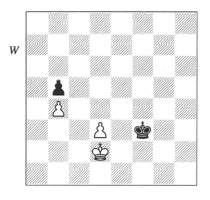

N. Grigoriev
K novoi armii, 1920

A position such as this would be an easy win for White if his king were on, say, d4, but here the win is difficult because of Black's active king position. The first point to note is that after 1 d4? ♔e4 2 ♔c3 Black does not play 2...♔d5?, when 3 ♔d3 forces the enemy king back, but 2...♔f5!. If White moves anywhere except to d3, then Black just returns to e4, but after 3

♔d3 ♚f4 White cannot make progress, e.g. 4 ♔d2 ♚e4 5 ♔c3 ♚f5!, etc.

It becomes apparent that White would be much better off in the diagram position if it were Black to play. If Black's king goes anywhere except to f4, then White wins by 2 ♔e3 or 2 d4, while after 1...♚f4 White plays 2 ♔e2 and the black king is gradually forced back. In fact the win is still not too easy, but we will return to this point later as the first step is to work out how to lose a tempo. If White plays 1 ♔c2, then Black must reply 1...♚f4 (since 1...♚e3 2 ♔c3 loses at once, and after other moves White wins by either ♔c3-d4 or 2 d4). Readers may now recognize a pattern emerging: the situation is basically the same as in the previous diagram rotated through 90 degrees, with c3-e3 taking the place of c5-c7 and c2-f4 the place of d5-c8. Now the solution should be apparent. While the white king remains adjacent to c3, Black's king must remain adjacent to e3; in other words Black can only oscillate between f3 and f4 (e2 and f2 are out because the d-pawn advances). White only has to triangulate c2-b2-b3-c2, all the time staying adjacent to c3, and he will lose a tempo. The solution runs **1 ♔c2 ♚f4 2 ♔b2 ♚f3** (2...♚e5 3 ♔c3 ♚d5 4 ♔c2 ♚e5 5 ♔d1 transposes) **3 ♔b3 ♚f4 4 ♔c2** (unlike the previous diagram, there is still quite a lot of play left in the position) **4...♚e5** (the most resilient defence; 4...♚e3 5 ♔c3 and 4...♚f3 5 ♔d2 lose more quickly) **5**

♔d1! (5 ♔d2 ♚d4 forces White to retrace his steps with 6 ♔c2) **5...♚f5 6 ♔e2 ♚f4 7 ♔f2 ♚e5** (after 7...♚f5 8 ♔e3 ♚e5 9 d4+ ♔d5 10 ♔d3 White wins by driving Black's king back) **8 ♔e3 ♚d5** (the critical moment; if White is to make progress he must give up the b4-pawn) **9 d4! ♚c4 10 ♔e4 ♚xb4 11 d5 ♚c5** (forced, or else White promotes before Black) **12 ♔e5** (White must spend a tempo supporting his pawn, so now both sides promote at the same time; however, ...) **12...b4 13 d6 b3** (interposing 13...♚c6 14 ♔e6 doesn't change the situation) **14 d7 b2 15 d8♕ b1♕ 16 ♕c8+** and **17 ♕b8+**, winning Black's queen.

Expect the unexpected

Readers will have noticed several odd king manoeuvres in the preceding positions. This is no coincidence; paradoxical king moves are quite common in king and pawn endings. It is very important to take into account the possibility of 'unnatural' king moves, both for you and for your opponent. It is impossible to give rules for finding such moves, precisely because they are often 'one-off' events which only work in that precise position. However, this won't prevent me from giving a few entertaining examples.

Shirov had headed for the position in the following diagram because it seems an obvious draw after, for example 1 ♔g5 ♚g2 2 f4 ♚f3 3 f5 ♚e4.

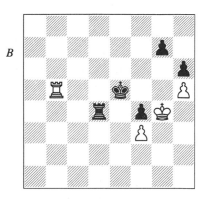

I. Rogers – A. Shirov
Groningen 1990

M. Hebden – G. Flear
British Championship, Brighton 1980

However, after the surprising **1 ♔g3!** Shirov resigned. The threat is simply to push the pawn to f6 and then run with the king to take the f7-pawn, *simultaneously defending White's own pawn.* Black can only try to extract his king from the box by 1...♔g1 2 f4 ♔f1 3 f5 ♔e2, but White can keep Black's king at bay: 4 ♔f4 f6 (or 4...♔d3 5 ♔e5 and wins after 5...♔e3 6 f6 or 5...♔c4 6 ♔f6) 5 ♔e4! ♔f2 6 ♔d5. The backward move of White's king is sufficiently counter-intuitive that even such a strong player as Shirov overlooked it.

In Hebden-Flear, Black had been a pawn up for most of the game, but here he abandoned his winning attempts and played **1...♖d5?!**, at which point the players agreed to a draw. Indeed, after 2 ♖xd5+ ♔xd5 3 ♔xf4 ♔e6 there is clearly no point in continuing. However, as soon as the draw was

agreed the players suddenly noticed that White could play 3 ♔f5! *(D)* instead of 3 ♔xf4.

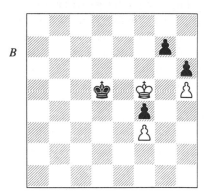

Suddenly Black is in trouble. After 3...♔d4 4 ♔xf4 ♔d3 5 ♔f5 ♔e3 6 ♔g6 ♔f4 7 ♔xg7 ♔g5 8 f4+ ♔xh5 9 f5 the f-pawn promotes, while 3...♔d6 4 ♔g6 ♔e6 (4...♔e5 5 ♔xg7 ♔d4 6 ♔xh6 ♔e3 7 ♔g5! ♔xf3 8 h6 ♔g3 9 h7 f3 10 h8♕ f2 11 ♕h1; in this line Black lost because he was not able to play his king to g2 at move 8) 5 ♔xg7 ♚e7 6 ♔xh6 ♚f6 is hopeless because White can extract his king by using up his one remaining tempo with the h-pawn: 7 ♔h7 ♚f7 8 h6 ♚f8 9 ♔g6 ♚g8 10 ♔f5 ♚h7 11 ♔g5 followed by 12 ♔xf4.

Having analysed both 3...♚d4 and 3...♚d6 to a loss, one might be tempted to assess the position as a win for White, but remember: 'Expect the Unexpected'. What does Black need to achieve in order to draw? First of all, he must be able to defend his g7-pawn if White plays ♔xf4 followed by ♚f5-g6. That means that his king must stay within three squares of f8. If White adopts his alternative plan of heading straight for g7 without bothering about the f4-pawn, then Black has to be able to answer ♚xh6 with ...♚xf3; one move slower and White will win as in the bracket given above. Since it takes three moves for White to reach h6, it follows that Black's king must stay within three squares of f3. The first criterion implies that Black must move to c5, c6 or d6 and the second implies that he must move to c4, d4 or c5. Luckily for Black, there is one square common to both these sets, namely c5. Thus 3...♚c5!! draws, e.g. 4 ♚g6 ♚d4, 4 ♚xf4 ♚d6 or 4 ♚e5 ♚c6.

It is quite hard to describe exactly what this motif depends on – it certainly has nothing to do with the opposition. Perhaps it is closest to the Réti manoeuvre, in that Black's king is trying to fulfil two tasks at the same time.

Chess is more than counting

One technique applicable in king and pawn endings, which is often recommended in textbooks, is that of 'counting'. This name refers to the method of working out how many moves both sides will take to promote a pawn. Of course, this is only useful in 'race' situations, where each king marches into the opposing pawn-mass with the aim of creating a passed pawn as quickly as possible.

I strongly advise *against* using the technique of 'counting'.

There are several flaws with this method, and its unrestricted application can result in dreadful blunders. The main problem is that this method cannot detect any of the finesses which make king and pawn endings so interesting and which arise quite often in practice.

The first cause of confusion is that you have to take account of who moves first. If White takes seven moves to promote and Black eight, when White promotes does Black reply by promoting or by pushing his pawn to the seventh? The answer is that it depends on who moves first. In the heat of battle it is quite easy to get this wrong and be 'out by one' (computer programmers know all about being 'out by one').

The second cause is that the counting method gives you no clue as to the relative whereabouts of the pieces at the end of the race. White may promote and give check, or promote on h8 and stop Black's promotion on a1. These things are obvious if you run the variation through in your head, but are not obvious if you are just counting. The simple fact is that you actually have to calculate the variation to make sure that one of these special situations doesn't arise at the end of the race and if you are going to do that, then you may as well not waste time on counting.

I will quote a position taken from *Chess: The Complete Self-Tutor* by Edward Lasker (it appears in all editions before 1997), a popular chess primer which advocates the use of the counting method.

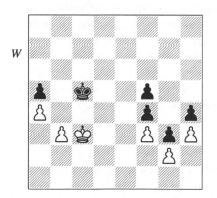

W

Lasker writes "In the position reached, the sequence 1 b4+ axb4+ 2 ♔b3 forces Black to leave his pawn unprotected, giving White a passed pawn. After 2...♔c6 3 ♔xb4 ♔b6 4

♔c4 it is all over. White captures the black pawns on f4, h4, and g3 while Black takes the a4-pawn and walks back to the kingside."

Lasker does not consider what happens if Black plays 2...♔d4. By counting (carefully!) one quickly finds that Black's g-pawn is still on the sixth when White queens and, moreover, it is White's turn to move – enough reason to abandon the position as lost, if one does not take the trouble to visualize the resulting position.

If we actually play over the moves 2...♔d4 3 a5 ♔e3 4 a6 ♔f2 5 a7 ♔xg2 6 a8♕ ♔h2 (D), then we arrive at the following diagram:

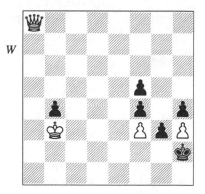

W

It only takes a few moments to realize that this is a special situation. The congested mass of kingside pawns prevents White from pinning the g-pawn diagonally and from giving check on the h-file. In fact the g-pawn is unstoppable and the best White can do is to grab as many kingside pawns as he can, hoping for a favourable queen ending. However, even this hope is in vain: after 7 ♕b8 (7 ♕h8 g2 8 ♕xh4 g1♕ 9 ♕xf4+ ♕g3 10 ♕xf5 ♕xh3 11 ♕g4!? ♕g3 and 12...♔g2 is also a draw) 7...g2 8 ♕xf4+ ♔h1 9 ♕xf5 g1♕ the ending is a sure draw.

Finally, if you don't calculate the whole variation, how can you be sure that the moves you are intending to play are actually possible? Here is a simple example.

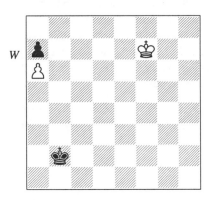

W. Schlage – C. Ahues
Berlin 1921

It takes White five moves to take on a7 and it takes Black five moves to reach c7, so Black can meet ♔xa7 by ...♔c7 and the position is a draw. This was borne out by the game, which duly finished 1 ♔e6 ♔c3 2 ♔d6 ♔d4 3 ♔c6 ♔e5 4 ♔b7 ♔d6 5 ♔xa7 ♔c7 ½-½. Right? Wrong! If White had played 2 ♔d5! then he could still take on a7 in five moves, but Black would take longer as the moves he wants to play are illegal, for example after

2...♔b4 3 ♔c6 ♔a5 4 ♔b7 he cannot move to b6.

There is far more to king and pawn endings than counting, and if you use this method you are asking for trouble.

Rook endings

Rook endings are the most common type of ending to occur in practical play. The reason is that if there are no open files, a relatively frequent occurrence, then exchanges of rooks are rather unlikely. Minor pieces and queens can be exchanged far more readily. The ability to play rook and pawn endings well is a great distinguishing feature between a master player and a club player. In simultaneous displays, it is noticeable how the club players routinely lose completely equal rook endings, and how easily the master manages to escape with a draw from lost rook endings.

Part of the reason for this is that rook and pawn endings are genuinely complicated, with a great deal of theory. Experience is perhaps even more important; the master will probably have encountered many rook endings in the course of his career, the club player far fewer. However, the situation for club players is certainly far from hopeless; indeed, this is one of those areas in which a few hours' study can provide great dividends. We start with the ending of rook + pawn against rook, which is fundamental to all rook endings.

Rook and Pawn vs Rook

This ending is sufficiently complex that your author was able write a 320-page book solely about this material balance (and even then several interesting positions had to be omitted!). However, many average tournament players have not studied even the fundamentals of this ending. In fact, a few basic principles can be quite effective in improving one's rook endgame technique.

If the defender's king can occupy the pawn's queening square, then the ending is almost always a draw. The only exception is when the pawn is already far advanced and the defender's pieces are badly placed. The general drawing technique is quite simple and is called the 'third-rank defence'.

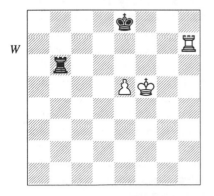

Here is a typical position. White appears to have made quite a lot of progress. His rook is cutting the enemy king off on the back rank and his king and pawn have advanced as far as the fifth rank. Nevertheless, the position is completely drawn because Black has positioned his rook on his third rank, thereby preventing the immediate advance of the white king. The only way in which White can get his king to the sixth is to play 1 e6, but then Black switches plans and plays 1...Rb1, preparing to bombard the white king with checks from behind. Now that the pawn is on e6, there is no hiding place for the king, and after 2 Kf6 Rf1+ 3 Ke5 Re1+ 4 Kd6 Rd1+, etc., the position is clearly drawn. If, in the diagram position, White waits with 1 Ra7 then Black does likewise by either 1...Rc6 or 1...Rh6.

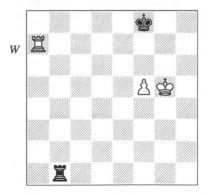

The second important principle is that of 'checking distance'. If the white king has no way to hide from a checking black rook, then the factor determining whether the checks are a minor nuisance or a serious problem is the distance between the king and the rook. The further apart they are, the better it is for the side with the rook.

The above example makes this clear. If it is White to play then he should continue 1 ♔g6, which creates the most awkward problems for Black. If White waits, then Black sets up the third-rank defence by ...♖b6. 1 ♔f6 ♖b6+ leads to the same thing, while 1 f6 ♖g1+ is an immediate draw (note the large checking distance).

After 1 ♔g6 it is easy for Black to go wrong, for example the passive line 1...♖b8 2 f6 ♔g8 fails to 3 ♖g7+ ♔f8 (or 3...♔h8 4 ♖h7+ ♔g8 5 f7+) 4 ♖h7 and White's plan of 'switching to the other side' leaves Black defenceless. Note that this line would be a draw if White's pawn were on g6 and his king on h6, because there would be no room to switch to the other side. This leads us to the important conclusion that in the type of position in which Black has been forced to defend passively with his rook on the first rank, the result is a draw with an a-, b-, g- or h-pawn, but lost with a pawn on one of the other four files.

Here we have an f-pawn so this defensive plan is not good enough for Black. Instead, he should play **1...♖f1**. This ensures that after 2 ♖a8+ ♔e7 White cannot play 3 f6+. White can only make progress by playing **2 ♔f6**, which threatens mate. Black has to choose between 2...♔e8 and 2...♔g8. One move loses and the other draws.

The correct choice depends on ensuring that Black has sufficient checking distance in the subsequent play. After **2...♔g8! 3 ♖a8+ ♔h7** White can

try **4 ♖f8** (4 ♔e6 ♔g7! and 4 ♖a5 ♔g8 do not help White) intending 5 ♔e7, followed by 6 f6. If Black keeps his rook in its current position then he will eventually lose, but Black can change direction by **4...♖a1!**. If White now plays a king move to free his pawn, then Black starts checking from the side. There is no shelter, so in view of the large checking distance White cannot effectively meet the barrage of checks. White can, of course, play other moves but they do not help, for example after 5 ♖e8 (to meet 5...♖a6+ by 6 ♖e6) the simplest draw is to return to f1 with the rook.

On the other hand, 2...♔e8? loses. After 3 ♖a8+ ♔d7 4 ♖f8, there is nothing Black can do to prevent White playing 5 ♔g7 (or ♔f7, if the rook leaves the f-file), followed by f6, and there is no way to stop the pawn. Black's problem is that he lacks the lateral checks which saved him after 2...♔g8. There is no space for his rook on the kingside, and he cannot give checks from the queenside because his own king gets in the way.

This principle is usually formulated as 'move the king to the short side' in order to leave the other side free for long-range rook checks, but in the end it all comes down to ensuring adequate checking distance.

Here is another example *(D)*:

Black is to play, and he faces the threat of ♔c4 followed by b5. If he plays 1...♖h5, then White advances his pawn by 2 ♔a4. The only possibility

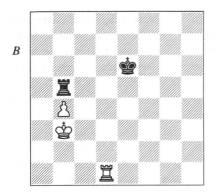

B

to defend is to retreat the rook along the b-file, so then when the white king moves to a4 or c4, Black can start checking. In order for this to work, Black needs to have the maximum possible checking distance and in fact **1...♖b8!** is the only move to draw. After **2 ♖d4** (2 ♔c4 ♖c8+ 3 ♔b5 ♖b8+ 4 ♔c5 ♖c8+ 5 ♔b6 ♖b8+ is pointless – the white king has to retreat; after the text-move, however, this line is a threat since White could play ♔c7 at the end) **2...♔e5** (dislodging the rook from the defence of the b-pawn) **3 ♖d7 ♔e6** (Black cannot wait; 3...♔e4? loses to 4 ♔c4 ♖c8+ 5 ♔b5 ♖b8+ 6 ♔c5 ♖c8+ 7 ♔b6 ♖b8+ 8 ♖b7, followed by b5; in this line White's rook effectively reduced Black's checking distance by being able to interpose on the seventh rank) **4 ♖a7 ♔d6 5 ♔a4 ♔c6** and Black is in time to prevent the pawn's advance. If the checking distance had been even one square less Black would have lost, for example 1...♖b7? 2 ♔c4 ♖c7+ 3 ♔b5 ♖c8 (trying to regain his checking distance;

3...♖b7+ 4 ♔c5 ♖c7+ 5 ♔b6 is hopeless) 4 ♔a6 ♖a8+ 5 ♔b7, followed by b5, and White wins.

We already saw in the analysis on page 126 how the defender must be prepared to use his rook flexibly and operate from different directions according to changing circumstances. Here is another, very important, example of this:

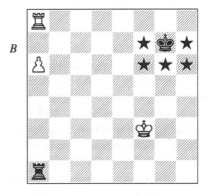

B

Black cannot move his king to the queenside because after ...♔e7 White replies a7 and the king is caught between two stools. After either ...♔d7 or ...♔f7 White replies ♖h8, winning the enemy rook. It follows that Black's king is trapped in an invisible box on the kingside, consisting of the marked squares in the above diagram (plus g7, the square the king is currently standing on). Black can only use his rook to defend, and he must counter White's threat of playing his king over to defend the pawn, releasing his rook and clearing the way for the pawn. If Black checks from behind, the white king hides on a7 (this is why White must not push his pawn to a7 prematurely) and again his rook is freed.

Black to play draws by being flexible with his rook: 1...♖f1+ 2 ♔e4 ♖f6!. This change of direction is the key; a7 is no hiding place when Black is checking from the side. Play might continue 3 ♔d5 ♖b6 4 ♔c5 (4 ♖a7+ ♔g6 5 ♔c5 ♖f6 is the same) 4...♖f6 5 ♔b5 (now White threatens to move his rook, so Black must start checking) 5...♖f5+ 6 ♔c4 ♖f4+ 7 ♔d5 ♖f6 and White cannot make progress. If White plays a7 at any stage, Black replies ...♖a6 followed by ...♖a1, and if the white king then approaches the pawn, Black draws by checking the king from behind (the nook on a7 is no longer available). This double change of direction (a1 to f6 and then back to a1) is quite hard to see, and in fact it was not discovered until 1924 by Vancura.

Several years ago I was asked to check some rook ending analysis, but I couldn't understand any of it – White, who had the advantage, seemed to be forcing Black to reach a drawn position, which Black then avoided! Finally, I looked at the date of the analysis – 1912 – and realized that because the Vancura draw wasn't known at that time, all positions of the type shown in the previous diagram were thought to be winning for White. Not surprisingly, this led to some odd moves.

I should add that if White's king is nearer to the a-pawn in the above diagram, then Black has no time to set up the Vancura draw. The precise details of how close White has to be to win are rather complicated and may be found in specialized endgame books.

The extra Pawn

One of the most common endgame situations in practical play is a rook and pawn ending with an extra pawn on one side of the board, and the position otherwise symmetrical.

Here is a typical situation:

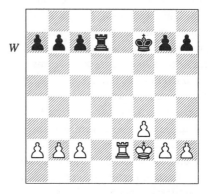

An ability to win positions such as this is fundamental to successful chess. White may have won a pawn with a combination, or perhaps Black had an isolated e-pawn which White picked up with subtle strategic play – whatever your chess style, situations in which you win a pawn for essentially no compensation are very common. The question then arises: how often do you convert the resulting positions into a full point?

I showed this position to some of the world's leading grandmasters, including Karpov, Kramnik and Andersson, and asked them to estimate their winning chances as White, assuming an opponent of equal strength. The answers were all in the range 80-90%. The general feeling was that such a position should objectively be a win, and the 'missing' 10-20% represented the probability of making a mistake oneself rather than the probability of running into exceptionally good defence.

A search of 500,000 games revealed 94 clear-cut examples of this type of structure (3 vs 3 on one side, 3 vs 2 on the other, no doubled pawns and pawns not blocked). The result was 72 wins, 19 draws and 3 losses(!). The 77% success rate was slightly lower than the GMs thought, but at their level technique is better and so, assuming that the position is objectively won, they would be more likely to round up the point. They probably also wouldn't lose a rook ending with a clear extra pawn!

Unfortunately, such situations are poorly covered in endgame theory books, which tend to concentrate on more simplified positions. While they devote a lot of attention to the situation with 3 vs 3 on one side and an outside passed pawn on the other wing, the situation in which there is a majority rather than a passed pawn is hardly covered at all. The massive *Encyclopaedia of Chess Endings*, with 1727 positions, doesn't contain anything

like it, nor do standard works on the endgame such as Levenfish and Smyslov's famous *Rook Endings*.

Fine's old *Basic Chess Endings* contains perhaps the most helpful advice. He recommended that if the defender's king is on the side where the pawns are balanced then you should adopt the following plan:

1) place the king and rook on the best possible squares;

2) advance the pawns on the other wing as far as convenient, without actually setting up a passed pawn;

3) transpose to a won ending with an outside passed pawn.

What he means is that you should not necessarily create the passed pawn as quickly as possible, as some positions with an extra outside passed pawn are drawn. Instead, you should continue to manoeuvre until the passed pawn can be created under favourable circumstances, for example with your rook behind it.

If the defender's king is on the side with the potential passed pawn, then the decisive manoeuvre is the penetration of the attacking king on the opposite wing.

Having played over all the 94 examples mentioned above, I failed to find any clear-cut examples of this winning plan. Either the ending was misplayed by one side or the other, or the defender seemed to assume that he would lose in the long run and embarked on a desperate bid for counterplay. Thus readers will have to make do with Nunn vs Fritz5 from the diagram on page 128:

1 h4

We are in the second of Fine's cases mentioned above, so White's long-term aim will be to penetrate amongst the queenside pawns with his king. However, at the moment this pawn structure offers no avenues of approach for the king, so White must find a way to induce the pawns to advance. One plan would be to play ♔e1 and then attack the pawns by ♖e3-a3, etc., forcing them to move forwards. Then White could play ♖d3 and ♔d2, cross the d-file with his king and then try to get amongst the pawns.

Perhaps this plan is the most systematic, but I decided on another idea, that of advancing the kingside pawns. If Black remains passive, White will gain a great deal of space on the kingside and should eventually be able to create a passed pawn there under favourable circumstances. If Black tries to generate counterplay by advancing his queenside pawns, then White will again have the possibility of switching his king to the other side of the board.

1...b5

I doubt that a human would defend in such forthright style! Fritz decides to gain space on the queenside, but it is creating precisely the sort of openings that will help White later on.

2 g4 a5 3 ♔g3 a4 4 a3

It is a good idea not to let the queenside pawns advance too far. Later on

the black rook may switch behind the pawns, and this could prove very awkward if Black has pawns on a4 and b4. Now that Black has advanced a pawn to a4, White can conveniently halt the pawns by a3 and c3, which also makes his queenside safe against an attack by Black's rook.

4...♖d1 5 h5

In rook endings it is quite often a good idea to have such a chain of pawns. If the white rook defends the base of the chain, then all the pawns are secure against enemy rook attack.

5...♖b1 6 c3 g5

An attempt to obstruct White on the kingside.

7 hxg6+ hxg6 8 ♔f4 ♖d1 (D)

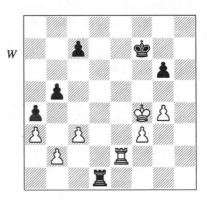

9 ♔e3

This is where Fine's advice came in helpful. The immediate attempt to advance with the king leads nowhere, since after 9 ♔e5 c6 Black is ready to drive the king back with ...♖d5+. Instead, White intends ♖d2, followed by ♔d4-c5. In fact Black can prevent this plan, but White loses nothing by trying it before considering other ideas.

9...♔f6?

An error, allowing White to execute his plan. 9...♖f1 was also bad since 10 ♖f2 ♖d1 11 ♖d2 ♖f1 12 ♖d7+ ♔f6 13 ♖xc7 ♖b1 14 ♖c6+ transposes to the game.

The correct move was 9...♔e6!, when 10 ♖d2 ♖e1+ 11 ♔d4 ♔d6 prevents the king reaching c5. Instead 10 ♔e4 is probably best, followed by f4 and the possible creation of a kingside passed pawn.

10 ♖d2 ♖f1

10...♖e1+ 11 ♔d4 ♖f1 12 ♔c5 ♖xf3 13 ♔xb5 is hopeless – Black's queenside pawns are too weak.

11 ♖d5

Now White can exploit the queenside pawns with the rook instead of the king.

11...c6 12 ♖c5 ♖b1 13 ♖xc6+ ♔f7 14 ♔f4 ♖xb2 15 ♔g5

This more or less forced sequence has left White very well placed. He will inevitably win the g-pawn, thereby gaining two connected passed pawns on the kingside, whereas Black cannot create two passed pawns on the queenside.

15...♖b3 16 f4!

A small finesse avoiding Fritz's trap. After 16 ♖c7+? ♔e6 17 ♔xg6 ♔d6! Black either perpetually attacks the rook or drives it away from the defence of c3, when Black can also gain two connected passed pawns (e.g. 18 ♖c8 ♔d7 19 ♖b8 ♔c7, etc.).

16...♖xa3 17 ♖c7+ ♔e6 18 ♔xg6 ♔d6 19 ♖c8 ♔d7 20 ♖c5

Black cannot continue his attack on the rook as the b5-pawn is hanging.

20...♖b3 21 f5 a3 22 f6 ♖b1 23 f7 ♖f1 24 ♖xb5 a2 25 ♖a5 ♔e7 26 ♖xa2 ♖f6+ 27 ♔g5 1-0

This, incidentally, provides an example of using computer programs for training purposes. It is possible to set up simplified, idealized positions and play them out against the computer. The best method is to play the same position several times for both colours, trying different ideas to see what works and what doesn't. This kind of experience cannot be gained in over-the-board play. We will return to this subject in Chapter 5.

Many endings with an extra pawn eventually reduce to the situation in which the pawns are equal on one side and one player has an outside passed pawn on the opposite wing. The remainder of the section deals with this common occurrence. For the sake of simplicity, let's assume that White possesses an extra pawn on the queenside. White's rook will need to defend the pawn, and there are three possible positions for the rook: behind the pawn, to the side of the pawn, and in front of the pawn. This list is arranged in descending order of desirability from White's point of view.

The situation in which White's rook is behind the pawn is a familiar one.

The pawn is continually threatening to advance, so Black has to block the pawn with his rook. Not only does the rook become tied down, but Black is left open to the possibility of zugzwang. The classic example of this situation is also one of the best:

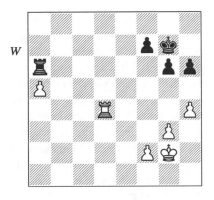

A. Alekhine – J. Capablanca
Buenos Aires World
Championship (34) 1927

54 ♖a4

In accordance with the above principle, the rook is better behind the pawn than to the side of it.

54...♔f6

White's immediate threat is to run his king to b5 and lift the blockade of the pawn. Black can prevent this using his own king, but he quickly runs into zugzwang.

55 ♔f3 ♔e5 56 ♔e3 h5 57 ♔d3 ♔d5 58 ♔c3 ♔c5 59 ♖a2

This is the reason why having the rook behind the pawn is so favourable. Since Black cannot move his rook, the situation is just as if he had lost the opposition in a king and pawn ending. After ...♔d5, White plays ♔b4 and supports his pawn with the king; after ...♔b5, White can head for the kingside pawns with his king. Black can only avoid these lines by playing pawn moves on the kingside, but White can always move his rook up and down, so that Black is sure to fall into zugzwang sooner or later.

59...♔b5 60 ♔b3

Black is helpless, so White can afford to gain time on the clock by repeating moves.

60...♔c5

After 60...♖xa5 61 ♖xa5+ ♔xa5, White wins by 62 ♔c4 ♔b6 63 ♔d5 ♔c7 64 ♔e5 ♔d7 65 ♔f6 ♔e8 66 f4 ♔f8 67 f5 gxf5 68 ♔xf5 and 69 ♔g5.

61 ♔c3 ♔b5 62 ♔d4

Now the king heads for the vulnerable enemy pawns. Black's king is too far away to prevent this, so Capablanca decides to use his king to blockade the a-pawn and his rook to fight against the penetration of the white king. This is indeed the best defence, but however Black plays he cannot overcome the fatal handicap of having one or other of his pieces fully occupied blockading the a-pawn.

62...♖d6+

If Black tries to arrange a perpetual attack on White's rook by 62...♔b4 63 ♖a1 ♔b3, then 64 ♔c5 ♔b2 65 ♔b5 wins.

63 ♔e5 ♖e6+ 64 ♔f4 ♔a6 65 ♔g5 ♖e5+ 66 ♔h6 ♖f5 (D)

The alternative is to defend the f7-pawn along the second rank by 66...♖e7 67 ♔g7 ♖d7 68 ♔f6 ♖c7, but White wins after 69 ♖e2 ♔xa5 70 ♖e7 ♖c2 71 ♖xf7 ♖xf2+ 72 ♔xg6 ♖g2 73 ♖f3.

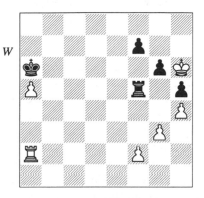

67 f4?!

By exposing the pawn on g3, Alekhine makes the win more difficult. After 67 ♔g7 ♖f3 68 ♔g8 f5 (the only chance, as 68...♖f6 69 f4 ♖f5 70 ♔g7 wins immediately) 69 ♔g7 f4 70 ♔xg6 fxg3 71 fxg3 ♖xg3+ 72 ♔xh5 ♖c3 73 ♖a4 ♔b5 74 ♖f4 ♔xa5 75 ♔g5 the h-pawn decides the game without difficulty.

As Speelman points out, White can even avoid the minimal counterplay of ...f5-f4 by continuing 67 ♔h7 ♖f3 (67...♖f6 68 ♔g8 ♖f5 69 f4) 68 ♔g7 ♖f5 69·f4, winning straight away.

67...♖c5 68 ♖a3 ♖c7 69 ♔g7 ♖d7 70 f5?!

Once again introducing unnecessary complications. 70 ♔f6 ♖c7 71 f5 (the ♖e3-e7 plan is less effective now, since Black can target the g3-pawn)

71...gxf5 72 ♔xf5 ♖c5+ 73 ♔f6 ♖c7 74 ♖f3 ♔xa5 75 ♖f5+ wins easily.

70...gxf5 71 ♔h6 f4 72 gxf4 ♖d5 73 ♔g7 ♖f5 74 ♖a4 ♔b5 75 ♖e4 ♔a6 76 ♔h6 ♖xa5

Black could have put up more resistance by 76...♔b7, but White can still win with 77 ♖e5 ♖xf4 78 ♔g5 ♖f1 79 ♖f5! ♖g1+ 80 ♔h5 ♔a6 81 ♔h6, and so on.

77 ♖e5 ♖a1 78 ♔xh5 ♖g1 79 ♖g5 ♖h1 80 ♖f5 ♔b6 81 ♖xf7 ♔c6 82 ♖e7 1-0

If you have an extra outside passed pawn and your rook is behind the pawn, then you should have very good winning chances. As with any proposed rule, there are exceptions (for example, a position with rook on a1 and pawn on a2 against rook on a3 would be far less favourable!), but in normal situations such positions are extremely favourable for White. The further away from the kingside the pawn is, the better for White, but even with a c-pawn his winning prospects would be good.

When the rook defends the pawn from the side (we will assume the rook is to the right of the pawn), Black will place his rook behind the pawn. Then much depends on the kingside pawn structure. The white rook is vulnerable to attack by Black's king, and the best situation arises when the rook can occupy an invulnerable square on the kingside where it is defended by a pawn.

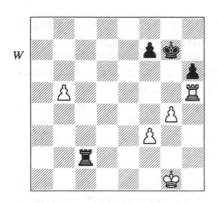

B. Spassky – Zhu Chen
Veterans vs Women,
Copenhagen 1997

Here White has an ideal position on the kingside. His rook can settle at f5, creating a cosy little cluster of pieces defending each other. Black can only break this up by playing ...h5 at a moment when both her rook is attacking the pawn on f3 and the white king is not defending it. However, it turns out that this possibility is of little value to Black.

White can win by simply playing his king to c1. If the black rook stays on the second rank, White pushes the b-pawn. Otherwise the king has to be released and it can then advance. The analysis runs 49 ♔f1 ♖c3 (49...♔g6 50 ♔e1 ♖b2 51 ♔d1 ♖f2 52 ♖f5 h5 53 ♔e1 wins a pawn) 50 ♔e2 ♖b3 51 ♖f5 ♔g6 52 ♔d2 h5 (the only moment when this is playable, but it is too slow) 53 ♔c2 ♖e3 (53...hxg4 54 ♔xb3 ♔xf5 55 fxg4+ wins) 54 ♖xh5 ♖xf3 55 b6 ♖e3 56 b7 ♖e8 57 ♖b5 ♖b8 58

♔d3 with an easy win as the king advances to support the b-pawn.

The course of the game is a warning against trying to be too clever in technical positions. If you see a systematic and safe winning procedure, don't worry about the fact that there may be a quicker win; just play it.

49 ♖h2??

The idea is that Black has to check, or else White switches his rook behind the pawn, but then White's rook can return to h5 and he has released his king from the back rank immediately.

49...♖c1+ 50 ♔g2 f5!

The point Spassky had overlooked. Black breaks up White's favourable pawn structure on the kingside and draws.

51 ♖h1

After 51 gxf5 ♖b1 52 ♖h5 ♔f7 53 ♖xh6 ♖xb5 54 f6 White has no winning chances as his rook is completely immobilized. 51 ♖h5 fxg4 52 fxg4 ♖b1 53 ♔f3 ♖b4 is no better because White's king cannot move to the queenside without immediately abandoning the g-pawn.

51...♖c2+ 52 ♔g3 ♖b2 ½-½

The final case, when the white rook is in front of the pawn, offers the fewest winning chances. Indeed, most positions are drawn. Even in the most favourable case (that of a b-pawn) it is unclear whether White can win unless he has an additional advantage, such as a weak enemy pawn structure on the kingside.

The situation with an extra pawn and all the pawns on the same side also occurs quite often in practice. Here is a typical position:

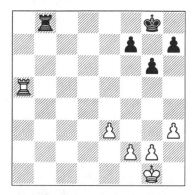

Black's ideal defensive pawn structure is f7-g6-h5. White's only chance is ultimately to create a passed pawn, and this pawn formation means that White can only make one at the cost of several pawn exchanges. First he must play g4, when Black can swap his h-pawn. Then White will aim for f5, but another pair of pawns disappears. It follows that once Black has achieved this optimal set-up, White's winning chances are minimal. Thus if Black is to play in the diagram, 1...h5! is the right move.

If White moves first, then of course he plays 1 g4!. While the resulting position is still theoretically drawn, there is no doubt that in practice Black's task is rather difficult. Black cannot prevent White from gaining a lot of space on the kingside (♔g2-g3, h4-h5, etc.) and his defence is not easy.

Endings with 3 vs 2 (and no passed pawns) on one side are also drawn; again the same principles apply. If you remove the pawns on e3 and f7 from the above diagram, Black's safest first move is again 1...h5!. White to play could try 1 g4, but here his winning chances would only be very small.

Positional advantage

We have already mentioned that piece activity is extremely important in rook and pawn endings (see page 92). A rook on the seventh usually ties the opponent's pieces down to defensive positions, while a king penetrating into the opposing pawn-mass can make mincemeat of them. Another point is that a passive rook is very often permanently passive. Here is an example, taken from Levenfish and Smyslov's classic book *Rook Endings*.

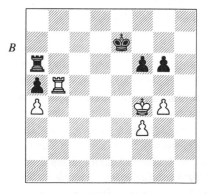

St Petersburg – London
Telegraph match, 1886-7

At this point London conceded the game. Chigorin gave analysis indicating that White could win and the position has been subject to considerable debate ever since. Levenfish and Smyslov gave the verdict that Black could draw, but only with very precise play.

The white rook can range freely across the fifth rank, while Black's is restricted to just three squares. First of all, defending passively is no good. White can move his king towards the vulnerable a-pawn and the defence eventually breaks down: 1...♖a7 2 ♔e4 ♖a6 3 ♔d4 ♖a7 4 f4 ♖a6 (or 4...♔d6 5 ♖b6+ ♔e7 6 ♔c5 ♖c7+ 7 ♔b5 ♖c1 8 g5 f5 9 ♖xg6 ♖f1 10 ♔xa5 ♖xf4 11 ♖f6 ♖f1 12 ♔b6 f4 13 a5 ♖g1 14 ♖xf4 ♖xg5 15 a6 ♖g6+ 16 ♔b7 ♖g1 17 ♖b4 and wins) 5 ♖b7+ ♔d6 6 f5 gxf5 7 gxf5 ♖a8 8 ♖b6+ ♔e7 9 ♔c5 ♖d8 10 ♖b5 and White wins the a-pawn while retaining both his pawns. With his pieces so actively placed, this means a sure win.

Very often in such situations, it is better to jettison the weak pawn and try to activate the rook, and here this plan just about draws for Black. Note that Black must not delay; if he allows White's pieces to become any more active before giving up the pawn, then the game will be past saving. The best line is 1...♖c6! 2 ♖xa5 ♖c4+ 3 ♔e3 ♔f7! (another difficult move to find; the king has the option to moving to h6 and g5 for a counter-attack against White's pawns, while being protected from rook checks by his own f- and

g-pawns) 4 ♖a8 (4 ♖a7+ ♔e6 5 a5 ♖a4 6 a6 ♔e5 7 f4+ ♔d5 8 ♖a8 ♖a3+ 9 ♔f2 ♔e4 is also a draw) 4...♔g7 5 a5 ♖a4 6 a6 ♔h6 7 f4 (trying to prevent the king's entry; 7 a7 ♔g5 is a clearcut draw) 7...g5 8 f5 (8 fxg5+ fxg5 9 ♔d3 ♔g7 is also drawn) 8...♔g7 and White cannot make progress. If White plays a7 at any stage, then there is no shelter for White's king on the queenside. However, if the pawn stays on a6 then Black can safely take the g4-pawn and return to a4.

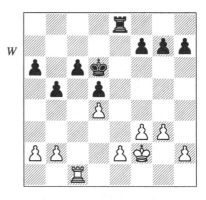

U. Andersson – R. Hübner
Johannesburg 1981

In this position White has a permanent positional advantage in the shape of Black's backward c-pawn. Nevertheless, it requires a high standard of endgame technique to convert this single positive factor into a win.

23 g4

It is moves like this that are the key to successful endgame play. It is not just a random pawn advance but part of a well-thought-out plan for putting White's central pawn majority to use. The obvious plan is to play e4 at some stage, but for this White needs the support of the king (note that the rook should stay on the c-file to prevent ...c5). White could try e3, ♔e2-d3 and then e4, but Black could counter this plan by playing ...f5 at some point. The move played not only makes it much harder for Black to play ...f5, but also opens up a second possibility for activating the white king, based on ♖c2 and ♔g3-f4.

23...a5 24 h4 g6 25 ♖c2 h6

After 25...f5 26 gxf5 gxf5 27 ♔g3, followed by ♔f4, White ties Black down to the defence of f5, and then plays e3 and ♖g2, when his rook can penetrate along the g-file.

26 ♔g3 g5

This is Black's counter-plan. He prevents White's king occupying f4.

27 h5

It would be wrong to exchange on g5 as Black's rook would be in a position to occupy the h-file.

27...f6 28 ♔f2

White now returns to the original plan of playing his king to d3, because the change in the kingside pawn structure has made ...f5 virtually impossible (if Black tries to prepare it with ...♖f8, then White plays e4 immediately).

28...♔c7 29 e3 ♔b6 30 ♔e2 ♖c8 31 ♖c5

Of course White prevents ...c5.

32...♖e8 32 ♔d3 ♖e7 33 e4 *(D)*

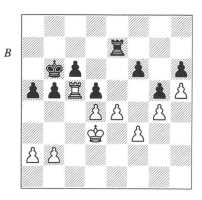

White finally achieves e3-e4, and gives Black a difficult choice. If he exchanges on e4, then White's rook gains access to f5 to attack the backward f-pawn, while otherwise Black has to defend the d5-pawn.

33...♖d7

After 33...dxe4+ 34 fxe4 ♖e6 35 ♖f5 ♔c7 36 e5 fxe5 37 dxe5 ♔d7 (37...c5 38 ♔e4 ♔c6 39 ♖f6 ♔d7 40 ♔d5 wins easily) White can pursue a policy of constriction, e.g. 38 ♔d4 ♔e7 39 b3 ♔e8 40 a3 ♔e7 41 b4 axb4 42 axb4 ♔e8 43 ♖f3 ♔e7 44 ♖a3 and White's rook penetrates.

34 a3 ♖d8 35 ♖c1

White's intention is to play b4 so as to provide further support for the rook, but for the moment he simply waits until the game is adjourned at move 40.

35...♖d7 36 ♖c2 ♖d8 37 ♖c3 ♖d7 38 ♖c2 ♖d8 39 ♖c1 ♖d7 40 ♖c5 ♖d8 41 b4

Now White undertakes positive action.

41...axb4 42 axb4

Black is in zugzwang.

42...♖d7

After 42...dxe4+ 43 fxe4, activating the rook by 43...♖a8 is too slow, as Black's kingside pawns are vulnerable and White would just play 44 ♖f5. Otherwise a rook move along the file is the only possibility.

43 exd5

Exploiting the absence of the rook from the first rank. Now 43...cxd5 loses to 44 ♖c8, for example 44...f5 45 gxf5 ♖f7 46 ♖h8 ♖f6 47 ♖h7! ♔c6 48 ♔e3 ♔d6 49 ♖b7 ♔c6 50 ♖a7 ♔b6 51 ♖g7, followed by ♖g6.

43...♖xd5 44 ♔e4

Making use of the extra support for the rook provided by b4.

44...♖d8 45 d5 (D)

White cannot penetrate to f5 as his d-pawn is hanging, but once it has been exchanged Black will be unable to defend his kingside pawns.

45...♖e8+

45...cxd5+ 46 ♖xd5 ♖e8+ 47 ♔f5 ♖e3 transposes to the game.

46 ♔f5 cxd5 47 ♖xd5 ♖e3

Black's only chance is to counterattack, but Andersson has everything worked out.

48 ♔xf6 ♖xf3+ 49 ♔g7!

This is the crucial finesse. Black draws after 49 ♔g6 ♖f4 50 ♔xh6 ♖xg4 51 ♔g7 ♖xb4 52 h6 ♖h4 53 h7 ♔a5.

49...♖f4 50 ♖d6+

The point behind White's last move. He takes the h6-pawn with his rook, and at the same time cuts the black king off along the third rank.

50...♔c7 51 ♖xh6 1-0

White wins after 51...♖xb4 52 ♖g6 ♖xg4 53 h6 ♖e4 (however Black plays, he has to give his rook up for the pawn within a few moves, for example after 53...♖h4 54 h7 White threatens ♖h6, so Black has to take the pawn immediately) 54 h7 ♖e7+ 55 ♔h6 ♖e1 56 h8♕ ♖h1+ 57 ♔g7 ♖xh8 58 ♔xh8 g4 (58...b4 59 ♔g7 b3 60 ♖xg5 ♔c6 61 ♖g3 wins) 59 ♔g7 g3 60 ♔f7 g2 (60...b4 61 ♖xg3 ♔c6 62 ♖g5) 61 ♖xg2 ♔b6 62 ♖g5 ♔a5 63 ♔e6 and the white king is easily in time.

Minor-piece endings

This is really four endings rolled up in one; knight endings, bishop vs knight endings and bishop endings, with either same- or opposite-coloured bishops. A detailed coverage of each of these endings is not possible here, so I will concentrate on the most useful information.

Knight endings

Here is a common situation – the knight is single-handedly holding back a passed pawn. There are three possible outcomes to such a struggle: either the knight loses the battle against the white king and pawn, and the pawn promotes. Then White wins. Alternatively, the white king cannot achieve more than a perpetual attack on the knight; then the result is a draw. Finally, it may be that the knight can not only restrain the pawn, but can do so while providing a continuous supply of spare tempi. Then Black has time to advance his h-pawn and win.

The diagram position is a draw. The knight can prevent the pawn's promotion but without providing any spare tempi: 1 ♔b7 ♘b5 2 ♔b6 ♘d6! 3 ♔c6 ♘c8 4 ♔c7 ♘a7 and so on.

If the pawn is on a7 and the knight on a8, then of course White wins by 1 ♔b7.

Moving the other way, with the pawn on a5 and knight on a6, the position is a draw since 1 ♔b6 again gives a perpetual attack on the knight. If the pawn is on a4 and knight on a5 then White loses even if he can attack the knight with 1 ♔b5 on the first move; Black just plays 1...♔g5 and when he promotes on h1, White is prevented from promoting on a8.

Now suppose that the pawn is on b7 and knight on b8, with Black to play. The position is drawn by repetition: neither side can deviate from the sequence 1...♘a6+ 2 ♔b6 ♘b8 3 ♔c7 (3 ♔a7? ♘d7 would win for Black) 3...♘a6+.

Now move the pawn to b6 and the knight to b7. Black to plays wins by 1...♘a5, because the white king takes far too long to make it round to attack the knight (note that even 1 ♔d6 is impossible because of 1...♘c4+). However, White's loss here was due to the poor initial position of his king on c7. If the king starts on c6, then the position is a draw since 1...♘a5+ 2 ♔b5 and 1...♘d8+ 2 ♔d7 both lead to repetitions.

With the pawn on b5 and knight on b6, it doesn't matter where the white king is; Black always wins since he can generate an unlimited supply of tempi. If White attacks the knight by 1 ♔c6, then 1...♘a4 wins as before, while 1 ♔c5 is met by 1...♘c8, and 2 ♔c6 fails to 2...♘a7+.

With a c-pawn, Black wins even with the pawn on the seventh rank. If Black's knight is on c8, he can meet ♔d7 by ...♘a7 and ♔b7 by ...♘e7, and the white king has to take the long way round to attack the knight again.

Moving on to knight vs knight endings, the most important point to note is the devastating effect of an outside passed pawn. The knight is such a short-range piece that if it is preventing the advance of a passed pawn on the queenside, then it cannot exert any influence on the kingside. Thus the side with the outside passed pawn will be effectively a piece up on the other side of the board. Knights are particularly ineffective against rook's pawns:

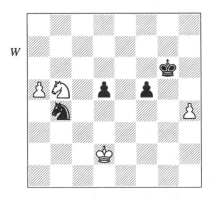

W

S. Dolmatov – A. Beliavsky
USSR Championship, Odessa 1989

Here Black is fighting against two rook's pawns. Despite material equality and the small number of pawns, White has a winning position.
57 ♘d4 ♘a6
White is normally happy to swap his h-pawn for Black's f-pawn, since his king will then be faster to reach the

queenside. Thus after 57...♔h5 58 ♔c3 ♘a6 59 ♘xf5 ♔g4 60 ♘e3+ ♔xh4 White wins by 61 ♘xd5 ♔g5 62 ♔c4 ♔f5 63 ♔b5 ♘b8 64 ♘b4 ♔e6 65 ♘c6 ♘d7 66 a6. The line 57...f4 58 ♔e2 ♔h5 59 ♔f3 ♔xh4 60 ♔xf4 is similar, for example 60...♔h5 61 ♔e5 ♔g6 62 ♔d6 ♔f7 63 ♔c5 ♘a6+ 64 ♔b6 ♘b8 (or 64...♘b4 65 ♔b5) 65 ♔b7 ♘d7 66 ♘b3.
58 ♔e3 ♘c5 59 ♔f4 ♘d3+ 60 ♔e3 ♘b4
If Black repeats by 60...♘c5, then White continues 61 ♘f3 ♔f6 (61...♔h5 62 ♔f4 ♔g6 63 ♔e5) 62 h5 ♔g7 63 ♘d4 ♔h6 (63...♔f6 64 h6 ♔g6 65 ♘xf5) 64 ♔f4 ♔xh5 65 ♔xf5 winning as in the previous note.
61 ♔f4 ♘d3+ 62 ♔f3 ♘b4 63 ♘e2 ♔f6 64 ♘f4 d4 65 ♔e2 ♔f7
Not 65...♔e5 66 ♘d3+.
66 ♔d1 ♔f6 67 ♔d2 *(D)*

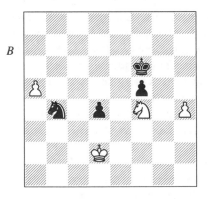

B

Black is in zugzwang and must go back with his king.
67...♔f7 68 ♘e2
Now the d-pawn is lost.

68...♚g6 69 ♘xd4 f4 70 ♚e2 ♚h5
71 ♚f3 ♚xh4 72 ♚xf4

This ♘+♙ vs ♘ ending is a simple win.

72...♚h5 73 ♚e5 ♚g6 74 ♚d6 ♚f7
75 ♚c5 ♘a6+ 76 ♚b6 ♘b4 77 ♘c6
♘d5+ 78 ♚b7 ♚e6 79 a6 ♚d7 80 a7
♘c7 81 ♘e5+ ♚d8 82 ♘c4 ♘a8 83
♘b6

White avoids the trap 83 ♚xa8?? ♚c8 drawing.

83...♘c7 84 ♚c6 1-0

Bishop vs Knight endings

The relative value of the bishop and the knight is a familiar topic in every phase of the game, and the basic principles are the same in an ending.

On average, a bishop is worth a little more than a knight. A bishop is at its best in an open position with a fluid pawn structure. Pawns fixed on the same colour as the squares on which the bishop moves are an obstruction; the more such pawns exist, the more restricted the bishop is and the weaker the squares of the opposite colour.

Knights favour blocked pawn structures and like stable, invulnerable squares on which they can settle without being disturbed by enemy pawns. A typical such situation arises when a knight occupies the square in front of an isolated pawn, as in the following diagram.

We will not discuss this very complicated endgame in detail here. Capablanca, who was one of the greatest

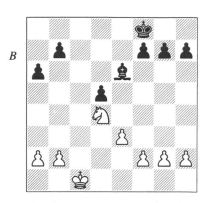

S. Flohr – J. Capablanca
Moscow 1935

endgame players of all time, just about managed to save the game, but I would doubt my ability to do likewise! He adopted what is undoubtedly the correct plan, namely to avoid allowing any more pawns to be fixed on light squares. He therefore played ...b6, ...a5, ...♗d7 and ...f6, and waited to see if White could make progress.

It is worth noting that if Black had a dark-squared bishop, then the position would be a comfortable draw. If, on the other hand, Black had a further pawn weakness, for example the pawn on b7 were on b5 (so that White could fix the queenside pawns by playing b4), then he would be lost.

It is worth adding one point which applies particularly to the endgame. Bishops prefer positions with unbalanced pawn structures. If both sides create a passed pawn, a bishop can support the friendly passed pawn while at the same time holding up the enemy passed pawn. Knights, being short-range pieces, have to be committed to one or the other task.

Players often underestimate the advantage which is conferred by having a bishop against a knight, even in positions with symmetrical pawn structures.

Z. Ilinčić – G. Čabrilo
Cetinje 1992

I suspect that many players would abandon the position as a draw, but in the game White won. Ilinčić annotated his game in both *Informator* and the *Encyclopaedia of Chess Endings*, claiming that the diagram position is actually winning for White. As we shall see, this claim is rather far-fetched, but it is true that White's advantage is sufficient to justify playing on.

26...♔g8 27 ♔d2 ♔f7 28 ♔e3 ♔e6 29 ♗c3 g6 30 ♔e4

White has two very slight advantages: his bishop is better than the knight in this open position, and his king is slightly more active.

30...h5

There is nothing wrong with this move. It allows a possible penetration by the white king via f4 to g5, but in itself this is not dangerous as the simple reply ...♔f7 secures the kingside pawn structure.

31 ♗e1 ♘e5 32 ♗f2 (D)

White aims to provoke a pawn move on the queenside, so as to provide a possible entry route for White's king on that side also.

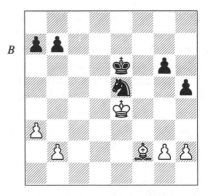

32...♘c4?

This leads to an exchange of pawns, which helps the defender, but allows the white king to occupy the fifth rank, which is a far more important factor. Ilinčić gives 32...a6 33 ♔d4 ♘d7 34 ♗g3 but stops here with the claim that White is winning. However, Black can just move his knight, meeting 35 ♔c5 by 35...♘d7+, and further progress is not easy.

33 ♗xa7 ♘xb2 34 ♔d4 ♔d6

Certainly not 34...♗f5? 35 ♔c3, winning after 35...♘d1+ 36 ♔c2 or 35...♘a4+ 36 ♔b3 b5 37 ♔b4.

35 ♗b8+ ♔e6

One of the problems facing the side with the knight is that a 'race' situation normally strongly favours the bishop. Here 35...♔c6 36 ♔e5 ♘c4+ 37 ♔f6 ♘xa3 38 ♔xg6 ♘c4 39 ♔xh5 b5 40 ♗f4 b4 41 ♔g6 b3 42 ♗c1 b2 43 ♗xb2 ♘xb2 44 h4 wins for White.

36 ♔c5 ♔d7

Black also cannot afford to let the white king get at the b-pawn, e.g. 36...♔f5 37 ♔b5! ♔e4 38 a4 ♔e3 39 a5 ♔f2 40 ♗e5 ♘d3 41 ♗d4+ ♔xg2 42 ♔b6 and wins.

37 ♔d5

By now Black is in serious trouble. White's main plan is to cover e7 with his bishop and then play ♔e5-f6.

37...♘d3 38 ♗g3 ♘b2 39 ♗e1 ♘d3 40 ♗d2 ♘b2 41 h3 (D)

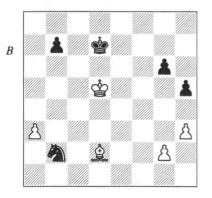

B

41...♘d3

After 41...♔e7 42 ♗g5+ ♔d7 White wins by 43 ♔e5 ♘c4+ 44 ♔f6 ♘xa3

45 ♔xg6 ♔e6 (45...b5 46 ♔xh5 wins as in the note to Black's 35th move) 46 ♔xh5 ♔f7 47 ♔h6! ♔g8 (or 47...b5 48 ♔h7 b4 49 g4 b3 50 ♗c1 ♘c4 51 g5 ♘e5 52 h4 ♘g6 53 h5 ♘f8+ 54 ♔h6) 48 ♔g6 b5 49 h4 ♘c4 50 ♗f6 b4 51 h5 b3 52 h6.

42 a4 b6?

This loses straight away, although the position was in any case very difficult for Black. After 42...♘b2 43 a5 ♘d3 44 ♗e3 ♘e1 45 g3 ♘d3, White continues 46 ♔d4! ♘b4 (46...♘c1 47 ♔e5 ♔e7 48 ♗g5+ ♔f7 49 ♔d6) 47 ♔e5 and Black cannot play 47...♔e7.

43 ♗e3 ♘b2

43...♔c7 44 ♔e6 is also an easy win.

44 ♗xb6 ♘xa4 45 ♗d4

The knight is trapped and can only be rescued at the cost of both Black's kingside pawns.

45...h4 46 ♔e5 ♔e7 47 ♔f4 ♔e6 48 ♔g5 ♔d5 49 ♗f2 ♘b2 50 ♗xh4 ♘d1 51 ♔xg6 ♘e3 52 g4 ♔e4 53 ♗g5 ♘c4 54 ♗f6 ♘e3 55 ♔g5 ♔f3 56 ♗d4 1-0

Bishop endings

Considering the case of same-coloured bishops first, the outside passed pawn is again a very powerful force, even if not quite so effective as in knight endings. I would therefore normally expect endings with 3 vs 3 on one side and an extra outside passed pawn on the other side to be winning, although if the passed pawn is not too far away from the remaining pawns there is a small chance of a blockade.

With all the pawns on the same side, a 3 vs 2 or 4 vs 3 ending with fluid pawns should normally be a draw. Since bishops are heavily influenced by fixed pawns, one of the most important questions is how many pawns are fixed on the same-coloured squares as one's bishop. The more there are, the worse it is, all the more so in that the opponent's bishop will automatically be a 'good' bishop. Two pawns fixed on the same colour as one's bishop may be a fatal weakness, especially if they can both be attacked simultaneously by the opposing bishop. This completely immobilizes one's own bishop, and zugzwang may not be far away.

Opposite-coloured bishop endings are often quite tricky because many of the principles that apply in a wide range of endings break down in this case. Here are some of the main differences:

1) Material advantage is less important than usual. Endings with one extra pawn are usually drawn. Even two extra pawns may not be sufficient to win. For this reason reduction to an opposite-coloured bishop ending is often a useful drawing resource in a desperate situation.

2) What is important is the ability to create passed pawns. If you can create two passed pawns, then you have good winning chances. Connected

passed pawns are better than passed pawns with only one file between them, but two widely-separated passed pawns are best of all.

3) If you are trying to draw an opposite-coloured bishop ending, then it is better to have your pawns on the same-coloured squares as your bishop. *This is practically the only type of position in which this reversal of the normal principle applies.* The reason is that your drawing chances depend on setting up an unbreakable fortress. Everything has to be defended, and a pawn which is capable of being attacked by the enemy bishop will just drop off.

Here are a couple of examples illustrating these principles:

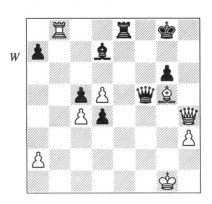

Y. Piskov – J. Nunn
Bundesliga 1992

Black is in a difficult position because his king is more exposed. While there are still heavy pieces on the board, the opposite-coloured bishops pose a particular danger for Black.

37 ♗f6

Threatening mate in two. 37...♖xb8 is no defence because of 38 ♕h8+ ♔f7 39 ♕g7+ ♔e8 40 ♕e7#.

37...♕h5!

This is the safest move. Even though Black loses two pawns, the resulting opposite-coloured bishop ending is a clear draw. It is possible that Black might have got away with 37...♔f7 38 ♖h7 ♕xf6 39 ♖xd7+ ♗e7, but the advantage of opposite-coloured bishop positions is that if they are drawn, then they are usually completely drawn.

38 ♕xh5 gxh5 39 ♖xe8+ ♗xe8 40 ♗e7 ♗g6 41 ♗xc5 ♔f7!

Not 41...♗d3? 42 d6 ♗f5 43 ♗xa7 and White obtains three passed pawns.

42 ♗xd4

After 42 ♗xa7 ♗b1 43 a4 d3 44 ♔f2 ♗a2 Black wins one of the white pawns, again with an easy draw.

42...a6

Threatening to win a pawn by means of ...♗d3 followed by ...♗c4.

43 a3

White has two extra connected passed pawns, and if he could support them with his king then he would be winning. However, his king is too far away and by attacking the pawns with his bishop, Black can force them to advance to dark squares, when it is easy to blockade them. The defender must keep his pawns on the same-coloured squares as his bishop, but the opposite holds true for the attacker. He must try

to avoid the blockade of the pawns, and so they should occupy squares of the opposite colour to his bishop. This usually means that they must be defended by the king.

43...♗d3 44 c5 ♗c4 45 d6 ♔e6 46 ♔f2 ♔d7

The blockade is set up. The a- and h-pawns can be defended by the bishop, and the passed pawns are totally immobile.

47 ♔g3 ♗e6 48 h4 ♔c6 ½-½

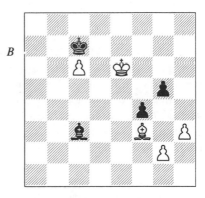

B

This is a slight modification of a game I played in a simultaneous display during 1977.

Black defended the g-pawn in the only way possible, by heading for h4.

1...♗e1

At first sight this is a dead draw. If White's king attacks the g5-pawn, then Black plays ...♗h4 and waits with his king, while if White's king approaches the c-pawn, then Black's bishop is freed and so he can just keep his king on c7. This is in accordance with the principle that you need two passed pawns to have a chance of winning an opposite-coloured bishop ending.

2 ♔f6!

White's plan is to force the bishop to h4 and then play g3. If Black replies ...♗xg3, White continues ♔xg5 and has his second passed pawn. If Black replies ...fxg3, White plays ♗g2 and the black bishop is imprisoned. When the white king approaches the c-pawn, Black will be forced to release his bishop by ...g4, again giving White another passed pawn.

However, this plan must be implemented accurately. After 2 ♔f5 ♗h4 3 g3 fxg3 4 ♗g2 ♔d6 White experiences certain difficulties. He cannot move his king to f6 or e4 and after 5 ♔g4 ♔c7 he is not making progress. In fact, this is very much like a king and pawn ending, since both sides can only move their kings (if White moves his bishop, then ...g2 draws at once). White can try to exploit the fact that d7 is not available for Black's king by 5 ♔g6 ♔e6 6 ♔h7, but his subtlety is to no avail: after 6...♔e7 7 ♔g7 ♔e8 White cannot 'by-pass' by 8 ♔f6.

The key is to lose a tempo *before* the bishop arrives on h4.

2...♗h4 3 ♔f5 ♔d6

White has lost a tempo and now the g3 plan works.

4 g3 (D)

4...fxg3

After 4...♗xg3 5 ♔xg5, the win is still not straightforward as Black has a possible drawing plan of covering c7

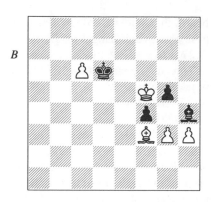

with his bishop and running to h8 with his king. Then it will not matter if Black has to surrender his bishop for the c-pawn, as he has a 'rook's pawn and wrong bishop' draw. However, White can win by 5...♗e1 6 h4 ♔e7 7 h5 and now:

1) 7...♗c3 (using the bishop to hold back the h-pawn, but the passed pawns are too far apart for this to work) 8 h6 ♔d6 9 h7 ♗e5 10 ♔f5 ♗h8 11 ♔xf4 ♗b2 12 ♔f5 ♗c3 13 ♔g6 ♔e7 14 ♗d1 ♗b2 15 ♗a4 (threatening 16 c7) 15...♔d6 16 ♔f7 winning the bishop for the h-pawn.

2) 7...♗a5 8 ♔g6 ♔f8 9 ♗d5 (of course White must prevent ...♔g8 at all costs) 9...f3 10 h6 f2 11 h7 f1♕ 12 h8♕+ ♔e7 13 ♕e5+ ♔f8 14 ♕d6+ ♔e8 15 ♕d7+ ♔f8 16 ♕g7+ ♔e8 17 ♗f7+ ♔d8 18 c7+! ♗xc7 19 ♕f8+ ♔d7 20 ♗e8+ winning the queen.

5 ♗g2

Black is in zugzwang and must go back with his king.

5...♔c7

Or 5...♔e7 6 ♔e5.

6 ♔e5 g4

Otherwise the king reaches d6 and that would really be Black's last chance to play ...g4 before White promotes his pawn.

7 hxg4

White wins easily by supporting the passed g-pawn with his king.

It is worth noting that Black only loses in the diagram as he cannot defend the g5-pawn from d8 or e7. If his king were on the apparently inferior square b8, then 1...♗a5 would draw.

I must emphasize that the special principles mentioned above apply only to pure opposite-coloured bishop situations. As soon as extra pieces are added to the equation, normal service is resumed. Many players assume that endings with rooks and opposite-coloured bishops are almost as drawn as pure opposite-bishop positions, but this is not so. An extra pawn in an ending with rooks and opposite-coloured bishops normally confers good winning chances; adding a pair of knights is similar. If even more pieces are added then the attacking potential of opposite-coloured bishops starts to come into play, and then one cannot talk about a drawish influence at all.

Queen endings

Queen and Pawn vs Queen

Of all the fundamental endings with piece + pawn vs piece, this is the second most common in practice (the most common being rook and pawn vs rook). It is also by far the most complicated, so much so that it has proved too daunting for the majority of authors and very little has been written about it. Before the advent of the computer database, Averbakh provided the best coverage. However, the complexity of the ending was only emphasized by the fact that his seventy pages of analysis dealt almost exclusively with certain simple cases of the pawn on the seventh rank.

Now that the oracle of a perfect database has been constructed, one would have expected someone to provide a far more detailed explanation of the principles behind the ending. However, the database has revealed that Averbakh's efforts only scratched the veneer of this ending and most of the real work remains to be done.

I suppose I could stop here with the comment 'nobody understands ♕+♙ vs ♕', but this does seem a little cowardly.

The first point to make is that if the defending king is in front of the pawn then the position is almost always drawn. There are exceptions in which a winning exchange of queens can be forced, but they are very few indeed.

Thus the only interesting case is when the defending king cannot move in front of the pawn. Dealing firstly with the a-pawn, this not surprisingly offers the fewest winning chances of any pawn. The diagram below shows a typical situation with the pawn on the sixth.

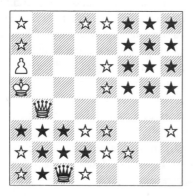

We will display several diagrams of this type, the aim being to convey a great deal of information in a visual form. The various stars indicate the result when the black king stands on that square. A white star indicates that the position is a win with White to move, but a draw with Black to move. A black star indicates that it is a win whoever moves first. Unmarked squares are drawn whoever moves first.

In the case of squares that are under attack by White, then the position is only legal with Black to move and a black star indicates that it is a win; no star indicates that it is drawn.

A few positions are illegal because the kings stand next to each other; these are also unmarked.

Readers should note that we take no account of the 50-move rule in our discussion. With optimal play, some of the positions are drawn only because of this rule, but who is going to play optimally over the board? Our objective is only to establish some general principles helpful in practical play and for this the 50-move rule is not especially relevant.

This diagram already reveals many of the important principles governing ♕+♙ vs ♕. We can ignore the 'special case' squares a7 and a8, which are only marked because White to play can mate in one. There are basically two drawing zones. One lies near to the pawn and these squares are drawn because with the enemy king so close to the pawn, Black can very often exchange queens and catch the pawn with his king. Virtually all ♕+♙ vs ♕ positions (except those with the pawn on the seventh) have such a zone, which we call the *proximity zone*. When the black king lies in the proximity zone, White is restricted in his attempts to avoid perpetual check, as he can only interpose his queen in favourable circumstances. There is a popular myth that when defending ♕+ ♙ vs ♕, it is always best to have your king as far away from the pawn as possible; as we shall see, this is true only in certain circumstances.

The second drawing zone is in the lower right-hand corner, i.e. diagonally opposite the pawn. White's main weapon in preventing perpetual check is to interpose his queen in such a way as to force the exchange of queens, either by checking or by pinning the enemy queen. When the black king is poorly placed, for example on f7, then there are many chances to achieve this and Black's options are consequently restricted. White can set up a position with his king on b7 and queen on c6. Then 1...♕e7+ is answered by 2 ♕c7, 1...♕b4+ 2 ♔c8 ♕f8+ 3 ♔c7 ends the checks, 1...♕b3+ 2 ♔c8 and 1...♕b1+ 2 ♔a8 likewise. The toughest check to meet is 1...♕b2+, but even in this case White can manoeuvre so as eventually to force Black to give one of the inferior checks mentioned above. In the end Black's checks dry up, and White can push his pawn. This problem afflicts Black whenever his king is in the top right-hand corner. The lower left-hand corner is also not ideal, but this largely depends on Black's queen position. If Black can occupy a good square with his queen, then this is sufficient to draw. The bottom right-hand corner is the best of the distant areas; White has very few chances to interpose with check and so Black has few problems drawing.

While much of the play is governed by general principles, there are a few anomalies. The isolated loss with the black king on h3 (when 1 ♕d4! is the only winning move) is hard to explain, as is the loss with Black to move when his king is on c2.

The point about the two drawing zones is emphasized if we imagine the black king starting somewhere on Black's fifth rank. With the king on d4, the only drawing move is 1...♔d5!, entering the proximity zone. When the king is on h4, the only move is

1...♔g3! (although it would be amazing if anyone realized over the board that 1...♔h3? is losing). If the king starts on e4, there is a choice between 1...♔d5 and 1...♔f3, but I would always go for the proximity zone if possible, as the draw is far simpler.

Summing up, the proximity zone is the best location for the black king, then the bottom-right corner, then the bottom-left corner. The top right corner is by far the worst.

If we move the pawn back to a5, the drawing zones expand enormously:

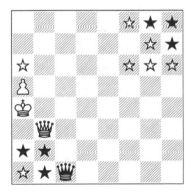

The lower-left squares are marked only because White has the possibility of ♕a3+, forcing an immediate exchange of queens, so we can fairly say that Black is only in danger if his king is in the upper-right corner.

We can summarize by saying that with an a-pawn, the pawn needs to be on at least the sixth rank in order to have decent winning chances.

Not surprisingly, the b-pawn offers far more winning chances. There are two main reasons. First of all, the white king has the squares on the a-file to aid him in his efforts to avoid perpetual check. Secondly, an exchange of queens is much less likely to lead to a draw, even when Black's king is quite close to the pawn, so the proximity zone is much reduced in size. Here is a typical case with the pawn on b6 *(D)*:

We can see how vastly different this situation is. If White is to move then he wins no matter where Black's king is located. With Black to play there is a small drawing zone in front of the pawn, and a slightly larger one in the bottom right-hand corner.

With the pawn on b5 White's winning chances are of course less than with the pawn on b6, but still greater than with the pawn on a6 *(D)*:

Here we see the familiar pattern emerging, but with some differences. The proximity zone is much smaller than with the a-pawn; it includes all the squares in front of the pawn, but little else. Black can draw with his

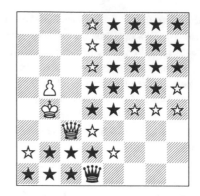

king on certain d-file squares, but only if it is his turn to move, and even then the draw requires great accuracy. With the king on d8, Black's unique drawing move is 1...♕g1!, with the king on d7 again there is only one move, 1...♕h1!, and with the king on d6, 1...♕d5! is the only saving possibility.

The drawing zone in the bottom-right corner is relatively large, and it is clear that against a b-pawn, if you cannot bring your king in front of the pawn, then this is the area to head for. We do not give the details in the case of the pawn on b4; the situation is somewhat similar to that of the pawn on a5, i.e. White can only win if the black king is near to the top-right corner.

To summarize, with a b-pawn the pawn should be on at least the fifth rank to provide good winning chances.

The c-pawn provides the greatest winning chances of any pawn. One reason is that the drawing zone in the bottom-right corner disappears when the pawn is on at least the fourth rank, so in this case Black is left only with the proximity zone.

The situation with the pawn on c6 needs no diagram, because Black is losing except if his king is in front of the pawn. When the pawn is on c5, the drawing chances are still very slim, except if the king is in front of the pawn:

Even with a pawn on c4, White's winning prospects are surprisingly good:

It follows that if you have various methods of liquidating to ♕+♙ vs ♕, the c-pawn is the one to go for. The defender's only chance is to bring his king near to the pawn, but even with the pawn as far back as the fourth rank there are still good winning chances.

Central pawns offer significantly fewer chances than with the c-pawn. Once again, there is no distant drawing zone and the defender should have his king somewhere near the enemy pawn. Here are two typical diagrams:

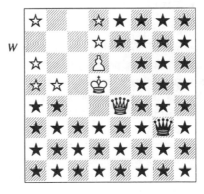

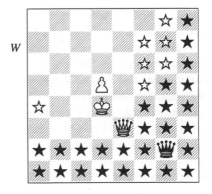

In the second diagram the drawing zone has expanded considerably and encompasses quite a large part of the board. The square a4 is rather anomalous (White to play wins only with 1 ♔c5!).

Just as with the c-pawn, the defending king should be as near to the pawn as possible. It is worth noting that it is much better for the defender to have his king on the short side of the pawn than the long side.

The extra Pawn

Just as in the case of rook endings, queen endings with an extra outside passed pawn are relatively common. It is hard to say whether the winning chances are greater or less than in the case of rooks. Objectively speaking, I suspect that they should be greater, but there are far more chances for things to go wrong with queens on the board! The main danger is that of perpetual check, so king safety is an important factor.

Unlike the corresponding situation with a rook, a queen is capable of shepherding a pawn to the promotion square all on its own. Suppose, for example, White has a passed pawn on b4 supported by a queen on b1, and that Black has blockaded the pawn with his queen on b5. If the queens were replaced by rooks, then the pawn could not advance without either zugzwang or the approach of White's king. With queens, however, White can continue

♕b3-c3-c5 and drive the enemy queen away. The pawn can then be advanced and, if necessary, the manoeuvre can be repeated all the way down the board.

This would be the winning technique in the case that the kings are on the kingside and White's king is safe from perpetual check. Note that we are assuming that Black cannot exchange queens. This is normally a safe assumption, but there might be cases in which Black could swap on c5, take the c-pawn with his king and return to the kingside in time to save the game. In that case White might do better to play ♕b3-a3-a5 in order to advance the pawn. The problem with this is that it badly decentralizes the white queen, and while the queen is away, Black's own queen can take up an active post, increasing his chances of perpetual check.

If the white king is not safe from perpetual check, then the win is much more complicated, if indeed it is possible at all. The plan is again to try to push the pawn using the above manoeuvre, and when the black queen starts checking, the white king will run to the queenside, where his pawn and queen stand ready to provide shelter. It is important to bear in mind that a barrage of random checks from the enemy queen very rarely amounts to a perpetual, provided that one's own queen occupies a central position and there is at least one pawn for shelter. Therefore White should have no hesitation about running with his king to the queenside. Here is an example:

G. Kieninger – E. Eliskases
German Championship,
Bad Oeynhausen 1938

It is Black to move and he first of all brings his queen nearer the centre with gain of time.

49...♕c2+ 50 ♔g1 ♕d1+ 51 ♔g2 ♕e2+ 52 ♔g1 ♕e3+ 53 ♔g2 ♕e2+ 54 ♔g1 c4

Black has achieved all he can with checks and now takes the opportunity to push his passed pawn. This allows White to start his own barrage of checks, but Black's king can eventually evade the checks by moving to the queenside. One unusual feature of the position is that Black is prepared to leave his h6-pawn undefended. Normally, every pawn has to be protected to avoid being gobbled up by the enemy queen, but in this special case the possibility of ...♕e3+ provides an indirect defence.

55 ♕g8+ ♔f3 56 ♕g3+

Black wins after 56 ♕f8+ ♔e4 57 ♕xh6 ♕e3+ 58 ♕xe3+ ♔xe3.

56...♔e4 57 ♕g6+ ♔d4 58 ♕d6+

Once again the h6-pawn is invulnerable.

58...♔c3

With a slightly different version of the same idea: 59 ♕xh6 ♕d1+ 60 ♔g2 ♕d2+.

59 ♕a3+ ♔d2 60 ♕a2+

Or 60 ♕b2+ and the checks run out after 60...♔d3 61 ♕b1+ ♔d4 62 ♕b6+ ♔c3 63 ♕a5+ (or 63 ♕f6+ ♔c2 64 ♕f5+ ♔d2 65 ♕d5+ transposing) 63...♔d3 64 ♕f5+ (64 ♕d5+ ♔c2 65 ♕f5+ ♔d2) 64...♔d2 65 ♕d5+ ♔c1, for example 66 ♕c5 ♕e1+ 67 ♔g2 c3 and the pawn edges forwards.

60...♔d3 61 ♕a6

Realizing that there is no perpetual check, White decides to halt the pawn's advance by pinning the pawn: this is also a typical motif in queen and pawn endings.

61...h5

As a matter of fact, this position would be a win even without the h-pawns, but their presence certainly makes Black's task simpler. White has no threat, so Black simply creeps forward with his h-pawn. When it arrives on h3, White will have mating threats to contend with in addition to the passed c-pawn.

62 ♕b5 ♔c2! *(D)*

The immediate 62...h4 would be a mistake because of 63 ♕b1+ ♔d4 64 ♕b6+ ♔c3 65 ♕f6+ ♔d2 66 ♕d4+

and the h4-pawn is vulnerable. It is true that Black's position is so strong that he might win even after losing his h-pawn, but understandably he does not wish to test this theory.

63 ♕a4+

White must start checking, as Black threatened to check on g4 and then play ...c3.

63...♔d2 64 ♕a2+ ♔d3 65 ♕a6?

This makes life easy for Black as his h-pawn is able to advance another square. 65 ♕b1+ would have offered more resistance, but Black would escape from the checks in the end: 65...♔c3 66 ♕a1+ ♔b4 67 ♕b1+ ♔c5 68 ♕f5+ ♔d4 69 ♕d7+ (69 ♕f6+ ♕e5 70 ♕b6+ ♔c3 and 69 ♕f4+ ♔d3 70 ♕f5+ ♕e4 71 ♕f1+ ♔d2 72 ♕f2+ ♔d1 also win for Black) 69...♔c3 70 ♕g7+ ♔c2 71 ♕g6+ ♔d2 72 ♕d6+ ♕d3.

65...h4 66 ♕b5

After 66 ♕d6+ Black wins as in the previous note: 66...♔c2 67 ♕g6+ ♔d2 68 ♕d6+ ♕d3.

66...♕e3+

Black decides to improve his queen position before advancing the c-pawn further. If Black plays ...h3, he must start to take care about possible stalemates.

67 ♔f1 ♕f3+ 68 ♔g1 ♕g4+ 69 ♔f2

Or 69 ♔f1 ♔e3 70 ♕c5+ ♔d4 71 ♕e7+ ♕e4 72 ♕c5+ ♔f4 73 ♕d6+ (73 ♕c7+ ♔g4 74 ♕g7+ ♔h3) 73...♔g4 and the checks run out.

69...♕d4+ 70 ♔f1 ♔d2 (D)

70...♔e3 71 ♕e8+ ♕e4 would have been a little quicker.

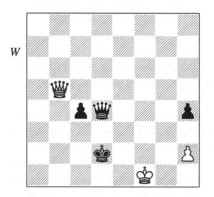

71 ♕b4+ ♕c3 72 ♕b5 ♕d3+ 73 ♔f2 ♕e3+ 74 ♔f1 ♕f3+ 75 ♔g1 c3

Although the process is rather slow, the pawn gradually advances. White can give several checks between each pawn move, but there is no perpetual.

76 ♕a5

The alternative pin 76 ♕b4 loses after 76...♕e3+ 77 ♔f1 ♕e2+ 78 ♔g1 h3 79 ♕d4+ (79 ♕d6+ ♕d3) 79...♔c2 80 ♕a4+ ♔b1 81 ♕b4+ (81 ♕b3+

♕b2) 81...♕b2 82 ♕e4+ ♔a1 83 ♕a4+ ♕a2.

76...♕e3+ 77 ♔f1 ♕e2+ 78 ♔g1 h3 79 ♕d5+ ♔c1 80 ♕g5+ ♔b2 0-1

Where the pawns are on one side of the board, the winning chances with an extra pawn are probably greater than with rooks. An ending with 4 vs 3 offers fair winning chances, and even 3 vs 2 is sometimes won in practice, although I have no doubt that theoretically it should be a draw.

Common endings without Pawns

Rook vs minor piece

The ending rook vs bishop (without pawns) arises occasionally. There are three important things to know about this ending. First of all, in a general initial position this ending is totally drawn. Secondly, if the defender's king is trapped in the corner then he can draw if his bishop moves on squares of opposite colour to the corner square; otherwise it is lost. The reason is quite simple (D).

Here White can try 1 ♖a8+, but after 1...♗g8 he must lift the stalemate. This involves either letting the black king out of the corner, or unpinning the bishop. The only other reasonable winning attempt is 1 ♖h7+ ♔g8 2 ♖b7, attacking the bishop and threatening mate on b8, but Black has the saving move 2...♗c2+. However, it is

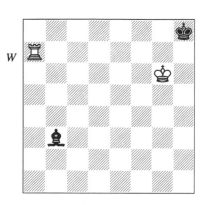

W

worth noting that after 1 ♖a8+ ♗g8 2 ♖a7, for example, 2...♗e6? would allow 3 ♖h7+ ♔g8 4 ♖e7 and White wins (checking distance again).

If we move the bishop from b3 to b4, then White wins even if Black moves first, for example 1...♔g8 2 ♖a8+ ♗f8 3 ♖b8 and mate next move.

The third important point is the following position.

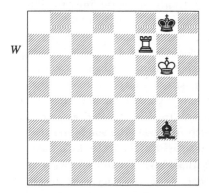

W

In this case Black's king is near the 'wrong' corner and in fact the position is lost whoever moves first. The important point is that the result is the same no matter where Black's bishop is positioned, so long as it is on a dark square.

The winning method runs **1 ♖f1 ♗h2** (1...♗h4 2 ♖f3 ♗d8 3 ♖f4 forces the bishop to a bad square, winning after 3...♗e7 4 ♖a4 or 3...♗b6 4 ♖b4 ♗c7 5 ♖c4) **2 ♖f2 ♗g3** (Black tries to keep the bishop sheltered behind the white king for as long as possible; 2...♗g1 3 ♖g2 also drives the bishop out) **3 ♖g2 ♗d6** (3...♗h4 and 3...♗f4 are impossible because White wins the bishop with a discovered check) **4 ♖d2 ♗e7 5 ♖a2** and again White wins the bishop.

Rook vs knight is another ending which occasionally arises in practice. It can even result from some endings of rook vs pawn in which the pawn has to underpromote to avoid mate. While the details of the ending are significantly more complicated than with rook vs bishop, the one basic principle is clear enough: if the king and knight are not separated, then this ending is almost always a draw. Even if the defending king is on the edge of the board (this situation arises automatically in the underpromotion cases), then the position is usually drawn.

Black's king is in a relatively unfavourable position near the corner of the board, but there is just enough space to hold the draw. However, accurate defence is required. Play might continue **1 ♔f6 ♘h7+ 2 ♔g6 ♘f8+ 3 ♔h6 ♔h8 4 ♖f7** (4 ♖g7 ♘e6! 5 ♖f7

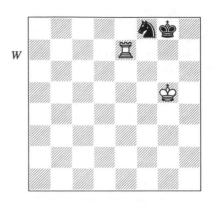

♔g8! is also a draw) **4...♔g8! 5 ♖g7+ ♔h8 6 ♖g1** (this is the key moment; Black must play carefully) and now:

1) 6...♘h7? 7 ♔g6! ♔g8 (7...♘f8+ 8 ♔f7) 8 ♖g2 (purely a waiting move) 8...♘f8+ 9 ♔f6+! ♔h8 10 ♔f7 wins.

2) 6...♘e6? 7 ♔g6! ♘f4+ (after 7...♘f8+, 8 ♔f7 wins) 8 ♔f7 wins.

3) 6...♘d7! (the drawing move, because it allows Black to meet ♔g6 by ...♔g8) 7 ♔g6 (7 ♖d1 ♘f8!) 7...♔g8! 8 ♖f1 (8 ♖g2 ♔f8) 8...♘f8+! 9 ♔f6 ♘h7+! 10 ♔e7 ♔g7! and Black draws.

Whilst this marginal position requires accurate play, the general situation (king and knight next to each other and away from the edge of the board) is a comfortable draw.

Lost positions of the type that arise in over-the-board play generally fall into two categories. The first arises when the king and knight are next to each other, but are poorly placed. One obvious case is when Black's king is trapped in a corner. A less obvious possibility is when Black's king is on the edge of the board and the knight occupies g7 (b7, b2 and g2 are equivalent, of course). The position with the black king on g8 and knight on g7 is one of the worst defensive formations and is quite often lost if the white king is nearby (for example, with the king on f6 and rook on a1 Black loses even if he moves first).

The second category consists of positions in which the king and knight are separated and cannot join up. Sometimes the win is quite simple, but in others subtle play is required to keep the king and knight apart while at the same time making progress. If the knight cannot be trapped directly, then it is important to keep the defender's king restricted. The attacker sometimes has to use his own king for this purpose, even though it is counter-intuitive to move it away from the enemy knight.

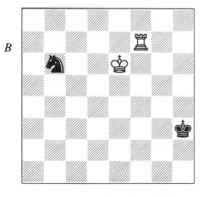

A. Karpov – L. Ftačnik
Thessaloniki Olympiad 1988

83...♘c4

Or 83...♔g3 84 ♖c7! ♔f3 (84...♘a4 85 ♔d5 ♘b2 86 ♖c1! ♘a4 87 ♔d4 wins) 85 ♖c3+! (a surprising winning move, but a typical motif in such endings; moving to either the second or fourth rank allows White to chase the knight) 85...♔e2 (85...♔e4 86 ♖c6! ♘a8 87 ♔d6 followed by ♖a6) 86 ♖c6! ♘a4 87 ♖c4! ♘b6 88 ♖b4 ♘c8 89 ♔d7 and the knight is trapped.

84 ♖f3+! ♔g4

White wins easily after 84...♔g2 85 ♖c3! ♘a5 86 ♔d5 ♘b7 87 ♖a3 ♘d8 88 ♖a7, followed by ♖d7.

85 ♖d3 ♔g5

The knight cannot move, for example 85...♘a5 86 ♔d5, 85...♘b6 86 ♖b3 ♘c8 87 ♖b7 or 85...♘b2 86 ♖d2!.

86 ♔d5! ♘b6+

The alternative is 86...♘b2 87 ♖d4 ♔f5 88 ♔c6! (not 88 ♔c5? ♔e5! with zugzwang; White must use triangulation to ensure that this position arises with Black to move) 88...♔e5 89 ♔c5! ♔e6 90 ♔b4 ♔f5 91 ♔b3! (not 91 ♔c3? ♔e5 and again White is in zugzwang) 91...♔e5 92 ♖d8 and wins.

87 ♔e5 ♘c4+

Black has little choice, for example 87...♔g4 (87...♘c8 88 ♔e6 ♘b6 89 ♖d4 wins similarly) 88 ♔e6 ♔g5 89 ♖d4 ♔g6 90 ♖b4 or 87...♘a4 88 ♖b3 ♘c5 89 ♖b5 ♘a6 90 ♔d6+ ♔f6 91 ♖b6.

88 ♔e4 (D)

Karpov could have won more rapidly by 88 ♔e6, e.g. 88...♔g6 89 ♖g3+ ♔h5 90 ♔d5 ♘b6+ 91 ♔e5

♘c4+ (alternatively, 91...♔h6 92 ♖d3 ♔g7 93 ♖d4 ♔f7 94 ♔d6 ♔f6 95 ♖f4+ ♔g5 96 ♖b4) 92 ♔f4 (keeping the black king confined is more important than running after the knight) 92...♘d6 93 ♖g7 ♔h6 94 ♖e7 ♘c4 95 ♖c7 ♘d2 96 ♖c2 ♘b3 97 ♔e5 ♔h5 98 ♔d5.

88...♘b6?

Ftačnik collapses. He should have tried 88...♔f6, when White can only win with extremely precise play: 89 ♖d4! ♘a5 90 ♖a4! ♘b7 91 ♖a6+! ♔g5 92 ♔e5! ♘d8 93 ♖f6! (this position would be a draw with White to play) 93...♘b7 (93...♔g4 94 ♔d5 ♘b7 95 ♖a6 wins) 94 ♖f8 ♘c5 (94...♘a5 95 ♔d5 ♘b3 96 ♖f1 ♔g4 97 ♖d1 ♔f4 98 ♔c4 ♘a5+ 99 ♔b5 picks up the knight) 95 ♖d8 ♔g4 96 ♖d5 ♘b3 97 ♔e4 ♘c1 98 ♔e3 and wins.

89 ♖d8 ♘c4

White threatened 90 ♔d4, and if 89...♘a4 then White wins by 90 ♔d4 ♘b6 91 ♔c5 ♘a4+ 92 ♔b4.

90 ♖d4 ♘b6

Or 90...♘b2 (90...♘a3 91 ♔d3) 91 ♔e3 ♔f5 92 ♔d2 ♔e5 93 ♖b4 and wins.

91 ♔e5 ♘c8 92 ♔e6 ♘a7 93 ♔d7 1-0

Rook and minor piece vs Rook

This occurs quite often in practice. The general position is a draw, whether the minor piece is a bishop or a knight, but the practical winning chances depend very much on which minor piece is involved.

The ending of ♖+♘ vs ♖ should be a simple draw as there are only a few winning positions. Almost all of these have the defending king badly placed near a corner, and nothing like this can be forced from a normal starting position. The general feeling amongst GMs has been that there is no point in carrying on this ending because there are no real winning chances.

However, the following ending may cause this judgement to be modified *(D)*:

70 ♔h5

A perfectly reasonable move, but 70 ♖f8+ ♘f4 71 ♖g8 would have been slightly more comfortable for Black. After 71...♖h1+ 72 ♔g5 ♖g1+ 73 ♔h4 the result is either stalemate or the white king escapes from the edge of the board.

70...♘g3+ 71 ♔h6

Thanks to the unfortunate position of White's rook, her king cannot escape from the edge: 71 ♔g6 ♘e4+ and

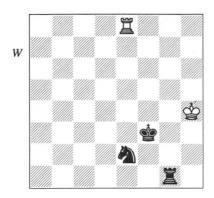

J. Polgar – G. Kasparov
Dos Hermanas 1996

now 72 ♔f5 and 72 ♔f7 drop the rook. However, 71 ♔g6 ♘e4+ 72 ♔h6! was probably safer than the text, as on e4 the knight is less well placed to shield Black's king.

71...♘f5+ 72 ♔h7 ♔f4 73 ♖b8 ♖g7+ 74 ♔h8

White's king is now uncomfortably placed in the corner of the board. The position is still drawn, but care is needed.

74...♖d7 75 ♖e8

As an example of how close White is to losing, 75 ♖f8? would lose after 75...♔g5 76 ♖a8 ♔g6. One line runs 77 ♖g8+ ♔h6 78 ♖g1 ♖d8+ 79 ♖g8 ♖d3 (this square is chosen to avoid tricks such as 79...♖d2 80 ♖g2) 80 ♖g1 ♖f3 81 ♖g4 ♘e7 82 ♖h4+ ♔g6 83 ♖h6+ ♔f7 84 ♖h7+ ♔f8 85 ♖h1 ♘g8 86 ♔h7 ♔f7 87 ♔h8 ♘f6 with a quick mate to come.

75...♔g5 76 ♖e6 ♘d4 77 ♖e1 ♔f6 78 ♖d1?! *(D)*

78 ♖f1+ was simpler, for example 78...♘f5 79 ♔g8 ♖g7+ 80 ♔f8 ♖a7 81 ♔e8.

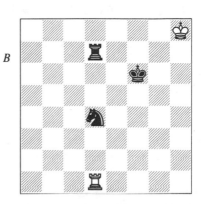

78...♖d5! 79 ♖a1??

This is actually the losing move. The only move to draw is 79 ♖f1+! and after 79...♘f5 one line runs 80 ♖f2 ♖d4 81 ♔g8!.

79...♘e6!

Kasparov, once given his chance, finds the only winning move.

80 ♖a6 ♔f7 81 ♖a7+ ♔g6 82 ♖a8 ♖d7 83 ♖b8 ♖c7 84 ♔g8 ♖c5 85 ♖a8 ♖b5 86 ♔h8 ♖b7 87 ♖c8 ♘c7

87...♖b6 is the winning idea. The plan is to play ...♘g5 without allowing White to check on the sixth rank. Then ...♘h7-f6 (possibly with ...♖e6 to keep the king confined) will fatally restrict the white king.

Kasparov's move retains the win, but loses time.

88 ♖g8+ ♔h6 89 ♖g1

It would probably have been a better practical chance to try 89 ♖f8 and see if Kasparov could find the winning idea (89...♖b6!) mentioned in the previous note.

89...♖b8+ 90 ♖g8 ♘e8 0-1
As 91 ♖f8 ♔g6 92 ♖g8+ ♔f7 wins.

It is up to the individual whether to continue this ending, but I would only regard it as worthwhile in the case of a quick-play finish.

If one is the defender, then the main advice is perfectly obvious: try to keep your king away from the edge of the board or, failing that, try to keep it away from the corner. However, even if you do find yourself in a less favourable position, don't despair – even with the king in the corner many positions are drawn.

The ending of ♖+♗ vs ♖ is one of the most common pawnless endings to arise in practice. In general it should be a draw, but the defence requires considerable accuracy and grandmasters have been known to lose it even in the days of adjournments. There are two basic drawing techniques, and it is worth knowing both of them because the position you find yourself in may be more suited to one rather than the other.

The following diagram is the basic position of the 'Cochrane Defence'. The black rook is pinning the enemy bishop and this prevents the white king approaching its counterpart. The only way to unpin is to play ♔d5 or ♔d3, but then the black king moves

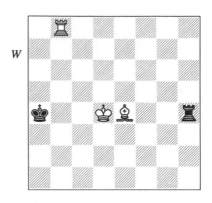

I. Rogers – M. Illescas
Spanish Team Championship 1996

along the edge of the board away from the white king. Thus Black avoids the most dangerous situation, that in which White creates mating threats by having his king directly opposite Black's.

78 ♔d5
Of course 78 ♔d3 is answered by 78...♔a5.

78...♔a3
It is worth pointing out that the Cochrane Defence is most effective when the black king is near the mid-point of one edge. If, for example, the same formation were set up along the third rank, then the corresponding move would take the black king to a2, dangerously near the corner.

79 ♗d3 ♖b4
Black takes the chance to release his king from the edge.

80 ♖h8 ♖g4 81 ♗c4 ♔b4 82 ♗e2 ♖g7
Now Black can meet 83 ♔d4 by 83...♖d7+. Black should try to maintain

a good checking distance for his rook, and it is helpful to position the rook so that it can check along both files and ranks.

83 ♖b8+ ♔c3 84 ♖c8+ ♔d2 85 ♗f3 ♔e3 86 ♖c3+ ♔d2 87 ♖a3 ♖d7+ 88 ♔c4 ♖c7+ 89 ♔d4 ♖d7+ 90 ♗d5 ♖d8 91 ♖a2+ ♔d1 *(D)*

All White's efforts have only resulted in the Cochrane Defence reappearing on the lower edge of the board.

92 ♔e4 ♔c1 93 ♗c4 ♖d2 94 ♖a8 ♖d7 95 ♗d3 ♔b2 96 ♖b8+ ♔c3 97 ♖c8+ ♔b4 98 ♗c4 ♖h7

Ensuring the maximum checking distance.

99 ♗e6 ♖h4+ 100 ♔d5 ♖h5+ 101 ♔d6 ♖h6

Even when there is no Cochrane Defence, pinning the bishop is an effective defensive tactic.

102 ♖c4+ ♔a3 103 ♖c3+ ♔b2 104 ♖g3 ♔c2 105 ♔e5 ♖h8 106 ♗f5+ ♔d2 107 ♖a3 ♖e8+ 108 ♔f4 ♖f8

Again a useful pin.

109 ♖d3+ ♔c1 110 ♖d5 ♔b2 111 ♔e3 ♔c3 112 ♗e4 ♖h8 113 ♖c5+ ♔b4 114 ♔d4 ♖h4

Cochrane again.

115 ♖c1 ♔b5 116 ♖b1+ ½-½

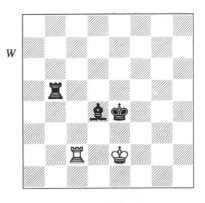

J. Norri – S. Atalik
*European Team Championship,
Pula 1997*

In this position White is in no position to use the Cochrane Defence. Any attempt to switch the rook behind the black king would lose, for example 87 ♖c8? ♖b2+ 88 ♔f1 ♖f2+ 89 ♔e1 ♔d3 would lead to a lost 'Philidor position' (see the next diagram). Therefore White has to use the second of the two drawing techniques, the 'second-rank defence'.

87 ♖d2

The basic idea is to defend passively with both king and rook on the second rank. White will just oscillate with his rook between c2 and d2 until Black undertakes positive action.

87...罝h5 88 罝c2 罝h2+ 89 ♔d1

This is the first of the two main points behind the second-rank defence. Black can drive the enemy king to the edge of the board with a check, but then his own rook is attacked so he has no time to approach with his king.

89...罝h1+ 90 ♔e2 罝h2+ 91 ♔d1 罝h3 92 ♔e2 ♗c3 (D)

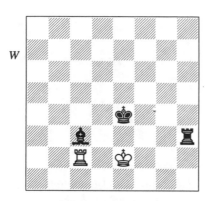

This is Black's other winning attempt. At first it seems that White is in zugzwang as any rook move loses instantly (93 罝c1 罝h2+ 94 ♔d1 ♔d3).

93 ♔d1!

Now 93...♔d3 is answered by the stalemate defence 94 罝d2+ and the king has to retreat.

93...罝h1+ 94 ♔e2 ♔d4 95 ♔f3

Given the chance, White's king slips away.

95...罝f1+ 96 罝f2 罝a1 97 ♔g4 罝a8 98 罝g2 ½-½

If you have the rook and bishop, there is one winning position which you must be aware of – the 'Philidor

position'. This winning position arises relatively often as a result of inferior defence, but it is quite tricky to win. If you don't know the correct method, it is easy to go round and round in circles, until you give up in frustration.

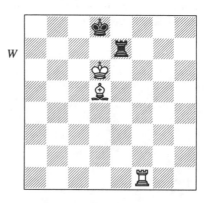

Philidor, 1749

This is the characteristic Philidor position. The kings face each other with Black's king trapped on the edge of the board, and his rook restricted to one file by mating threats.

1 罝f8+! 罝e8 2 罝f7!

First White improves the position of his rook with gain of tempo, and confines Black's king to the first rank. The immediate threat is 3 罝a7.

2...罝e2

White can force Black's rook to c2 by playing 罝a7 and this side-to-side switch, with possible checks on d7 thrown in, gives rise to so many possibilities that confusion is easy. What is hard to grasp is that White can only win by means of appropriate bishop manoeuvres; the bishop appears ideally placed on d5, so the idea of moving it away is counter-intuitive.

Black cannot run with his king, as 2...♔c8 loses to 3 ♖a7 ♖d8+ 4 ♔c6 ♔b8 5 ♖b7+ ♔a8 6 ♖b1 ♔a7 7 ♔c7, forcing mate or win of the rook. Thus he must play his rook down the e-file, in order to meet ♖a7 by a switch to the c-file. It turns out that e2 is the best square for Black's rook and e3 is the worst; e1 is somewhere in between. The win after 2...♖e3 runs 3 ♖d7+ ♔e8 (3...♔c8 4 ♖a7 wins at once, because 4...♖b3 is impossible) 4 ♖a7 ♔f8 5 ♖f7+ ♔e8 (White has forced the king from d8 to e8 with gain of tempo) 6 ♖f4 (threatening 7 ♗c6+) 6...♔d8 (6...♖d3 fails to 7 ♖g4 because Black lacks the reply ...♖f3) 7 ♗e4 (the final blow for Black; d3 is covered) 7...♔e8 8 ♗c6+ and mates in two more moves.

If Black plays 2...♖e1, then 3 ♗f3 is a reflection of the position after White's fifth move in the main line.

After 2...♖e2, White's ultimate aim is to force Black's rook to the third rank.

3 ♖h7

A waiting move to force Black's rook to the slightly inferior square e1. After 3...♖e3 White wins as in the previous note.

3...♖e1 4 ♖b7

White's winning line only works when his rook is on f7 or b7. The side-to-side manoeuvres are typical of this ending; Black is forced to follow suit and oscillate with his own rook

between e1 and c1, but this gives White the chance to transfer his rook from h7 to b7 with gain of tempo.

4...♖c1 *(D)*

4...♔c8 loses to 5 ♖b2 ♖d1 6 ♖h2 ♔b8 7 ♖a2.

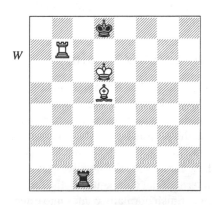

5 ♗b3

This is the key idea, without which White cannot make progress, and it explains why e1 is an inferior square to e2. This position is a genuine zugzwang and if White were now to play, his quickest win would be 1 ♗e6 ♖d1+ 2 ♗d5 ♖e1 3 ♗b3, passing the move to Black.

5...♖c3

Or 5...♔c8 6 ♖b4 (threatening 7 ♗e6+) 6...♔d8 7 ♖h4 ♖e1 (7...♔c8 8 ♗d5) 8 ♗a4 ♔c8 9 ♗c6 ♖d1+ 10 ♗d5! ♔b8 11 ♖a4 winning.

6 ♗e6

Now that Black's rook has been forced onto the inferior third rank, White transfers his bishop back to d5 with gain of tempo.

6...♖d3+ 7 ♗d5! ♖c3

Here the win is analogous to the note to Black's second move.

8 ♖d7+ ♔c8

8...♔e8 9 ♖g7 and f3 is out of bounds.

9 ♖h7 ♔b8 10 ♖b7+ ♔c8 11 ♖b4 ♔d8 12 ♗c4 ♔c8 13 ♗e6+ and White mates.

Quick-play finishes

These days the normal method of finishing a long game is the 'quick-play finish' in which, from a certain point on, the players have a fixed amount of time to complete the game, no matter how many moves this might take. In international competitions, the quick-play finish normally comes into effect at move 60, and players are generally given half an hour (sometimes an hour), in addition to any time they still have, to complete the game.

Quick-play finishes only affect a relatively small percentage of tournament games, but it is important to be aware of the impact such a finish may have on certain endgames. There are many endings in which the odds would favour a draw at a traditional time-limit, but in a quick-play finish the balance of probabilities is changed. Quick-play finishes also put a premium on memorized knowledge; after the exhaustion of six hours' play, and with limited time on the clock, working out a complex ending is very difficult – you just have to know how to play certain positions.

It should be noted that in most cases the speeding up of play will favour the side trying to win, because he can go round and round several times, each time hoping for a mistake, whereas the defender only has to go wrong once. Here is a quick round-up of the most common endings where the result might be affected:

1) Rook and bishop vs rook. The drawing techniques are fairly well-known, but to apply them in practice requires considerable thought. I would not care to defend this in a quick-play finish.

2) Rook and knight vs rook. Should be comfortably drawn at a normal time-limit, but in a quick-play finish it might be worth continuing (as Kasparov showed).

3) Queen and pawn vs queen. Of course, some positions are objectively lost, but even many of the drawn positions require very accurate defence. I imagine that the 'marginal' drawn positions would be almost impossible to defend in a quick-play finish, and even some of the fairly comfortable draws would probably be difficult.

4) Rook and pawn vs rook. Positions which are drawn by the standard 'third-rank' defence would still be drawn in quick-play. In more complex positions, there would of course be more errors, but in these endings the attacker also has to play accurately, so the accelerated tempo probably makes the task equally difficult for both players.

If one can liquidate to a variety of different endings, then the fact that there is a quick-play finish might affect one's decision as to which to aim for. If one evaluates ♖+♗ vs ♖ as an 80% chance of a win (which seems reasonable) then one might prefer that to a line in which one has a clear positional advantage but not necessarily a win.

It is perhaps unfortunate that modifications to the time-limit can cause what amounts to an alteration in the evaluation of certain endings, but that is the price one has to pay for the elimination of adjournments.

5 Using a Computer

Computers are wonderful tools. In half a century they have moved from a few specialized applications to occupy a central position in our society. Modern civilisation probably could not function without them, so dependent have we become on their services. With the growth of the Internet, a further communications revolution as great as the introduction of radio and television is upon us.

Computers have also had an impact on chess. Early chess computers were laughably weak but, after Deep Blue's defeat of Kasparov in 1997, nobody is laughing now. For a relatively small price, you can buy a chess program in a shop which, running on a standard PC, can defeat virtually anybody except for IMs and GMs. You can also purchase a database of up to a million games.

The question arises as to how these tools can best be used for personal improvement. The discussion that follows refers to the database program *ChessBase* and the playing program *Fritz*. This is not because ChessBase have paid me a wad of money to mention their products, but because these are the products I am most familiar with. The discussion is as general as possible and doubtless applies to other, similar, products.

Game databases

When non-chess players think of a grandmaster making use of a computer, they probably think of playing programs. However, at this level the main use of a computer is to access a large database of games.

There are two main uses for a database. For the professional, examining the games of prospective opponents is part of the job. If you are participating in a round-robin tournament, some of this may be done before the event, but in a Swiss event it can only be done when the pairings are known, which normally does not allow much time for preparation.

The second use is to look at the games played in specific opening lines. If you are intending to play a particular variation in the afternoon, a quick scan of the database to see if there are any recent games is very helpful. You might get a new idea, or you might see something potentially dangerous for your opponent. For home preparation, a database is also extremely useful. Instead of searching through dozens of *Informators*, *New in Chess Yearbooks* and other standard references, you can call up all the games in a particular line with a few keystrokes. The games can then be merged into a single game with variations, so that you can easily see the general structure of the variation. If the database program has an interface to a playing module, then at a keystroke you can set the computer to work analysing any given position.

The range of features available is truly astounding, and these days any serious player is virtually obliged to use a database.

The main features which I regard as essential for a database program are:

1) It should handle databases of up to a million games without struggling. Of course, you will need a powerful computer to handle such large databases, but even so operations on very large databases can be rather slow.

2) It should have facilities for entering both variations and text annotations, and manipulating these.

3) It should run under the current version of Windows. DOS is dead; forget anything running under DOS. Mac users will have to make do with what is available.

4) It should support openings keys of unlimited depth, and should have facilities for users to modify and expand these.

5) The ability to merge several games into one game with variations is critical. Once you have used this feature, you will not want to do without it.

6) There should be an interface to a playing program, so that you just have to hit a key to see the analysis of the current position. A method of pasting this analysis into the game is highly desirable.

That deals with the program, but what about the data? Nobody is going to enter a million games by hand, so one is utterly dependent on commercial offerings. However, here the situation is much less satisfactory than with the programs. Even the best databases contain a significant number of errors. Poor-quality data is commonplace; indeed, sometimes it is so poor as to make the data practically useless. Some 'commercial' databases are little more than games collected from every available source, and just lumped together – the 'kitchen sink' approach.

Typical problems are:

1) Inconsistent spelling of names. This is perhaps the most irritating. If you are considering buying a database, have a look to see if Korchnoi is spelt more than one way in the database. If it is, then just forget it. There is nothing more irritating than missing a critical game because you have failed to guess whether the player is 'Korchnoi', 'Korchnoj', 'Kortschnoi' or any of his other close relatives. The same applies to tournaments; you may find games from the same tournament described as 'Wijk aan Zee', 'Wijk', 'Hoogovens', 'WaZ', etc.

2) Duplicate games. This is often a result of problem 1. Sometimes whole tournaments are duplicated because of some minor difference in the spelling of the event name.

3) Incorrect results. This is one of the most common errors. When entering data, most programs have a default option. If the operator forgets to enter the result, you will just get the default result – with a two-thirds chance of being wrong. You may even find combinations of these errors, for example Korchnoi beat Bareev, but in an amazingly similar game Kortschnoj lost to Barejew.

4) Incorrect moves. The above errors are often fairly noticeable, but incorrect moves are trickier to spot. Of course, if the error is such as to leave one player's queen *en prise* then you might be a bit suspicious, but if it is the wrong rook to d1, then you might never know unless you compare the game with another source. Once, when dealing with a collection of games that contained many errors, I came across a particularly grotesque example. I later mentioned it to the grandmaster concerned:

"Do you know how your game was mangled in this game collection? According to their score, your opponent could have mated in two, but instead left his queen *en prise* with check", I laughed.

"But that really happened", he replied.

Employing a poor-quality database causes immense frustration and waste of time; the small amount of money saved is not worth it. 'But they are both databases with the same games...',

you may say. Well, a Trabant and a Rolls-Royce are both cars with four wheels. Unfortunately, the defects of a database are not visible by looking at the shiny surface of the CD-ROM; you actually have to use it before you spot the problems.

At the end of the day much of the blame for this situation must be laid at the door of the chess players themselves. Copying of data is commonplace. Why should a company invest thousands of man-hours producing high-quality data if it is just going to be stolen (because that is what copying is in this case)? Software piracy is illegal – don't do it.

Once you have a database you will probably want to keep it up to date. There are various commercial services which offer regular 'top-ups' for your database. These days much of the information can be downloaded from the Internet, although then you have all the problems of inconsistent names, forgetting which tournaments you have already included, etc. For really up-to-the-minute material, the Internet is unbeatable, but it requires considerable effort to keep on top of the flow of data. Unless you really need new games on a week-by-week basis, the pre-packaged commercial offerings are probably better. The Internet is wonderful for e-mail, news and specific enquiries for which you can use a search engine. Otherwise it strikes me as being a great time-waster.

Playing programs

The availability of cheap but very strong playing programs for the home PC provides many new opportunities for training and self-improvement. If you already have a computer, I would strongly recommend buying such a program. The most obvious use, that of checking over one's own games, is also one of the most useful. It is amazing how often a computer check reveals missed tactical ideas. Even if nothing shattering is found, the computer often suggests interesting alternative ideas which were overlooked during the game. It is important not only to play over the game itself, but the tactical lines on which your decisions were based. For this reason, you should only consider buying a program that supports the entry of variations, and can afterwards store the games and variations in a database. You may well find a pattern in the ideas you have missed, and this will provide you with useful information about which areas of your game need special attention.

Another use is to play out training positions against a computer. The famous Russian trainer Mark Dvoretsky recommends the method of 'playing out' interesting positions. The idea is that if, for example, one of his students is weak in tactics, Dvoretsky would set the student to play tactical positions against a strong opponent. Afterwards they would go over the course of the 'game' and see where the student could have played better. Most players don't have a suitable opponent on hand for such exercises, but the computer can perform a similar job and can also help in the post-mortem analysis. Even though computers play endings less strongly than the middle-game, they can still be useful. As discussed on page 131, if you have trouble winning rook and pawn endings with an extra pawn, play out such a position against the computer. It is a good idea to play out the same position several times, trying different plans. You will soon develop a feeling for which plans work and which are ineffective. If you experience trouble winning at all, you may get some ideas by reversing the colours!

The computer does have several limitations; in the areas of positional judgement and plan-forming it is of practically no help, and long-term sacrifices are almost always rejected by the machine. Analysing the Najdorf Poisoned Pawn with the aid of a computer is a futile exercise; White's compensation is so long-term that the computer does not see it at all, and resolutely assesses every position as winning for Black.

Curiously, I find playing normal games against computers much less helpful. Computers have a particular style of play and one soon learns how to avoid their strengths and exploit their weaknesses. This knowledge is of no value against human players, who (normally!) have a very different set of strengths and weaknesses. Moreover, it is quite easy to become depressed playing against the computer. All one really learns is that it is common to overlook tactical points. Playing programs are just starting to have a major impact on grandmaster chess. Here is one example:

A. Shirov – L. van Wely
Monaco Amber (rapid) 1997
Sicilian, Najdorf

1 e4 c5 2 ⟨f3 d6 3 d4 cxd4 4 ⟨xd4 ⟨f6 5 ⟨c3 a6 6 ⟨e3 e6 7 g4 h6 8 f4 b5 9 ⟨g2 ⟨b7 10 g5

This move was introduced in the game Ivanchuk-Topalov, Las Palmas 1996 as an improvement over the previously played 10 a3.

10...hxg5 11 fxg5 ⟨h5

The Ivanchuk-Topalov game continued 11...b4 12 ⟨a4 ⟨h5 13 0-0 ⟨d7 14 g6 ⟨hf6 15 c3 ⟨e5 16 gxf7+ ⟨xf7 17 cxb4 ⟨h4, and now 18 ⟨f4 would have been clearly better for White; in the game Ivanchuk played 18 ⟨b3 and lost quickly. The text is a counter-improvement by Gavrikov.

12 g6 ⟨f6 13 gxf7+ ⟨xf7 14 0-0 ⟨bd7 (D)

Now Kulaots-Gavrikov, Hallsberg 1996/7 continued 15 e5 ⟨xg2 16 exf6 ⟨xf1 17 ⟨xe6 ⟨xf6 18 ⟨g5+ ⟨g6 19 ⟨d5 and here Black could have gained a large advantage by 19...⟨h4 20 ⟨ce4 ⟨g4+ 21 ⟨g3 ⟨xg5 22 ⟨xg5 ⟨xg5 23 ⟨xa8 ⟨h3.

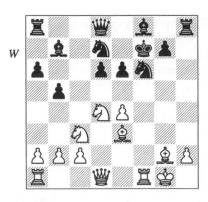

15 ⟨xe6!!

An absolutely stunning innovation, which gives White a clear advantage in every variation. After the game Shirov announced that this move had not been discovered by him, but by *Fritz*. Sure enough, when I set up the position on my *Fritz*, the program found ⟨xe6 in less than a minute. It is perhaps slightly surprising that Shirov used up his innovation in a rapid event, but he probably felt that since anyone with a *Fritz* could find this move, it would only be a matter of weeks before someone else played it.

15...⟨xe6 16 e5 ⟨xg2

Black is lost after 16...⟨xe5 17 ⟨xb7 ⟨b8 or 16...⟨c7 17 exf6 ⟨xf6 18 ⟨d5 ⟨xd5 19 ⟨xf6+ ⟨xf6 20 ⟨xd5.

17 exf6 ⟨xf6 18 ⟨xg2 ⟨c8

18...⟨e8 is no improvement, owing to 19 ⟨xf6+ ⟨xf6 (19...gxf6 20 ⟨d5+ ⟨e7 21 ⟨b7+ ⟨e6 22 ⟨e1 wins) 20 ⟨d5 ⟨g6 (20...⟨xe3 21 ⟨e4+ ⟨e7 22 ⟨xd6+ ⟨e8 23 ⟨e6+ ⟨d8 24 ⟨d1+ mates) 21 ⟨d3+ ⟨f7 22 ⟨f1+

♔g8 23 ♕d5+ ♔h7 24 ♖f3 ♗e7 25 ♖h3+ ♔g6 26 ♕e6+ ♗f6 27 ♖g3+ ♔h7 28 ♕f5+ and wins.

19 ♕f3 ♗e7 20 ♖ae1 ♔f7 21 ♕d5+ ♔f8 22 ♕f5 ♕c7 23 ♗d4 ♕b7+ 24 ♔g1 *(D)*

Of course 24 ♘d5 ♖xc2+ 25 ♕xc2 ♕xd5+ 26 ♕e4 ♖h5 27 ♕xd5 ♖xd5 28 ♖f4 is also good, but Black could put up considerable resistance in the ending.

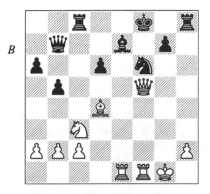

24...♖c4 25 ♖f4 ♕c8 26 ♖e6

All White's pieces are in perfect central positions, while Black's are scattered randomly around the edge of the board.

26...♖xd4

Losing at once, but after 26...♔f7 (or 26...♖h6 27 ♘d5) 27 ♘e4 ♖xc2 28 ♘xd6+ ♗xd6 29 ♖xf6+ gxf6 30 ♕xf6+ ♔e8 31 ♕f7+ the result would be the same.

27 ♖xf6+ 1-0

It isn't clear if this is the first instance in which a top-level opening line was refuted by a computer, but it may be the first in which the human 'innovator' was honest enough to admit it! The question naturally arises as to how many opening innovations are capable of being found by a computer. Every four months a panel of leading grandmasters votes on the most important opening innovations. The results are published in *Informator*. At the time of writing, the most recent issue for which the results of this vote are available is *Informator 68*. I set Fritz4 to work on the positions in which the top 15 novelties of *Informator 68* were played, to see how many the machine would find. In each case I allowed sufficient time for a complete analysis down to 11 ply (although many lines were taken far deeper, of course). The result: Fritz found 3 of the 15 innovations.

Of course, there are many problems with such a test, for example some of the 'innovations' may in fact not be good, and will perhaps be refuted in the near future. Another point is that sharp, clear-cut innovations tend to head the *Informator* list, because a subtle finesse which can only be appreciated by specialists in a particular opening line will not score well in 'democratic' voting. In a couple of cases the innovation was Fritz's second choice, which would certainly alert a human operator to the fact that there was something of interest present. However, to summarize I would say that Fritz was only of value for finding opening innovations in certain types of position. Having said that, to find 3 of the world's top 15 innovations in less than a day is quite an achievement!

Here are two of Fritz's successes and one of its failures.

V. Miluydas – S. Muraviov
corr 1994

Here Fritz took less than five seconds to find the innovation **24...♘h3+!!** (exclamation marks as given in *Informator*; 24...♘xe6 would have been good for White) **25 ♔g2 ♘g5!**. The game concluded in spectacular fashion with **26 ♕f2! ♗f3+ 27 ♔f1 f4 28 g4 ♕h3+ 29 ♔e1 ♘xe6 30 ♘e5 ♘g5 31 ♖xa6!! ♗xg4 32 ♗c4!! ♘e4 33 ♕f3!! ♕h4+** (33...♗xf3 34 ♘f7+ ♔g8 35 ♘h6+ is also a draw) **34 ♕g3** and the players agreed to a **draw** in view of 34...fxg3 35 ♘f7+ ♔g8 36 ♘h6+.

In the following position from the French Defence, **20 ♘f5!!** was already

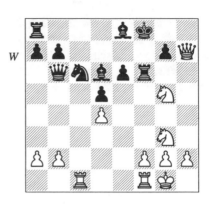

O. Korneev – Y. Piskov
Linares Open 1996

at the top of Fritz's list within 2 seconds, and in 75 seconds it was being assessed as winning for White. The game concluded **20...♖xf5 21 ♘xe6+ ♔e7 22 ♕xf5 ♘xd4?! 23 ♘xd4 ♕xd4 24 ♖fe1+ 1-0**

In the following example, Fritz failed to find Timoshenko's innovation although, as we shall see, it is not clear that the new idea was any improvement over the move previously played.

G. Timoshenko – B. Itkis
Baile Herculane 1996
French Defence

1 e4 e6 2 d4 d5 3 ♘c3 ♘f6 4 e5 ♘fd7 5 f4 c5 6 ♘f3 ♘c6 7 ♗e3 cxd4 8 ♘xd4 ♕b6 9 ♕d2 ♕xb2 10 ♖b1 ♕a3 11 ♗b5 ♘xd4 12 ♗xd4 ♗b4 13 0-0 a6 14 ♖b3 ♕a5 15 ♖fb1 ♗a3 (*D*) **16 f5!!**

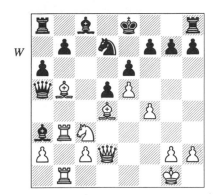

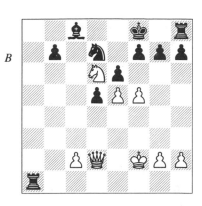

The innovation (with *Informator's* exclamation marks), deviating from 16 ♗xd7+. Fritz probably failed to find it for two reasons: firstly, it is not clear if it is really better than taking on d7; secondly, the combination would be simply too deep for Fritz, even were it sound.

16...axb5 17 ♖xa3! ♕xa3 18 ♘xb5 ♕xa2 19 ♘d6+ ♔f8 20 ♖a1 ♕xa1+ 21 ♗xa1 ♖xa1+ 22 ♔f2 *(D)*

This is really the critical moment of the whole combination, and we are already 12 ply away from the starting point. Fritz still feels that Black can survive after the obvious 22...♘xe5, but unfortunately this move isn't mentioned at all in Timoshenko's notes. I cannot see anything better than 23 ♕c3 ♘g4+ 24 ♔e2 ♖a8 25 ♘xc8 h5 26 ♕b4+ ♔g8 27 ♕xb7 ♖a2 with a likely draw.

22...♖a8? 23 ♕g5!

Now Fritz agrees that White is winning.

23...f6 24 ♕h5 g6

Or 24...♔e7 25 ♕f7+ ♔d8 26 fxe6!.

25 ♕h6+ ♔g8 26 ♘e8 ♔f7 27 ♘d6+ ♔g8 28 ♘e8 ♔f7 29 ♕g7+ ♔xe8 30 ♕xh8+ ♘f8 31 exf6 1-0

Index of Names

Numbers refer to pages

Adams 36, 55
Ahues 124
Alekhine 132
Anand 12, 25
Andersson 55, 136
Atalik 161
Averbakh 147

Beckemeyer 52
Beliavsky 140
Bellon 84
Botvinnik 103
Browne 89

Čabrilo 142
Capablanca 132, 141
Chandler 52, 110
Chekhover 103
Chernin 102
Chigorin 136
Christiansen 52
Cochrane 160
Conquest 47
Cook 51
Cox 50
Crouch 7

de la Villa 59
Dolmatov 140
Dvoiris 99

Eliskases 153

Filguth 58
Fine 129
Fischer 56, 57
Flear 121
Flohr 141
Ftačnik 157

Gelfand 26
Giddins 54
Grigoriev 119
Gunst 10

Hebden 121
Hort 40
Howell 111
Hübner 136

Ilinčić 142
Illescas 160
Itkis 172

Kamsky 25
Karpov 52, 157
Kasparov 64, 159
Khalifman 99
Kieninger 153
King 8, 14
Korneev 172
Kosten 71
Kotov 7
Kuligowski 11
Kuzmin, G. 12

Lasker, Ed. 123
Lautier 12
Levenfish 129, 135, 136
Ljubojević 107
London (city) 135

Mandler 117
Mellado 30
Mestel 55
Meszaros 45
Miles 107
Miluydas 172
Muraviov 172

Neustadtl 116
Nimzowitsch 98
Norri 161
Nunn 11, 15, 19, 22, 30, 40, 47, 50,
    58, 59, 62, 84, 89, 94, 101, 144

Onishchuk 36

Petrosian, T. 82
Philidor 162
Piskov 144, 172
Plaskett 94
Polgar, J. 159
Portisch 28
Přibyl, M. 22
Prokeš 118
Psakhis 8, 14

Ragozin, E. 111
Réti 117
Rogers 121, 160

St Petersburg (city) 135

Sax 105
Schlage 124
Seirawan 15, 53
Shirov 26, 64, 121, 170
Short 64, 102
Smyslov 129, 135, 136
Soltis 76
Sorri 79
Spassky 53, 134
Speelman 133

Stean 105
Stefanova 54
Sveshnikov 12

Tal 56
Tarrasch 98
Timman 64
Timoshenko 172
Tisdall 5, 9

Unzicker 57, 82

Van der Sterren 19
Van Wely 54, 55, 170
Vydeslaver 101

Wahls 111

Xie Jun 62

Ye Rongguang 54
Yudasin 110
Yusupov 28

Zhu Chen 134
Zimmerman 45

Index of Openings

French Defence 30, 172
Giuoco Piano 22, 40, 76
King's Gambit 53
King's Indian Defence 15
Latvian Gambit 71
London System 54
Nimzowitsch-Larsen Attack 45
Ruy Lopez 19
Sicilian, Dragon 107
Sicilian, Najdorf 56, 89, 94, 170
Sicilian, Pelikan 50
Sicilian, Scheveningen 105
Sicilian, Velimirović Attack 110
Torre Attack 54
Trompowsky 55
Two Knights Defence 36